BROWN SHOE/ BLACK SHOE

BROWN SHOE/ BLACK SHOE

Memories Of Two Air Forces, Two Wars And One Military Occupation

Troy Thompson Jr.

Copyright © 2003 by Troy Thompson Jr..

Library of Congress Number: 2003095878
ISBN :   Hardcover   1-4134-2714-6
              Softcover   1-4134-2713-8

All rights reserved. No part of this book may be reproduced or transmitted in any form or by any means, electronic or mechanical, including photocopying, recording, or by any information storage and retrieval system, without permission in writing from the copyright owner.

This book was printed in the United States of America.

To order additional copies of this book, contact:
Xlibris Corporation
1-888-795-4274
www.Xlibris.com
Orders@Xlibris.com
20837

CONTENTS

Brown Shoe/Black Shoe 7
Keesler Army Air Base 13
University of Tennessee 22
Nashville 30
Maxwell 33
Carlstrom AAB 41
Valdosta AAB 48
Gunnery School 50
Navigation School 58
Miami Interlude 69
Boca Raton AAB 72
On to Nebraska! 76
Pyote AAB 80
Herington AAB 92
Kwajalein Atoll 100
Guam 1 102
Guam 2 110
Guam 3 118
Guam 4 132
Guam 5 136
Guam 6 143
Guam 7 150
Civilian Interlude 158
Back to College 163
Active Duty Again 167
Occupation Life 179
Family Life . . . Again! 188
A Long Flight 198
Police Action—The Beginning 207

Police Action—Days of Confusion 212
13th Bomb Squadron 217
Korea! 224
Korea 2 230
Tachikawa—Again! 240
Appendix 247

BROWN SHOE/BLACK SHOE

During World War II, what is now the US Air Force was part of the United States Army—"The Army Air Corps". At that time for the Uniform, the shoes were brown. When the US Air Force became a separate, independent service, the Uniform shoe color changed to black. In the military, especially at the working level, many individuals felt the need for a "put-down". In the old Army Air Corps (the Brown Shoe Air Force), the ultimate put-down was, "I've stood in more pay-lines than you've stood in chow-lines!" In the new US Air Force, the put-down came to be, "Don't tell me! I was in the Brown Shoe Air Force." Of course, this could be used two ways, and a younger troop could put-down his elder with, "What does an old gaffer like you know—you were in the Brown Shoe Air Force."

Before it began I was hooked on airplanes. While I was in elementary school and high school in the latter '30's, aircraft were in the news frequently as they advanced their capability. At the same time politics grew murkier and murkier in Europe and, less reported, in the Far East. My father was a fan of detective magazines for recreational reading. I didn't share this taste, since his magazines were "crime reporter" accounts of actual crimes. But he had a swap relationship with one of his friends which I did find more interesting. The friend was Mr. Robert Rosson, publisher of one of our two small-town weekly newspapers. Mr. Rosson had been an Army pilot during World War I. I believe he was an instructor pilot who instructed pilots in their final flight training before going into a combat squadron. He was an avid buyer of pulp magazines about World War I flying. He and Daddy would occasionally swap the magazines which they had finished reading and I found Mr. Rosson's Flying Aces magazines much more interesting than

Daddy's crime report magazines. Daddy had been an Infantry Lieutenant in World War I and I guess he held the Infantry view "Infantry is the Queen of Battle". Probably a true statement even now but for me I'm talking flying! He had attended Mississippi State College shortly before that war and 'State was run as a military school, like The Citadel or VMI.

While in school (high school), I made model airplanes. Sometimes the solid ones which aimed for a realistic look. And, sometimes flying models made of balsa, rice paper, acetone dope, and a rubber band motor. The motor never did give enough power to make realistic flights any more than an occasional thing. My most realistic looking flying model unfortunately never made a decent flight, since it suffered major battle damage at the hands of a five year old son of one of Mama's visitors. Mama was chagrined for my sake because she was aware of all the time I had put into making it. She was very sympathetic to me after her visitor left but the little model of a Navy dive bomber biplane was hopelessly wrecked.

I guess my first hint of troubled days ahead was around the mid-30's on a family trip to Birmingham. We were on our way home, driving through the streets of North Birmingham. This was long before the day of the interstate road which cut North Birmingham out of the through-traffic picture. We had stopped at a railroad crossing for the passing of a long, heavily loaded freight train which crept slowly through the intersection. Most of the train's load was scrap iron and steel. Daddy's terse comment was "I guess it will be made into artillery shells that will be shot at our boys." The impact of his comment passed over my adolescent head but it did linger with me to be remembered later in different circumstances.

Second hint came several years later. In September 1939 I had just started my Senior year at Cullman High. Walking home through a residential area with several classmates, we passed a young boy (probably pre-high school age). He was walking in the opposite direction, across the street, shouting "Extra! Extra! War in Europe!" This was unheard of. In Cullman, small-town peaceful Cullman, paper carriers did not shout "Extra!" They just delivered papers to their customers and let the customer decide if it was truly Extra news. I guess I wanted to show off my awareness of events to impress my friends so I shouted out to him "What did England do?" He didn't answer and I doubt if that first paper's report would have given much information to answer that question.

Like most Americans my age I guess that I (or we) followed the stories in the paper about the war with varying degrees of interest. Cullman, my home town, had been settled in the 1870's by German immigrants and my classmates, probably about a third of them, were from German families. But Germans assimilate readily into a population and we all considered ourselves a hundred percent American.

At the end of Senior year I had a stroke of luck. Birmingham-Southern College, a small Methodist College in Birmingham decided that they were tired of trying to maintain a successful intercollegiate football team. With their remaining football scholarship money they decided to offer regular scholarships, one in each Congressional District. I was fortunate enough to win the one in our District. A real blessing for me, since it would have been very difficult for my father to send me to college out of his current income and I hadn't shown a great deal of aptitude toward working my own way through. At that time the country was in the final pangs of the Great Depression and jobs a high-schooler would do in present days were being held then by full-grown adults, some with families.

Freshman year at 'Southern was completely removed from the war for me. A few months of dating Lynelle; necessarily low cost dates, usually an afternoon matinee in the balcony of the Alabama Theater, Birmingham's leading movie theater. (Lynelle reentered my life as my wife many years later as Lyn when we both were coping with widowhood).The other big event in the Freshman year was the discovery that my choice of Chemistry as my major was a very poor choice! I had made the decision in High School while watching Miss Downey, a lovely and inexperienced teacher struggle to work out valence problems on the blackboard. I thought that that would be all there was to chemistry and I could do that. Chemistry 101 at 'Southern under Dr. Jones, followed by Qualitative Analysis convinced me that Miss Downey's problems at the blackboard were far from being all that there was to Chemistry! So, I changed my major to Geology. I loved Geology and still do but found that a major in Geology required some serious Physics courses and in the Physics courses I discovered that I had little talent at all for math higher than College Algebra. So, I changed majors again to become an English major. This one I liked.

Meanwhile, the War spread, our country became a major combatant and I received my preliminary draft registration. I immediately saw that some of my fraternity brothers, along with other students, who were pre-Med or studying for the Ministry, would probably be deferred from serving. That was not true for English Majors! Soon I would be receiving my letter "Greetings From the President. You have . . ."

I had a strong aversion to being in the infantry, having watched "All Quiet On the Western Front" and probably several lesser World War I movies. Maybe the Artillery might not be so bad but they would probably put me in the Infantry anyway. And who likes sleeping in the mud?

I decided that if I would be in the war, I would much rather it be in the air. Initially I believed it would be the Navy. But at that time I think that Navy wanted college graduates in their pilot training and I was only a college Junior. A good many years later when I was doing a tour as a Navigator in B-26's and contemplated making a night landing in a B-26, which touched down at around 150 MPH, on a frost slicked five thousand foot runway in Korea, I thought about my early Navy thoughts. And thanked God I hadn't gone into Navy pilot training. The short runway, made of pierced steel planking and covered with frost might be daunting to consider but I was glad it was that instead of landings on an aircraft carrier as regular routine.

About that time, the Army offered a tempting program. Sign up immediately and they would let you continue in school as long as the needs of the Army would permit. Then, enter the Army as first an Aviation Student, stationed in an Army unit on a college campus. After that next become an Aviation Cadet. That was for me and I signed up. When she learned of my decision, it didn't appeal to Mama at all and she was a little difficult about it. She had a fear of flying and couldn't accept the fact that I had an equally compelling distaste for being in the Infantry. But the fact that I continued on at 'Southern from the date I signed on for the program (May 1942) until I was called in nearly a year later (April 6, 1943) may have tempered her dislike for the idea.

The "nearly a year" was the most enjoyable of my whole college career. Several formal dances—tuxes, long gowns for the date with the obligatory corsage. Interesting classes—creative writing, Chaucer and his Canterbury Tales (you could read the bawdy tales in a translation in the library—they weren't covered in class!); playing my trombone in the annual Gilbert and Sullivan operetta.

'Southern was on the quarter system instead of the semester system. Very shortly after I registered for the Spring Quarter (1943) I received the call which I expected from the Army: report on April 6 to Keesler Army Air Base in Biloxi, Mississippi.

The Army included a TR (Transportation Request) with my order to report. I'd never heard of TR's but found that I could take it to the L&N Railroad Station and the man at the ticket counter would give me a train ticket to Biloxi. He did and I was ready to prepare to leave. It was both sad and exciting to do so. After all, it would be an entirely different world for the next part of my life.

I'm sure it was a sad and fearful time for Mama but she put up a brave front. I'm grateful for that, more so now than then because, for me, there was that undercurrent of fear and dread which you hope will stay as only an undercurrent. The flying I eagerly anticipated but not the probably eventual fighting. If she had broken down emotionally, it would have been much harder for me to stay calm.

KEESLER ARMY AIR BASE

(Biloxi, Mississippi)

Biloxi at last! The train trip, though comfortable, had been tedious as many train trips are when you travel alone. We left Cullman in early afternoon and passed through Birmingham, then Montgomery, then Mobile. It was around midnight when we passed through Mobile.

After leaving Mobile, the track which had been leading mostly southwest, turned more to the west as we ran along the Gulf Coast. The conductor went through the coaches, briskly pulling down each seat's window shade. I asked him "Why are you pulling all the shades down?"

His reply was brief. "Submarines!"

That was explanation enough for me. I assumed that he did it so any lurking sub might not be able to fire its deck cannon at us. Many years later I learned that was an oversimplification and we were not the potential target. German subs were prowling around in the Gulf at that time, looking for ships to sink, preferably oil tankers. If you are outside a town at night on a clear night and look toward the town, you will usually see that the sky over the town is much lighter than it is over areas which are wooded or open country. If a sub was lurking out in the Gulf at night and the skipper was looking toward the town, he would see that sky shine. And, if a ship passed between the sub and the sky shine on shore, it would be silhouetted and the sub skipper would have a good target. The conductor's move was our little part in reducing the sky shine. This answer made more sense to me later on when I read about it than I found at the time in the conductor's pulling down our train's shades.

It was the beginning of dawn when we arrived at Biloxi. The train station itself was very tiny, looking even more so in the dim light. I stood on the platform wondering what to do. Everything seemed to be gloom and shadows. There was a wisp of a fog, not enough to be a problem but it did remind you that the Gulf was nearby.

In my relatively sheltered young life, I had not been very often in the position of deciding what to do with a selection of unfamiliar choices. Standing there, indecisively looking around in the gloom, I realized that I was not alone. There were other people there. All males. And, as I looked more closely, males about the same age as me. Slowly, it dawned on me that a lot of the other passengers in my coach were these same young males, all of us headed for Keesler.

Before I could select one of these other passengers to talk to, there was suddenly a loud male voice, calling out instructions in a voice tone which didn't seem to expect anything but cooperation. Immediate cooperation! The voice ordered us to "Fall in!" Since we weren't even raw recruits yet, he had to explain that fall in meant to line up in several lines in front of him.

After this individual had arranged all of us passengers into a vaguely organized group, he had us march to his government truck. I use the term "march" with some degree of charity. It turned out that we were all college kids destined for the same program and most of the guys had never done any marching at all. I had only done a little in our high school band but that little made me feel like a pro.

Things now started to happen as group-things, not things that affected me as an individual. First Army chow, sometimes berated but really pretty good, especially when you're hungry from the vigors of basic training. Issue of uniforms, that clothing which would be our only type of dress for a long time. A blouse (read jacket) and trousers of wool, colored Olive Drab (OD's as they came to be called.) Shirts and trousers of khaki colored cotton, now to be called "Class A's". Underwear. Shoes, big high-top lace-ups. And dark green work clothes we were taught to call "fatigues", two sets. For the duration of Basic Training, it was the fatigues for wear every day but Sunday. And then the little personal near-ceremony where you packed all your civilian clothing into one bundle for the Army to mail to your home for you. No more civvies for a long time!

Soon there were individual interviews with clerk-typists who started your own record for the Army's benefit. And encounters with medical people; people who examined you and stuck needles into your arms. The war had started to become global and the Army tried to protect you from every disease you might be exposed to later on. Smallpox. Tetanus. Plague. Yellow fever. An occasional wise-guy would crack, "They have a shot for every disease except venereal disease and that's the one that they need most!" Some only hurt from the needle's prick; a few were rather uncomfortable.

This processing of us prospective troops took several days. But, after only a day or two of it, I guess we started to feel like we were real veterans. Every day or so, there would be the arrival of new batches of soon-to-be troops, marching, or more accurately straggling down the streets. For many of us razzling the newcomers became a new amusement. Most of my group were from the same general area of the country—North Alabama, East Tennessee, North Georgia, and South Carolina. Since we had arrived April 6, essentially Spring in our region, we had all arrived wearing only light jackets or sweaters. Occasionally a group of newcomers would be burdened down with long overcoats. To us, all Southerners, this identified that group as "Yankees". For most of us that didn't make all that much difference. But not to some of us, the Georgia boys, who seemed to want to start the Civil War all over again! The rest of us, Southern enough to stand whenever "Dixie" was played, felt that the Georgia boys might just be a tad too emotional about the past. We had signed up with fighting Germans and Japanese in mind, not Yankees.

The favorite razzle, though, was not one out of regional differences. In the early forties radio was well established as the big home entertainment medium, as TV became much later. The grand-dad of a still popular program format was a quiz show. The quizzer would ask the quizee a question and if the answer was correct the quizee won a dollar. On to the next question where the quizee would get twice as much for a correct answer. The questions would get more difficult as the quizee progressed, up until the last question where the prize would be sixty four dollars. The quizmaster would milk the suspense for all he could, building up the drama while the quizee debated whether to take his winnings or try to answer the sixty four dollar question. If the quizee said he would try the last question, in most cases a voice from what sounded like the very rear of the studio audience would shout out "You'll be sorry!" This always brought a laugh from the studio audience. Now, at Keesler, whenever a group of us old pros would see a new group straggling down the street from the train station, we would give them the customary razzle: "You'll be sorry! You'll be sorrrrreeeee!!" In a very few days the stragglers themselves would be pros, just as we were and would continue the tradition. (Reading this many, many years later you should remember that, in 1943, $64 was a respectable little prize.)

After the first few days of interviews and shots had run their course, the routine got down to the real stuff of basic training: drilling and physical training! PT was never a favorite of any of us except for the minority of jocks who lived and breathed athletics and athletic competition.

PT usually involved the customary starting calisthenics, push-ups, sit-ups, side-straddle-hops, running in place, etc. etc. etc. Fortunately none of the dreary soft ball games of college PT where if you were not a jock you were put out in right field where nothing was expected to happen and seldom ever did. After the organized calisthenics, for a finish there would be the obstacle-course run. Actually this was more fun than the organized stuff was. Each base had its own variation of the course, usually with some intimidating name, like "Burma Road", or "Ledo Road", names taken out of the jungle war in Southeast Asia.

Drill never did become better than a chore. And there was lots of it, hours and hours of it. The drill field was a dirt field, sandy dirt that floated up into the air around your face when many feet stirred it. The easy part of it was in drilling as a flight—four lines wide, about eight or ten men deep. After we had learned the basic commands, various members of the flight would take turns calling out the commands (saving the trainer's voice!). It became disagreeable when practicing with a squadron size group, eight or twelve or sixteen men across. Turns were a special problem for squadron size groups and required much more practice. The men on the inside line (or file) had to take half steps while those men in files toward the outside of the turn had to continue taking full steps until all the files on that rank had made the turn. With about 150 pairs of feet shuffling through a turn on dry dusty ground, the dust soon rose to the point where it was hard to see beyond the man in front of you. Though it had not been rainy, there was the usual Gulf-Coast humidity and before long your fatigue suit would be wet with sweat. When the sweat dried later, if you had been taking salt tablets like most of us did, the salt in your sweat would create interesting patterns of white on the dark green of your fatigues when it dried. With only two pairs of fatigues to your name you had two choices later: wear dirty, salt-encrusted fatigues or wash them yourself.

Washing fatigues was not a simple matter of dropping them into the laundry sink and running water in. There were no laundry sinks. The usual method was to take them into the shower room, get a GI brush and a bar of GI soap, wet the garment under the shower, then put it down on the floor and scrub it with the brush. There always was a plentiful supply of GI soap. We used to make jokes about it at later bases, saying that the Army ran on GI soap and six-by-six trucks. This was not a great way to do laundry but it did have advantages. Usually in the shower room you were nude and several sessions under the shower head were refreshing after the heat and dust of the day.

Normally during basic training you were entirely separated and isolated from family, friends or anything else of the civilian world. At Keesler, you also could not leave the base. I had a break about mid-way through Basic. Daddy was working for the US Department of Agriculture in a job which involved frequent traveling. On this Sunday afternoon I was relaxing on my cot in our barracks, not having anything to do and throughly enjoying that feeling. The CQ (Charge of Quarters, a man detailed to the job for the day), told me to go to the MP (Military Police) entrance gate to see a visitor. I went and found Daddy there. He wangled permission for me to leave the base for a couple of hours in his custody and we spent the time walking around residential streets of Biloxi. It was good to see a family member and I was thankful that he was able to talk me out of the base for our short time together.

The traditional picture of a drill sergeant in movies is a person with a fiery disposition coupled with hair-trigger impatience. I guess we were shortchanged when we got ours. First of all, he was not a sergeant, only a corporal. He was a very quiet, soft-spoken individual with a bit of a hill-billy accent. Everybody in our flight thought he was great. No shouting at us, no scenes of irate nagging. He spoke softly, gently, yet we all obeyed more quickly than if he had shouted at us. I guess he was a devout church-goer because we never heard a profane or obscene word out of him. Not so with a sergeant several notches up in the chain of command. That individual couldn't say five words without two or three of them being profane or obscene. I think he was from one of the New York City boroughs. We were all Southerners and not used to being talked to that way. I found later that men from the New York-New Jersey area could sometimes get into the loudest of shouting arguments and never come to blows. That's not the way it was in our area of the world—a loud shouting argument in the South frequently led to either a shooting or a cutting encounter. We were all in a subservient position as recruits and it rankled until by a sudden, common agreement we staged a sit-down revolt. The captain in charge of our overall unit fortunately (for all of us) decided to negotiate. Two or three of our guys acted as spokesmen. They told the Captain that the only thing we couldn't take was being cursed at; that we had been following all the sergeant's orders and would continue to do so, provided he didn't curse at us. Probably if we had been a bunch of draftees, the captain and the sergeant would have lowered the boom on all of us as a group. But we were in a group of volunteers, selected to be potential air crew officers and the captain must have decided that it would be much better for him if he could quietly defuse the situation. A little more quiet discussion followed; our leaders promised that we would do everything we were ordered to—if the orders did not include cursing at us—and the captain said he would have his sergeant control his language. End of mutiny!

No account of Basic Training, at least World War II Basic Training would be really complete without KP (Kitchen Police) stories. Yes, we all pulled KP. The old movies about KP always showed the KP peeling huge piles of potatoes with a little paring knife. We were spared that, thank goodness. All of the mess halls were large consolidated mess halls, each feeding several hundred men. The potatoes were all peeled by a large institutional potato peeling machine. What a blessing! A blessing because hash browned potatoes were very frequently on the menu and the Army hash browns were a delight to a potato fan.

KP's reported to their assigned mess hall about an hour before serving time for that mess. Usually this was about a quarter to five (AM!). The first thing to happen was that the mess sergeant would assign you to one of the work teams. Dining room crew organized the tables, served the food from the steam table, cleaned up the tables after the meal and then mopped the floor. It was mopped after every meal! China Clipper crew (usually one or two men) manned the China Clipper—the big dishwashing machine. Kitchen Crew helped the cooks in all the helper-type chores. Pots and Pans washed pots and pans (surprisingly one of the easiest assignments). Garbage detail did what the name implies—kept scraps and other debris in the proper cans and took the cans out to the garbage can rack outside. Except for one tour on Pots and Pans, I usually ended up on the dining room crew. That one seemed to keep you busier than the others, since you always seemed to be tidying up, on the steam table, or manning one of the mops! As an occasional detail, KP was not all that bad, though it could grow wearisome on an every-day basis. As Daddy often said, "Gets common in a hurry!"

In the early planning days for the Army, the planners decided that instead of using chinaware in the dining room, they would adopt a stainless steel serving tray. It was stamped out of a sheet of stainless steel and had several compartments of various sizes for the items in the menu. After eating his meal, a troop would dip his used tray into a 32 gallon can of hot water and then hand it to the China Clipper crew. The trays' trip through the China Clipper did not take much time and the Clipper crew would put the newly washed tray on the rack for the next diner. The Clipper used very hot water and the last step was probably a blast of live steam. Consequently all the trays in the rack were very hot. While this is good for hygienic reasons and kept the meat and gravy nice and hot, it was bad news for the dessert, especially if the dessert was Jell-O or ice cream. After eating several meals in the mess hall, you frequently would find yourself eating your Jell-O while you were still going to your table. Even then it was half melted. It was almost as bad for ice cream, though it did last just a little longer than Jell-O.

In the Basic Training for the Infantry or the Marine Corps, recruits were probably introduced to their future weapon, learning its care, firing, and ceremonial use. We were Air Corps and the only weapons we ever saw was either the pistol in an MP's holster, or the pistol which was ostentatiously placed next to the pile of money by the Captain paying us on payday. (Months later and several Bases later when I went to Gunnery School I had weeks of nothing much except guns.)

The routine of PT, Drill, and KP seemed to go on for a long time but actually it covered only four weeks and that included the time spent establishing our personnel records. Then it was time to move on to CTD—the College Training Detachment!

Of course the move would be by troop train. Practically all the transfers were by troop train if you were in an enlisted status as we were. Even some of the later moves for officers were by troop train. This meant that when you were on a troop train you didn't deal with the conductor on tickets and the whole train, or at least your whole coach, was for your group. World War II was the last major war where trains were used extensively to move people. Aircraft were just beginning to come into use and weren't all that numerous.

Trains were numerous then. But the job of moving so many people strained even the railroads' inventory of equipment and you never knew what kind of a railroad car you would be riding in. On one later move we guessed that the cars might have been of a vintage of around 1910—the passage between cars was not enclosed and you could look down at the track passing under you. One later move used a very novel type car. The railroad (or maybe it was the Army) took freight box-cars and installed double-decker bunks in them. Fine for sleeping but boring in the day time. There were no windows, only the big open loading door which we kept open. With no windows it soon became a boring ride in the day time. One guy amused himself by singing endless versions of "Ida Red, Ida Blue", a short country-music two line jingle. Examples:

> Ida Red, Ida Blue, prettiest gal I ever knew.
> Ida Red, Ida Green, prettiest gal I ever seen.
> Ida Red, Ida Brown, prettiest gal in town.
> Ida Red, Ida Yellow, prettiest gal when she gets mellow.

Most of us gave up on hoping he would shut up and found ourselves trying to make up new verses. We blamed it on boredom.

We all happily boarded the troop train which would take us to our College Training Detachment. At the time we boarded the train we didn't know which College it would be. I guess I automatically assumed it would be my alma mater, Birmingham—Southern, since there had been a CTD established there before I was called to active duty. I'm sure many of the other guys in our group were assuming that it might be their alma mater. Before arriving at our destination we learned that it would be University of Tennessee at Knoxville. So, a few of us got their wish and we had several happy Vols in our group.

UNIVERSITY OF TENNESSEE

Knoxville

The College Training Detachment (CTD) concept, serious though it tried to be, was like a movie set for a Western movie, all front and no back. We had classes, though the classes didn't seem to have much reason for being given. They were about high school level and I can't remember that there ever were any tests. There was PT every day but aside from having to march every where we went there were no long periods of Drill as there had been in Basic Training. It was never stated as such but to me, the CTD was the Air Corps way of holding for the Corps men who had shown some interest in flying. And, during the holding period keep them in good physical shape. On the surface this might sound cynical but to become a pilot an individual needed, in most cases, an interest and desire to fly. While we were in the CTD, the Army was building up the many Divisions of ground troops that would be used in 1944 in Europe and Asia. It would probably have used those of us who wanted to fly along with the ones having no interest in flying if we had not been pigeon-holed already in the CTDs, The high point, to me, was that they told us that we would have ten hours of actual flying time. I had never been up in a plane.

After we left Keesler, our group became a little more diverse, gaining a good many fellows from Chicago and Ohio. The largest number of us were housed in one of the large gyms. I was not in this large group. My group was much smaller and we were housed in a three story, narrow frame building. I never could figure out what the building was used for originally but it seemed more like either a rooming house or a small apartment building. It had lost its original character and for us had nothing but a lot of double-decker bunks. This was my first experience with double deckers and in this place, as in most of the later ones, I seemed to always end up by being assigned the top bunk. At first I was a little apprehensive about sleeping in an upper bunk, afraid that I would fall out of bed in my sleep. But I never did fall. The guy in the lower bunk this time was a fairly short, stocky guy from Chicago, named Phil Roschung.

I can't remember exactly how one got into an upper bunk. As I remember it, I think you faced the bunks and put your hands on the side rail of your (upper) bunk. You gave sort of a vigorous upward jump and as your body was rising you would help the upward momentum of your body by pushing down on the side rail, then at the top of your jump, twist your body around so that your rump landed on your bed. If you were not heavy (I wasn't, 140 pounds max), and in fairly good shape it became easy to do. The only minor inconvenience was when you might get up during the night to go to the latrine (that's what we now were supposed to call a toilet.) Going out, you would try to avoid coming down on top of the lower bunkmate if he had his feet out and, coming back, for Mr. Lower there would be the frame shaking impact when you got back into the bed. I always felt that that was his problem, the small price he paid for the convenience of the lower bunk.

Phil (Mr. Lower in my case) was a rather quiet fellow. One night he had earned the privilege of a short pass which he probably used to go to a movie. A couple of the other guys in our room decided to play a practical joke on him. The beds had flat wire springs, connected at each end to a line of coil springs. These jokers disconnected the coil springs at the head of Phil's bed from the flat spring, then tied the flat spring to the end coils with a length of light string, put the mattress back, and remade the bed. We had Taps at ten o'clock and lights must be out by that time. Phil came in about an hour later and undressed in the dark; then got into his bed. The string broke of course, as it was supposed to do, and poor Phil lay there with the foot of his bed still attached to the coil springs while the head end of his mattress now rested on the floor.

As I said, Phil was a quiet fellow and, staying in form, he just lay there for several long seconds, muttering "Shit-eating dog! Shit-eating dog!!!" The conspirators felt sorry for him; someone had a flashlight and they helped him reconnect the coil springs so he could sleep on an even keel.

The biggest complaint many of us had against University of Tennessee was the hilly nature of the campus. This was not entirely new to me, since I had been attending Birmingham-Southern for three years and it had a hilly campus; in fact, one nickname for us was "Hilltoppers". Probably the hills of U.T. were not much more rugged but what complicated it for some of us was the fact that you had to march in formation most of the time when going from one area to another. As we learned at Keesler, before you started to march, you had to "Fall in", forming four lines facing to the side. The flight commander would then order "If the man to your right is shorter than you, then swap places." A few minutes of shuffling around would ensue until the flight was neatly arranged with the tallest men in front and each rank progressively shorter toward the rear. The very tallest guy—the guide— was in a rank by himself in the file which would be on the right. The shortest guys would be in the last rank. Then at a command to "Right Face!"; everybody turned to their right in place and the leader gave the command to march. This was fine at Keesler with its flat terrain and nobody suffered. But at Knoxville the terrain was fairly hilly and if a fairly tall guy was the guide you would usually hear some of the shorties in the last rank plead "Hey! Shorter steps so we can keep up!" The flight leader set the frequency of the steps but the tall guide would be setting the length of the steps.

This hilliness gave birth to what became one of our favorite marching songs, sung to the tune of "When the Saints Go Marching In." We sang it:

> "Oh when we leave this hilly place,
> Oh when we leave this hilly place,
> Oh Lord I want to be in that number, when we leave this
> hilly place!"

The Army did try to keep a little more Army tradition in our routine than living on a college campus would in itself provide. They had us stand guard duty. At the lowest level, the actual guard was a "Sentry". Next level up was "Corporal of the Guard." Each sentry was assigned a position to guard, his post. The posts were numbered: "Post Number One. Post Number Two." Etc, Etc. If a guard wanted some help, he would call out: "Corporal of the Guard! Post Number One (or whatever his post was)". The Corporal of the Guard, when he heard this, was supposed to come over and relieve the Sentry or find what he wanted. I think I pulled Guard only once; ours was a quiet barracks. But apparently things were different at the Posts guarding the big gymnasium where the largest number of our men were quartered.

The stories of the guards at the gym probably were exaggerated some in retelling but apparently there was some basis of fact behind them. Apparently a young teen-age girl, reputedly a nymphomaniac, had discovered the gym's occupants and the system of guards and made the area her stalking grounds. I hesitate to use the girl's name, assuming that the stories about her were true. Let's just call her H____. After Taps for the guys in the gym, she would go to one of the guard posts and strike up a conversation with the guard. Apparently neither would mince words and when they reached a quick agreement, he would call out "Corporal of the Guard! Post Number (his post number)". When the Corporal came to the Post, he would relieve the sentry who would adjourn to the shadows with H____. She reputedly would approach several other sentries the same night. H____ never got around to our building. Like I said, it was one of the smaller buildings and she probably felt it would not be a fertile hunting ground. How true these stories were I can't say but at a later base I did room with a guy who claimed he had spent a week-end with H____.

At the CTD there were no GI mess halls for our meals. The University was responsible for feeding us and we had a choice between two eating places. One of them was in a large University-owned building. It was a large institutional type cafeteria on the ground floor of what was apparently a women's dormitory. (We were there during the summer months so there were few coeds there—the few coeds were mostly school teachers—probably married—who were there to pick up a course or two in the summer). The other dining choice was our favorite, Briscoe's. Briscoe's was more of a small commercial type restaurant, operating for us as a small cafeteria with a menu more approaching a GI Mess—meat and potatoes, good gravy; substantial things to appeal to healthy active young males. We usually chose Briscoe's.

I had been raised as a Southern Baptist and while I attended church fairly regularly, I tended to get bored during the sermons. At college I discovered that I enjoyed the Episcopalian service more. Not having been to church at all while in Basic Training and during the first weeks at UT, I decided to go to the large Episcopal Church near the campus. I guess I picked an unusual Sunday to go. The Church had their regular service and the liturgy and music were beautiful. Then, there were two more events scheduled for the same sitting. I believe one was either a Baptism or a Confirmation and I believe the other one might have been an Ordination of a new Priest. All very enjoyable but a rather long while to sit. Afterwards one of my fellow students and I were standing outside the Church, trying to decide what to do. We felt that Briscoe's or the Cafeteria were probably closed by then and so where could we eat?

An older couple (probably late fifties) approached us and asked "Would you young men like to have Sunday Dinner with us?" Both of us being Southerners, we knew we would be missing a good experience if the couple called it "Sunday Dinner". We also knew she meant the noon day meal, not the evening meal. Before we could answer, the woman said, "I'm sure my granddaughter would like to meet you." We were getting ready to accept anyway and her added inducement clinched the deal. It turned out that the granddaughter was about eleven years old, a nice girl but still only eleven. The food was sumptuous, though, as only a real Southern Sunday Dinner, prepared by a real chef of a black lady, can be. It reminded me of the Dinners put together by my grandmama in Southern Mississippi! It was almost a heavenly reward for sitting patiently so long in church.

One Saturday night, about forty-five minutes before we were due to be back in our quarters, there was an unusual little incident. Three or four of us were standing around on the corner nearest our quarters. One of the streets was mostly just one of the streets of the Campus. The other apparently was a through-road, leading out into the countryside. Everything was fairly quiet and there was no one in sight other than our little group. A car came up the street from the direction of the open country. Inside were several women who broke into cries of "Hey! It's soldiers! Hi, Guys!" The car didn't even slow down. One of our group asked "Who in the world was that?" Another of our group—who lived in Knoxville before being called into the Army—said, "Oh, it's just some of the workers from that big project."

"What kind of project?" someone asked.

"It's out at Oak Ridge. Something big but it's so secret no one knows what they're doing there." Group reaction was a shrug, then talk turned to another subject.

The time for our ten hours of flying finally came. Originally it was planned to be the full ten hours but I guess the University's resources didn't permit ten hours, so it was scaled back to four. Actually, I think I only got about two hours. Even so, it was something of a disappointment because the planes were not all that exciting. They were either Taylorcraft or Piper Cubs. High-wing monoplanes, constructed of metal tubing and covered with doped fabric. I guess that they probably might be fun for a pilot to fly. But the passenger seat was not a fun place to be. You sat immediately behind the pilot, your feet on either side of his hips. The seat was almost on the floor and there were no passenger windows, just the doped-fabric skin of the fuselage. You could see a little bit of sky over the pilot's shoulders but you saw little of the ground except when the pilot put the craft into a steep banking turn. The engine was a little noisy but not impressively noisy. And since there was only the pilot's flight controls a passenger couldn't feel the controls at all during the flight. The plane was not what I had expected but I knew it would have to be different in other planes. About all you could say for the rides was that you had been up in a plane.

Collectively for all of us there was not much overall effect from the flights. We did learn, though of one individual where that was not the case. Among the overall group of students (we couldn't call ourselves Cadets yet) was one individual who stood out from all the rest of us for his impressive military bearing. He had been named Student Commander (or some empty title like that) and would be the student commander for any of our parades or reviews. He supposedly had been going to The Citadel in South Carolina and I'm sure he had some high ranking cadet rank there. When he went up for his plane ride he found out that he absolutely, positively did not like to fly. Even in an inoffensive little Cub plane. So, he was taken out of the program at his own request. No reflection on him; it's just that some people like to fly and some don't. I didn't know him or what happened to him later. I would guess that he probably had a better time of it in one of the ground elements of the Army.

Living together in a large group, there would usually be some individual or individuals who had a recurring mannerism which you would tend to remember. I remember one individual, a guy whose last name was Wilhelm. He was a slow-riser and hated to get up early. After our reveille, he would stretch leisurely, then say, "I know what I want to be when I get out of the Army. I want to be a Kept Man." To him this meant that he could always get up when he felt like it.

Another fellow liked to start the day with a little couplet of his own. He would stretch leisurely, look around, then say "This is June____, nineteen hundred forty-three; another day nearer to Victoree!" After a week or two, it first started being boring. Then, as we became accustomed to it, it was like the proverbial man in bed waiting for the guy upstairs to drop the other shoe.

There was PT every day; very strenuous PT. The man who conducted the PT session was not an Army person. He was University of Tennessee's football coach, or one of them. Apparently several of UT's football team members were among us Aviation Students and we were firmly convinced that the coach was making a determined effort to keep his former football members in good physical shape in case the war suddenly ended and he would be trying to put together a winning team. We did our calisthenics in the football stadium and he usually asked for more than the PT leaders at Keesler had asked for. Then, after nearly wearing us out, he would come out with the big finish. Whereas at Keesler it had been the Burma Road, UT had no Burma Road. The coach would order that we would run up the steps of the stadium to the top level, then down, then repeat the trip several times. A real sadist and we disliked him enthusiastically.

CTD finally came to an end and I was not disappointed. I did not particularly like University of Tennessee, though it never went so far as hating it. I guess it was some lingering disappointment that the CTD had not been the one at Birmingham Southern where I still had strong interests.

NASHVILLE

We had been told—at Keesler, I believe—that the CTD period of our training would be for about five months. It actually lasted approximately three months. I assumed that we would go next to Maxwell Army Air Base in Montgomery, Alabama, for the first phase of our cadet training, called Pre Flight. I was looking forward to being at a base in Alabama but we found out that we had to go to another base first for about a month. This base was located at Nashville, Tennessee. I'm not sure what the base's name was but I think it was something like "Nashville Army Air Classification Center". It was a fairly small base whose sole purpose (at least to my knowledge) was to classify us as either Pilot Cadets, Navigator Cadets, or Bombardier Cadets. I had never even considered the last two alternatives.

"Going to Nashville" gave me no thrill of anticipation. Country Music was pretty far down on my list of entertainments, even though Nashville was the home of the Grand Ole Opry. Aside from an occasional Patsy Cline record, I leaned much more toward either The Big Band Sound (Tommy Dorsey, Benny Goodman, Glenn Miller, etc.) or Opera (Wagner, Verdi). To me, Nashville was just another large town. Getting there involved the inevitable troop train ride, this one about six or eight hours long.

The base, as might be expected, was like most World War II Army bases. Built in minimum time, they were all made with wood frame buildings, unimpressive to look at but reasonably comfortable and functional. There would be no more college cafeteria or Briscoe's for us. It would be GI mess halls and guess who would be the KP's!

I never learned what the Army's basis was for classifying us into the different Cadet categories. Personal preference was probably one factor. There were several psychological tests. Some involved doing intricate hand movements while at the same time ignoring conflicting distractions. I assume that doing well on that one showed aptitude for being a bombardier. I could never see any connection for the other tests. My classification pegged me as number one for pilot training and number two for navigator training.

Unlike our stint at Keesler, we weren't confined to the Base during our whole stay. Going off base never did involve going into downtown Nashville. I don't know why, since I never had any clear knowledge of how close to downtown the base was. Maybe it was too long a bus ride, if there was any bus service. We could go off base on week-ends, though it was never anything memorable.

I guess my most vivid memory of Nashville was the KP tour I was hood-winked into. I was detailed the job once or twice and I don't remember much about those legitimate stints. The one I do remember was one tour I had to pull, even though I had not been detailed for that particular tour. You were detailed to the job when your name showed up on a roster for the next day's duty. We had the usual double decker bunks, and, as usual, I ended up in a top bunk. The individual in the lower below me was also named Thompson. To get up early for KP detail, the Charge of Quarters, usually a Corporal, would wake up each person detailed a couple of hours before Reveille. For this particular KP detail, the other Thompson (Mr. Lower Bunk in my case) was detailed for KP. Although the other Thompson had gone to bed at Taps, when time for the CQ to wake him up, his bunk was empty.

The CQ woke me up and asked where the guy was. Sleepily I said he's probably in the latrine. The CQ went into the latrine, looked around and finding no one, came back to the bunk.

"What's your name?" he asked me.

"Thompson."

"Get up. You're on KP!"

"But I'm not the one on the schedule!"

"Your name is Thompson, isn't it?"

"Yes, but . . ."

"Shut up! Get up! You're on KP."

I was probably shrewd enough to realize that it was an unwinnable argument, got up, and reported to the mess hall for duty. When I tried to pin the other Thompson down later he would only give me evasive answers. Obviously he had slipped out of the barracks and had hidden in the darkness until the CQ rounded up his crew of KP's. Thankfully this was the only time I was in the same immediate flight with another Thompson, even though it's a common name.

The time at the Nashville base seemed to pass quickly without generating any significant memories, other than my unexpected stint of KP duty. Then the usual troop train ride to Montgomery.

MAXWELL

Montgomery, Alabama

Maxwell Army Air Base was going to be different. Keesler was one of the new Air Bases, constructed during the big Army build-up shortly before and at the beginning of World War II. But Maxwell was one of the few old ones with lots and lots of permanent buildings. It was built in the days of the old Army Air Corps Bases—Langley in Virginia, Bolling in District of Columbia, Mitchell on Long Island, Randolph and Kelly in Texas, March in California. Lots of permanent buildings and lots of grassy lawn. I had passed the base several times; US 31 passed along the western side. But I had never been inside the base.

We were a little surprised by our quarters. I don't know if they were called barracks or cadet quarters. They were long one-story buildings with a long porch passageway connecting a number of pairs of rooms. Each room was paired with another room with a connecting bath/shower. I suspect that our assignment to our room was a little more crowded than the planners had originally intended. There were seven of us in our room—three double-decker bunks around the room and one single decker cot in the room center. There was a row of lockers along one wall. Built-in. No living out of a barracks bag at this base! I don't remember the names of all my room-mates. I was closest friend with one, Frank Trebisky, and there was one named Smith and another named Webb.

One of the first and most important—to us—things to happen to us was getting our "Cadet Issue". We all still wore the uniforms which we had been issued at Keesler. They were army uniforms but there was little distinctive about them. Very apt for our nonentity status as Aviation Students. But now we were going to become Aviation Cadets. Not too long before, I believe, Cadet Uniforms were the same material as officers uniforms, i.e., "pinks" and greens. That practice had been discontinued long before we arrived. For us, it would still be the same OD's (Olive Drab, remember?). But military uniforms don't rest entirely on the cloth; a lot depends on the added hardware and other frills. We kept the OD's and khaki chinos but now were issued the hardware and frills.

The big item was the "Mister hat." A regular Olive Drab enlisted billed cap but without the enlisted brass button with its superimposed eagle (a replica of the eagle on the back of a dollar bill). The eagle would be gone now. In its place would be the Air Corps symbol—a set of wings with a propeller superimposed on the wings. The same design that Air Corps officers wore on the lapels of their blouse to denote their service branch. Only, the one on the Mister hat was a much bigger rascal, the wings about four inches from tip to tip and the propeller correspondingly long. When in uniform and not wearing the Mister hat there was also the usual overseas cap, a more comfortable headwear. It had the wing and propeller Corps insignia but of the size worn on blouse lapels.

The other items were smaller. Cadet patches—circles of cloth with an embroidered background and embroidered Corps design. These went on the sleeves. And, not to be forgotten, a couple of pairs of white cotton gloves. These were to be worn when participating in Parades.

One of the first and most useful skills I learned, right away, was how to tie my tie while running. We had to wear a tie when outside our quarters at all times. Not with the current Ascot knot but with the simpler old four-in-hand knot and the tie's end had to be tucked inside your shirt in the space between the second and third button down from the collar. Most of the things we did were reached and left by marching there in the usual flight formation. There were fairly frequent returns to our quarters between different activities. If you ever spent any time in Montgomery, Alabama, you would really get to know what high humidity is! Our quarters were not air-conditioned of course (in case you were not around in the nineteen forties, it should be noted that hardly any places beside movie theaters were air conditioned!) When you got back to the quarters on one of these break intervals, the first thing you did was take off your tie and shirt. The quarters were all connected to the Orderly Room by a loudspeaker system. End-of-break was a call to assemble in the street by the Orderly Room—IMMEDIATELY. You threw your shirt on, tucked it in, and as you ran to the assembly area you finished buttoning the shirt and tying the tie. Were you expecting maybe a compliment for responding so quickly? Forget it!

Being a bunch of recently ex-college kids, you might expect that someone would try a practical joke. One of the guys in our room—I forget who it was—pulled one which among practical jokers might be called a classic. As I noted, each room was connected to the orderly room by a loudspeaker system. Naturally it was a one-way system, incoming messages only. The speaker for our room was mounted on the wall above the row of built-in lockers. That wall was the common wall with the room on the other side of our connecting bath and their speaker was located just as ours was. This genius-joker of ours managed to climb up on top of the built-in lockers and put his mouth against our speaker, cupping his hands around his mouth to direct the sound into the speaker. Surprisingly, it must have sounded in the other room like an announcement from the Orderly Room. Our Master-Joker made an announcement, something like: "Attention all Cadets! Attention all Cadets! Raincoats will be carried at all formations today. Repeat: Raincoats will be carried at all formations today." Then he quietly hopped down. Our raincoats were the standard GI rubber raincoats which we had been taught to fold into a neat bundle. When we got the call to fall-out, all seven of the guys in our adjoining room were carrying their folded up raincoats. It was a beautifully sunny day and nobody else in the flight had a raincoat. There were several of these in-and-out episodes and all during most of the day, the poor souls from next-door faithfully carried their raincoats.

Although we were tempted to tell them; we never did have the heart to tell them of the trick. Why should we? That would put the ball in their court and they would have to pay us back.

I believe that in the cadet program of earlier years, there was much of the system in effect at the Academies (West Point; Annapolis), i.e. hazing of the lower or newer classes by the earlier classes. This had been discontinued before we arrived but they tried to continue the remnants of the device used to instill the honor system. The remnant of the system was a modern version of a "Drum out". There were two or three of these during our 9 weeks at Maxwell, always a surprise when one was held. You would go to bed at your usual time—the loudspeaker would sound the bugle call "Call to Quarters" a little before ten, then at ten "Taps" and you'd better have the lights out by the time the bugle call finished. About two hours later, the loudspeaker system would call everyone to an immediate formation outside in the assembly area. You fell out quickly and formed into a formation and were called to attention. Then the loudspeaker system would read out an announcement that a certain cadet had been guilty of a grave violation of the honor system and as a consequence, he was being dishonorably expelled from our cadet corps. It was moderately impressive the first one we were called out for. But there were a couple more during our stay and I got the feeling that they were being staged for effect. Who knows? Most of our daily routine didn't seem to present that many opportunities to violate the code.

What hadn't been relaxed though was the frequent quarters inspections. There was the usual likelihood of a daily inspection, consequently your bed had to be made up according to specifications as soon as you were up. The floor had to be swept and the latrine tidied up after everyone had shaved, brushed and tended to any other necessary chores there. Failure to meet the requirements could result in gigs and over a certain number of gigs meant no open post on Saturday or Sunday. This was daily routine. But the biggie was the Friday night GI Party. After your first one, you knew that a GI Party was not a party in the manner you might hope for. It meant you had to GI your quarters area—clean every possible nook and corner that might harbor dust or a dust-bunny or smudge on a window. It was a battle of wits between the Cadets and the eye of the inspecting officer at Saturday Morning Inspection. The most eagle-eyed of the inspecting officers was a Captain Turner. He had been known to prowl through the area during the GI Party, making sure that everyone was showing full diligence. The rooms were heated by steam heat and the steam came into the room via a large, asbestos covered pipe which was suspended a foot or so lower than the ceiling. On one SMI (Saturday Morning Inspection, remember?) Capt. Turner, who prided himself on his athletic ability, leaped up and caught onto the steam pipe, held on for a few seconds, then dropped down to look at his snow white inspection gloves to see if they had picked up any dust from the steam pipe. I doubt if he had ever done this more than once or twice but the story of it was part of our lore. On one GI Party night, it was summer time and all the windows were open, being diligently cleaned. One Cadet called out to one of his room mates, "Hey. You better clean off the steam pipe. If you don't, Tarzan Turner will swing on it!" In the story, Tarzan Turner (better known as Captain Turner) was prowling around outside the back windows of the quarters and overheard the reference to him. The story tellers report that he never did try swinging on the pipes again.

We did no drill practice, on the assumption that we had learned how to march during basic training. In basic training there had been hours of drill, first in flight size formations (i.e., four men across.) That was the basic formation for moving a group from one point on a base to a destination point. Now we were introduced to "Parades". Parades were a regular feature at Maxwell, one at the end of the day on about three of the days of the week, and a Saturday Morning Parade every other Saturday. I guess that parades can be a fairly impressive sight if the troops march well; if there is a good band; if the weather is pleasant, and if you didn't have something more pressing you would like to be doing. For the parade, you always wore the "Mister hat"—the one with the bill and the big cadet insignia and without fail your white gloves. The troops would line up about seventy five yards from the reviewing stand, facing the stand. You marched to the parade ground in flight formation, the first flight taking its position and halting. Then the next flight marched up and halted next to the first flight's position. You now had eight men abreast. There would be either one or two more flights joining the formation, giving a twelve or sixteen man front—a squadron. Then the next squadron would march into place, leaving a little open space between themselves and your squadron. This continued until all the squadrons were in place; all facing the reviewing stand, standing at parade rest. Each three or four squadrons would constitute a group and the group commander would stand about fifteen or twenty feet in front of his group. I don't know how many cadets were involved in our parades; at one time I guessed it was between five and ten thousand total. When all the troops had marched onto the field and had formed up the line, the band, which had been playing as we formed up, would usually play another march. Then, the reviewing party would move quietly into their reviewing place. When they were in place, the parade adjutant would march out to his place. This was especially funny if the adjutant moved at the old, traditional "adjutant's pace", a brisk walk with the arms rigidly down at his sides. He would halt, turn to face the troops and bellow out the order "Call your troops to attention." The Group Commanders, who had been facing the reviewing stand would do a formal 'about face' maneuver to face their squadrons, then bellow out "Group . . .", the squadron commanders in turn would 'about face' to face their squadron, and echo "Squadron . . ." Then the group commander would finish the order . . . "Attention!" which was echoed by the squadron commanders. And we would all snap from Parade Rest to Attention. This amusing little routine actually dramatized the chain of command and thus had an underlying serious purpose. A parade was an opportunity to dramatize some big order changing things, or recognize some particular person or feat. At most of our parades there was nothing dramatic to announce, so they would announce some very mundane announcement, such as "Officer of the Day is Lt. ____". When any announcements or other business were finished, the adjutant would shout out the order "Pass in Review!".

The Group Commanders would order "Pass in Review," and the Squadron Commanders gave the appropriate command—for the first squadron it was "Right Turn, March!" The order for the adjoining squadrons was "Stand Fast," which they did until the first squadron was on their way, then the next squadron would turn out and follow the first squadron. The first squadron would immediately make a left turn, march about thirty or forty yards and then make another left turn. This put them on course to pass right in front of the reviewing officer(s). A few yards before reaching the reviewer, the Squadron Commander would order "Eyes, right!" and as you marched past the reviewer, the Squadron Commander would salute for the whole squadron. Once the squadron was past the reviewer, the Squadron CO would order "Ready, front!". And the squadron would continue marching off the parade ground while the following squadrons were passing the reviewer in the same way. Usually as soon as you were away from the parade ground the squadron would break into flights which were much more practical for covering distance (and usually looked neater too!)

One of the pluses for my particular flight was that our squadron was the first to pass the reviewer. Our quarters were close to the parade ground and we would rush inside, shed the white gloves and exchange the Mister Hat for a flat flight cap. We would rush outside into a formation and march to the huge Cadet Mess while other squadrons were still waiting to pass in review. A very satisfactory arrangement for the chow hounds among us! (Weren't we all?)

About every second or third week-end, we would have a free Saturday and you could be gone from Friday night until Sunday night. On one of these, Frank Trebisky and I went to Birmingham for dates. Mine was with Mary Louise, who I had been dating while at 'Southern. She had gotten a date for Frank with one of her sorority sisters. We had a very quiet time of it and I guess it was more unusual for Frank who was from Ohio, since it may have been his first date with a southern girl (who was also a 'Southern girl!).

My more memorable long week-end was the one where I

planned to go back to Cullman by bus and see my family. I had been looking forward to that and had alerted Mama of the proposed visit. At the last minute my name showed up on the list of Cadets scheduled for guard duty on Saturday night. That pretty much squashed my plans for a visit home. I guess I must have walked around with a long face when an acquaintance in our flight asked me what was wrong. He was Frank Tuttle, from Illinois. I told him that I was planning to go home over the week-end by bus but being scheduled for guard duty made it impossible. With typical Mid-west friendliness, Frank said, "I'll stand guard for you. Just go. I'd like to see my family too but Illinois is a little too far for a week-end bus trip for me." So I was able to be home for Saturday and part of Sunday, seeing my Mother and brother for the first time in several months, thanks to Frank. Unfortunately Daddy's job kept him away most of the time but I had at least seen him for a couple of hours while at Keesler.

While the new cadet routine became a little dull after several weeks, the time spent in it was finite and we finished on schedule, ready for the troop train ride to the next phase, Primary Flight Training.

CARLSTROM AAB

Arcadia, Florida

In the late thirties and early forties, Arcadia, Florida, was a rather small south Florida town. I don't know what their economy was based on then but my guess is it would have been orange growing. They must have had a Congressman with a little more than average influence because the town, small as it was, actually had been selected as the site for two primary flight training bases. Carlstrom and another separate base, Dorr. Both were operated by contractors who contracted to run the base, maintain the aircraft, and instruct the students. There was also a small staff of uniformed Army Air Corps personnel who had military control of the cadets being instructed.

The field had been constructed wholly for the training mission. The aircraft were all PT-17 Stearman Trainers, a two-seater biplane. The Stearman had two open cockpits and a big radial air cooled engine. Like most aircraft of the period when they were designed, they had conventional landing gear instead of tricycle. That is, two main landing gear wheels up toward the engine and a small tail wheel underneath the tail. There was no runway; the flying field being a large flat grassy square, about a mile along each side. Along the side nearest the base buildings was a line of hangars. The hangars were for use in repairing the planes or doing routine maintenance; the planes themselves were parked in a long straight line in front of the hangars.

The quarters were one story concrete rooms, with a nice bathroom and concrete floor. They were not crowded as all our previous quarters had been, though we were expected to keep them as clean as we had kept the quarters at Maxwell.

There was one very distinctive feature about the base facilities at Carlstrom that was amusing at first, though it soon became annoying. The water. Sometimes with the water in a particular spot, Mother Nature decides to make it a mineral water. I guess that mineral waters may come in several flavors. This one was hydrogen sulfide. Hydrogen sulfide, that gas which gives rotten eggs their particular unpleasant odor. Since the base was located some distance from any town water supply, the builders apparently sank a well to provide water for the base water system. Bingo! The water they hit with the well was a strongly mineral hydrogen sulfide. After a few days of enduring the water whenever we needed a drink, someone found that out in a grassy field about fifty yards away was a lone outdoor spigot that flowed decent water when you turned it on. Since we all had canteens as part of our GI issue, everyone would go to the good water spigot and fill their canteen, using the mineral water only for shaving and bathing. Apparently the people who operated the Mess didn't feel like going to the good-water-spigot for the water for the Mess. Ever try ice tea or Jell-O made with hydrogen sulfide mineral water? It's a real taste sensation which you should pass up on trying.

Before our introduction to the airplanes there were several classes to be attended first; classes on theory of flight and safety procedures. These were to help keep us from killing ourselves in the air by doing something unsafe. They wanted us to learn what air speed was and how critical it was to keep it above the safe minimum; also what led to a tail spin and how to recover from it, points the flight instructor would emphasize as often as they thought necessary. These were the first classes of any the Army had put us in that I could see a reason for having. And, with this, a real reason.

Aircraft have been built with several different ways to start the engines. In World War I when the engines were much smaller, the usual procedure was for someone to stand in front of the propeller and give a vigorous pull down on it, usually several times before the engine caught and started running.

Later on, several approaches were used: inertia starters, electric starters, even a starter which used a shotgun shell to provide the energy. The Stearman used an inertia starter, a reliable way to start an engine, though a little tedious to use. The starter used a crank, inserted into a receptacle right behind the engine. When flying with an instructor, it was the cadet's job to man the crank. You would take the crank from its bracket in the rear cockpit; climb up on the wing alongside the fuselage near the engine, insert the crank into its receptacle and start cranking. Not like an old Model T Ford where your crank engaged the engine directly. This receptacle opened into the starter, an arrangement with a bunch of connecting gears and wheels. You would start turning the crank; which you could only move very slowly at first; then, as you kept cranking it would gradually move faster and faster. The train of gears inside the starter were slowly building up momentum, actually storing your cranking energy for release in a more powerful form when it engaged the engine. When the crank was turning fast enough the person starting the engine could engage the engine and it would start. It sounds like a bit of a "Rube Goldberg" arrangement but usually it started the engine right away. If you were flying with an instructor, he would engage the starter. But if you were flying solo, you had to come down off the wing, climb into the rear cockpit, replace the crank in its bracket, and then engage the engine with the starter. Once started, the engines were docile and did what you wanted them to do. However before moving the plane you needed to buckle the buckles on your parachute harness and, by all means the seat belt which kept you in the cockpit if the plane flew upside down. This latter item was an important personal point. Regardless of your personal or political or other viewpoints, your safety could depend on whether you had done the right mechanical things in fastening your parachute harness and the seat belt!

The Stearman was a simple piece of machinery and, generally a forgiving plane. The learning process involved a pilot trying to transfer a physical skill to an individual he was not in direct communication with. This was it! Not a complicated sounding requirement. But the communication was all one way—via the

Gosport. The Gosport was simply a speaking tube. It did not require the complicated electrical system of the Intercom system used in combat aircraft. There was no overall plane's electrical system; the engines got their firing spark from twin magnetos which were part of the engine. Stearmans were designed to be simple, rugged and uncomplicated. And the Gosport was simple, rugged and uncomplicated. First of all, you could barely hear or understand the pilot. It helped if you had an idea of what he was trying to say. Secondly, you may have already formed your own opinion of what might be necessary. No matter, what the instructor ordered was what was important. So, you did what the instructor ordered. And, sad to say for your ego—he was usually right!

I found that handling a Stearman was an unusual experience. The first thing was, you couldn't steer it on the ground except with the brakes. Turn right—toe the right brake down slightly. Turn left—toe the left brake down slightly. The brake pedals were both on the foot rudder pedals. The rudder itself was not effective at taxiing speeds, not until you were up to a certain airspeed. Although in later model tricycle gear planes you could see directly ahead, in a conventional-geared plane, such as the Stearman, the nose reared itself up in the air before you and you couldn't see what was directly ahead of you. Consequently, when you were taxiing, you had to constantly make a series of S turns to right and left to make sure that your propeller was not going to do bad things to anything directly ahead of you. Sort of slowed you down!

One aerodynamic thing I never did understand was the matter of torque. When you were ready to take off and had lined the airplane up onto the direction you wanted to take off, you then pushed the throttle full open. At the same time you had to push one of the rudder pedals to its full down position (I think it was the left pedal) to cancel out the engines torque. If you didn't, the plane would head off in a direction which you did not want it to go. I never understood this.

With a thundering horde of cadets wanting to get airborne at the beginning of the day and again at the end of the day with a horde of cadets trying to land, all at the same time, traffic could become something of a problem. Once I nearly came to grief at the landing time. I had progressed to the point where I was piloting the plane and the instructor pilot was observing. I was coming in to land, our plane and a bunch of others. I thought I was making a good approach; maybe a little too high but I would kill that with a little reduction in power which would cancel out being too high. Suddenly, the instructor took control away from me. He gave the engine full power and we picked up both airspeed and altitude, cancelling out my landing. He continued to control the plane; we flew around the landing pattern again and he made the actual landing. When I asked him what had happened, he said that there was another Stearman immediately below us which I had not seen. If I had continued on with the landing, I would have landed on top of the other plane. A real potential boo-boo which would have spoiled the day for both of us, maybe permanently!

I had logged about eleven or twelve hours of flight time with the instructor pilot when he signaled for me to land at one of our auxiliary landing strips. Once down, he proceeded to get out of his cockpit. "Take it off, fly it around the pattern, and land!" he ordered. This was my signal to solo, if I could.

"Do you think I can?" I asked, timidly.

"I wouldn't have told you to do it if I thought you couldn't," he said. Apparently he had more confidence than I did. But, I taxied over to starting position, gunned the engine, took off, flew around the field and then landed. All alone! I had soloed!

Although I didn't tell the instructor, a private triumph to me was that I had soloed an airplane before I had soloed an automobile! Since Daddy had always had a state-owned automobile, I couldn't drive it. He had given me one or two lessons in shifting gears with a manual shift, but I had never soloed with a car. Now I had soloed in an airplane! The Army didn't realize this but I did and it meant a lot to me. Whatever else came, they couldn't take that away!

Flight instruction continued. There were several flight conditions which I was supposed to learn to do according to the book. Stalls. Spins. Alertness as to what other planes were in the air near me. How much fuel was in the fuel tank and whether the engine was performing normally. And where I was in relation to the ground so I could find my way home.

Spins didn't present any real problems to me. A spin occurs when you have flown the plane into a condition where there is not enough wind flowing over the wings to give the necessary lift to hold the plane up. You then start to drop; the controls lose their effectiveness and the plane starts to nose down, usually spinning around the plane's horizontal axis which is now pointed straight down. Your instinctive reaction is to pull back on the control stick to try to make the nose of the plane lift. This is not effective when you're in a spin. The actual remedy is to put the control stick full forward, in the dive position. When you do this, air starts to flow normally over the wings and controls and you can control the plane, pulling back on the stick to get the nose up out of the diving position. Fortunately I didn't have any problems with spins.

Stalls were another matter. In a stall, you either have reduced the airspeed or changed the angle of attack of the wings to the point where there is not enough wind passing over the wings to give enough lift to keep you airborne. Then, the plane starts to drop. In a textbook stall, you proceed into a stall until the plane drops suddenly, falling into a spin unless you do the right thing promptly. In the textbook maneuver, it is supposed to be a fairly "crisp" motion. I could never do it with the right amount of "crispness", therefore I couldn't do stalls properly. I guess I always could feel the stall starting and wanted to maintain control, so I would ease off on the stick and the stall would lose its crispness. Not the way they wanted!

After accumulating about twenty-five hours of flight time (about fifteen with instructor; ten solo) the instructor(s) decided that I would not meet their standards for being a pilot. Therefore, no more pilot training. I would guess that the reasons were that I had required several more hours than usual of instructor training before soloing; my difficulty in learning stalls, and the near-disaster landing incident. Any way they decided it, there would be no more pilot training for me.

Naturally this was a big disappointment with me. I had wanted very much to learn to fly, really learn to fly. But, psychologically I could handle the disappointment—I could accept the fact that a disappointment wasn't the end of the world. Before leaving the base, I learned that I would likely go into training, still a cadet, as a navigator.

Before leaving Carlstrom, I had one more duty, the purpose of which I have never been able to understand. In aviation training, there is a training device called a Link Trainer. It had a cockpit like the cockpit of an actual plane and with the cockpit covered over by its cover; you "flew" it without actually leaving the ground. It had the full range of flight instruments to fly "blind", that is, relying only on the instrument panel. The instrument panel had a lot more "gages" which I didn't recognize. Instrumentation in the Stearman was Spartan-simple; airspeed meter, altimeter, a magnetic compass and a tachometer. That was it. I learned later when flying as a navigator what all the additional gages in the trainer were, things like the artificial horizon, needle and ball indicator, rate of climb indicator, directional gyro. Why in the world would they put a cadet who had been eliminated from pilot training into a trainer more complicated than a Stearman? For a full hour? My only guess was that it was to fatten up their record showing how much the trainer was used.

VALDOSTA AAB

Valdosta, Georgia

While I was at Valdosta, I don't know what its main mission or missions were. It was not us. I and my fellow washed-out pilot cadets were certainly not the base's main reason for existing. We were there to wait for the next phase of our careers to begin. We were still cadets, meaning we didn't have to do KP duty. But we were not in any kind of training. There weren't any real duties for us to perform, just keep up our normal cadet appearance, keep a low profile, and above all, stay out of trouble. By now it was December, 1943, the weather was cool and we were into the wool Olive Drab uniforms.

The biggest problem at this base was fighting boredom. No real duties and little in the way of base facilities for cadets. There was a nice Service Club for the base lower grade enlisted personnel. It was a place to go to sit and read, or write letters, or listen to music. A nice little place to go when you had nothing to do. Unfortunately, it was "Off Limits" to Cadets. Most of us could understand and even accept that situation without getting upset by it. Except for one individual. Every day or two the Captain who was responsible for us would have a formation where he would take questions from us. This one individual would, nearly every day, ask "Sir. Can we start going to the Service Club again?"

The Captain, a very patient man in spite of this persistent question, would patiently answer, "The Service Club is Off Limits to Cadets. Next question?"

Early in World War II, there was a humorous book published, "See Here, Private Hargrove!" The author was Marion Hargrove, I believe. The book told of the author's misadventures in going through Army training. Hargrove's brother, Rex Hargrove, was one of our group of washed out pilot cadets. Apparently Rex's current aim in life was to have as many misadventures as his famous brother. For example: The Post Exchange had a nice snack bar. We cadets were allowed to use it except during the noon-time rush when it was Off Limits to cadets. Not one to pass up any good opportunity, Rex decided to go there at noon-time for a milk shake lunch. When he went, he wore his Mister Hat, the billed cap with the huge cadet wing and propeller device above the bill. He sat at a table, blissfully slurping away; his hat telling even the people at the far side of the room that there was a cadet there and it was noon-time. I still believe that he was trying to be caught and follow in the foot-steps of Marion. Maybe he was looking to create an incident of his own which he could use to try to "one-up" his famous brother in a future family brag-session?

At Valdosta, Ed Yablonski and I became friends. Ed had been in pilot training at a base which I had never heard of. It was in Missouri, I believe. No matter, that base was past history for him, just as Carlstrom was now for me. Ed and I stayed in touch after the war and still communicate, usually about one letter a year for each of us and an occasional phone call. We were together at Christmas at Valdosta, both of us trying to cheer the other up about being away from our families. Ed was from New Britain, Connecticut. He started out calling me "Rebel". I think I finally convinced him that I thought that there was more to life than trying to relive the Civil War and all my family and relatives were fully reconstructed.

Ed and I knew that we both were scheduled for Navigator training and we kept wondering where that would be. We were a little surprised when we found that before going to Navigation School, we would be going to gunnery school first for training as aerial gunners. I don't think we even knew where this training would be, only that we would go there by the usual troop train. The few weeks in Valdosta soon passed and it was time to move on again. And this was the troop train with the ancient passenger cars, a real experience.

GUNNERY SCHOOL

Buckingham AAB

Fort Myers, Florida

Bored with sitting around in the washed-out cadet pool in Valdosta, most of us were ready for starting some serious training. Unfortunately, the gunnery school was not quite ready for us. They apparently had limited barracks space in permanent buildings, at least until they shipped out a group of students. What to do with this new group? Why, tents of course. The big, square old fashioned squad tent. We would stay in squad tents until space became available in wooden buildings. A squad tent can be made reasonably comfortable if it has a locally constructed wood floor, though it is still usually dark and gloomy inside. But these tents had just been erected, and the only floor was the grassy Florida sand of the base. Beds would be simple folding canvas cots with the usual issue of two OD Army blankets. This was not unbearably uncomfortable, even though it was now January. While South Florida doesn't get bonechilling cold, it does sometimes get rather chilly and worst of all, it's usually damp. But, this inconvenience passed after a few days and we were transferred into wooden buildings. Dry buildings with real wooden floors. And good old double-decker bunk beds with flat springs and mattresses.

The question might be asked that if we were scheduled for Navigator training, why would we be going to gunnery school? Very simple. When they started installing defensive machine guns all over the B-17 bomber (and the B-24 too, I guess) they put a gun or guns up in the nose compartment where the Bombardier and Navigator did their business. Not having been trained as a B-17 crewman, I would guess that the Bombardier would man the machine guns in the nose en route to the target area and then in the target area while the Bombardier was occupied with his bomb sight, the Navigator would man the nose machine guns. That would be reason number one for sending us to gunnery school. Reason number two was that if you washed out of Navigation School, you had been trained as an aerial gunner and could be sent immediately to a B-17 or B-24 training school as a prospective gunner on one of the two types of aircraft!

Classes began right away and they were not the usual class with a teacher talking and students trying to stay awake. The class rooms had a square made of rough wooden tables, one table to each student and a large open area in the center of the square for the instructor. No chairs; you had to stand in this class! The text was the standard air-cooled 50 caliber machine gun. You went to the door of the supply room to get your own gun. It was not like carrying a shotgun or rifle in one hand. These guns were heavy! You could carry it but you knew you had something massive in your two hands. The lesson we were to learn by endless repetition was how to take the gun completely apart and reassemble it again. This was called stripping the gun. There were two types of stripping and they differed in the degree of disassembly you went into. In "field stripping" you disassembled the gun into its major components. In "detail stripping" you disassembled the major components down to the smallest component parts that could be disassembled without shop equipment. After showing you how to do the two strippings, you were ordered to do them with your own gun. Many, many times; time after time. After doing it a lot of times, you could now disassemble and reassemble the gun without puzzling what to do next. Fine and good. On to the next subject!

The next subject was—more stripping. The same subject as before but now with a couple of refinements. You had to learn to field strip the gun and reassemble it while wearing a blindfold and a pair of leather gloves. Having mastered that, you had to learn to detail strip the gun while blindfolded, though on this one it was not necessary to wear gloves. After many, many hours of this you felt that you were intimately familiar with the construction of the 50 caliber machine gun. One other adjustment you practiced quite a bit also. That was the adjustment to change the rate at which the gun fired. A simple adjustment—the gun barrel screwed into the breech mechanism and as you screwed the barrel in, you could feel detent clicks. Normal adjustment was to screw the barrel all the way into the breech, then unscrew it for two clicks of the detent.

As the familiarization classes continued, we were introduced into other more active training. Although you did fire the machine gun several times while in school, most of your firing training was not with machine guns but with shotguns.

Before firing any shotguns we were given a safety lecture. The trainer for the safety lecture was introduced to us as "Sgt. Hatfield—you may remember the stories about the feud between the Hatfields and the McCoys." We were all sitting in a big circle on a grassy area around a central clear space. Sgt. Hatfield was a good talker, walking around the open area, talking quietly and earnestly, a shotgun cradled casually in one arm. We hadn't noticed but there was an empty wooden box on the ground; a box used for shipping and storing linked 50 caliber ammunition. These boxes were very sturdy, made of wood about one inch thick. As Hatfield continued talking, he stopped by the box, the shotgun cradled in his arm now casually pointed down at the box. Without interrupting what he was saying, he unobtrusively pulled the trigger of the shotgun. Naturally we all were startled and jumped accordingly. The point Hatfield was making was to demonstrate to us what a horribly deadly weapon a shotgun can be at very short range. The box now had a big gaping hole in its side, about eight or ten inches in diameter. I, for one, and probably most of the other men listening had a very dramatic impression of what we would be getting into. Also an image in our heads of the effect of a similar shot on a human body.

Some of our shotgun firing would be standard skeet shooting in a standard skeet shooting facility. This was a lot of fun and most of us got to be reasonably good at shooting skeet. I think I had a few rounds where I hit clay birds twenty one or twenty two times out of the full 24. The only dull part of this was that you had to take your turn in one of the trap houses, manning the trap that hurled the clay birds.

The school had a variation on regular skeet which was unusual and challenging. In the standard skeet shooting, you were standing still and shooting at a moving target—the clay bird. Much simpler than the gunner's job in a plane, where the gunner's plane would be moving at the same time he was trying to shoot a moving enemy plane. I don't remember if the school had a name for their solution to this training problem. I always thought of their solution as "race track skeet". The skeet range now would be an oval road, the oval being about a mile or a mile and a quarter on its long dimension. The trap houses were along the road at regular intervals. In standard skeet the trap man activates his trap when the gunner calls "Mark" or "Pull" (depending on which trap house he was manning). In the race track skeet, the skeet trap was activated by a trip-wire running across the road. But it was still necessary to have a person in each trap house to load the birds into the trap. The student gunner would fire while standing in the back of a big Army six-by-six truck. The gunner who was firing stood inside a circular brace made of iron, the circle being at waist level so he could lean against it and steady himself as the truck rolled. The truck driver would drive at a steady pace, around fifteen or twenty miles an hour. As the truck rolled over a trip wire it would activate the trap and a clay bird would sail out for the gunner to try to hit. Not an easy shot, since you were looking down and the bird would not be taking a predictable path as it did in regular skeet. Here again, as in regular skeet, it was fun if you were firing; boring if you were manning a trap.

Another variation was firing from a turret. In a B-17, two waist gunners would be holding the hand grips at the rear of their post-mounted machine guns. There also would be a gunner manning the plane's top turret which had two machine guns in it. The school had set up another range for this type of firing practice.

They used B-17 turrets in which the machine guns had been replaced with a shotgun. The traps were in a tall tower, about fifteen or twenty feet tall. The bird was hurled at your turret so that it would pass over you. You were supposed to track the bird's trajectory and fire the turret-shotgun at the clay bird. I don't think any of us ever got to be good at this one so I didn't feel bad when most of my shots were misses.

We did fire the machine gun itself several times at a firing range, after first being given a special cautionary warning. In the early forties Hollywood made an action movie (not a very accurate one) in which the hero picked up a machine gun in his hands and held it like a rifle, firing it at attacking Japanese planes. The range instructors emphasized that in the movie the actor was firing a 30 caliber machine gun. Our guns were 50 caliber, a much heavier gun with a tremendous recoil which conceivably could crush your chest if you tried to fire it like a rifle.

When I fired the gun, I quickly learned that the first two or three shots are the only really accurate ones. With its high muzzle velocity the gun was very accurate. But with a longer burst, the recoil made the heavy gun dance around on its post mount and it was hard to keep the sight centered on the target.

The firing range was way out in the boondocks (like the rest of the base!). It was originally forested with pine trees with trunks about ten inches in diameter. After the student gunners had finished firing, a couple of the instructors enjoyed showing off to us. They would aim at a spot on a pine tree about twenty feet above ground level. Then, they would "cut" the tree down with a machine gun. They were good shots and it only took a few shots to bring the tree down. But it seemed a shame to me to spoil a tree for a few second of shooting fun.

There was some practice firing of the machine gun while in the air aboard a B-17. Guns in a combat-flying B-17 were fired from several positions. Two waist guns, one on each side of the plane where the gunner held the hand-grips of his gun which was mounted on a post at the bottom edge of a large opening in the side of the fuselage. Not a bit uncomfortable when you were firing out over the Gulf of Mexico from a plane flying at around eight thousand feet altitude. But a miserable job in a B-17 flying at 25,000 feet altitude over Germany with the air a cold minus 25 (or so—sometimes even colder!). The plane also had other gunner positions, the tail guns, the top turret and that abominable position where the gunner was curled up in a tight little ball turret in the belly of the plane. In gunnery school we were firing only from the open-window waist position.

To have a target to fire at, we fired at a large cloth sleeve which was towed at the end of a long cable by a smaller twin engine bomber, frequently a Martin B-26. To make a half hearted effort to score each student gunner's accuracy, each gunner had his own stock of linked machine cartridges. Each gunner's cartridges had soft paint of a different color on the point of the slug to make a colored smudge when it hit the cloth sleeve. Our practice firing was in a designated square shaped area several miles out over the Gulf.

The gunnery instructions to the student gunners was, "Aim at the cloth sleeve. Don't aim at the towing cable." Guess what we all aimed at? I, as well as some of the others were lucky enough to hit the towing cable. I call it more luck than skill. But, if you hit the cable it broke the sleeve target loose and it fluttered down into the Gulf. I don't think that the gunnery instructor really cared when we hit the cable. Maybe he even felt a bit of pride whenever one of his students did cut a target loose. But I guess the crew of the tow plane had a different view; since they had to reel in the cable and attach it to a new target. Tedious extra work for them.

Firing at the towed target was fun, even if you didn't hit the cable. But after the firing was over the tedious work began for the student gunners. Where the earlier machine guns loaded the cartridges into a cloth belt, the guns we used had linked cartridges. Each cartridge was about five or six inches long before it was fired and the empty casing (the "brass") about an inch and a half shorter after being fired. Each cartridge was clipped to another cartridge by a small steel clip, and that cartridge was, in turn, linked to its neighbor and so on. The whole lot became a rather heavy, somewhat flexible belt. When the belt fed into the breech of the gun, the gun's mechanism fired the slug out the barrel and the recoil opened the breech, ejected the empty brass and linking clip which fell off to the side. As the breech closed, it inserted a new cartridge which fired, the sequence continuing as long as the gunner kept the trigger depressed. After all the student gunners had fired (about five or six), there was a lot of debris littering the floor of the plane. Our job was to pick up the spent brass and clips and load them into the packing boxes that the belts of ammunition had come in; then carry the boxes up to the planes radio room which was near the plane's center of gravity. On one flight (I was not on that one) one of the cadets was both enterprising and at the same time stupid. He thought, "Why take the boxes up to the radio room and then unload them from there when we land? I'll just throw the box overboard. After all, we're out over the Gulf and nobody will care." He had forgotten about the plane's slipstream. When he threw a box out the window, it did not fall directly. The 160 mile per hour slipstream carried the box back and slammed it into the horizontal tail plane, causing a big dent in the leading edge of the tail plane. I don't know what happened to the gunner but I'm sure he had a rough time when they grilled him back on the ground.

For some reason the curriculum planners thought that we students should have a brief firing experience with the Thompson sub-machine gun, that favorite gangster weapon. We each fired one magazine load on a firing range. I was not impressed with the accuracy of it. Sure, you can hit any target if you fire enough bullets at it. But after the first shot, the barrel wants to start climbing. I never could understand the reasoning of our firing this weapon. We would be firing the machine guns of the plane in the air and if we had to bail out, each of us would be carrying a pistol, not a sub machine gun.

The last type gun we fired in gunnery school was the standard 45 caliber Army automatic pistol. We were supposed to qualify with that weapon, meaning that we had to make a certain score. Our time on the pistol range was a Monday morning. Unfortunately for me, on Sunday my friend Ed Yablonski and I had gone in to town (Fort Meyers). I had fish for lunch in a grubby little restaurant. Then Ed and I took a bus out to the beach. Since it was January it was surprising that anything at the beach was open. But there was a little refreshment stand open and Ed and I had what was supposed to be our evening meal. I had a hamburger and Ed must have had something different, judging by later events. Either the fish or the hamburger was apparently spoiled because it gave me a violent case of food poisoning (the GI's) and I spent a very active night in the latrine. The misery had subsided by morning into only "upchucking" and instead of going on sick call, I decided to go out to the range with everyone else for our pistol firing. That was a memorable experience. When firing, I would fire a round or two, then turn around away from the firing line to upchuck, then turn back around to resume firing. Fortunately we kept our own score and I qualified with what I called my 45 caliber scoring pencil. The pistol range was our last shooting of any kind of weapon.

With classes now over the school conducted a simple little ceremony and gave each of us our enlisted wings, signifying that we were now gunners. Next phase would be Navigation School. By now we had been told which one of the Navigation Schools our group would go to. There was a school in Louisiana, one in Texas, and one at Coral Gables, Florida. Our's was to be the one at Coral Gables.

For a novel change, this move did not involve a troop train. This time it was a "Troop Bus Convoy." Probably a troop train would have involved a ride north to Tampa, then southeast from Tampa to Coral Gables. The Troop Busses went directly across the Everglades to Coral Gables and it was a much more enjoyable trip, to say nothing of being less time consuming. The one comfort stop was at an Indian trading post in the Everglades, an interesting break in the ride.

NAVIGATION SCHOOL

Coral Gables, Florida

Coral Gables, if you will pardon a tiny travelogue, is a suburb of Miami. A reasonably short bus ride put you into downtown Miami and from there, Miami Beach. Coral Gables was strictly a residential community, mostly upper middle-class homes, quiet and subdued. Also, it was where the University of Miami was located and that was where the Army's Navigation School was located. We checked into our quarters late on a Saturday afternoon and by the time we ate and were assigned beds, all of us were ready for sleep.

At military bases, Sunday was and probably still is a morning for sleeping-in, if that's one of your pleasures. There was already a class ahead of us at the school, about half-way through their training. The Army commander of the school had designated Cadet Officers from this class, something which we had not previously had at Maxwell or the subsequent bases. Bright and early on Sunday morning, the Cadet Commander sounded a strident wake-up call, ordering us to fall out in front of the building in PT clothes. When we were all assembled into formation, he then led us in a brisk morning run, probably about two miles through the residential streets of Coral Gables. Even though it was around six AM, he had us singing several times as we ran. He was something of a fitness fanatic and I guess he wanted to show off his own fitness and from us find out what kind of shape we were in. As a group, I suppose we were about his equal; at least he couldn't find anything about our condition he wanted to complain about. It was amusing later when the school commander (a real Army officer this time) said that someone in the city government of Coral Gables complained about formations of cadets singing in the streets that early in the morning. The commander said he enjoyed telling them "You should be happy it's our troops singing and you weren't listening to jack-booted troops singing in German." But apparently he decided not to press the issue beyond that and that was our only early Sunday morning run.

Our quarters were comfortable, though quite unusual. We were billeted in the Santander Hotel. I believe the hotel had been quarters for either teachers or visitors to the school before the Army arrived. It was a three story building, roughly triangular around a nicely landscaped interior courtyard. On the ground floor was a fairly large dining room where we ate.

The room I was in had three single-decker cots and one double decker. In a little alcove was another single decker. As usual I ended up as "Mr. Upper" in the double decker and Dave Swiss was "Mr. Lower". In the three singles were, first Noah Sweat (nicknamed "Soggy"); then Martin Swetsky (very much a New Yorker); and a guy named Smart (a sports fanatic). In the little alcove was Dave Thomas. We came from all over: me from Alabama, Swiss from Pennsylvania (I think), Sweat from Mississippi. I don't remember where Smart was from. Thomas was from Georgia. You might notice that all of our names began with either the letter "S" or "T"—we had been assigned quarters in alphabetic order.

As we were first getting organized as a group, Dave Swiss earned a new nick-name. The person calling the roll from a written roster tentatively pronounced his name as "Swees" first, then "Swyss".

Dave quietly answered, "Just plain Swiss, sir. Just plain Swiss." From then on he was frequently called "Just Plain," by his roommates or, more briefly, "J.P."

The school had an unusual assortment of sponsors. The quarters, as well as the class rooms were from the University of Miami. The housekeeping and mess facility were by a commercial corporation, Embry-Riddle. The navigation classes as well as the flight instructors were all from Pan American Airways. The Army provided military command and instruction. It all seemed to work very well, at least it appeared that way to us. There was one quirk which I found amusing. On payday, when we were paid, we were paid at one table by a Captain (with the ever-present pistol on the table by the money). We were paid considerably more than our normal payday gave us. But right next to the pay table was another table with a representative of Embry-Riddle who expected and received the extra which we had been paid. One wit in our group made up a little jingle:

> Hey diddle-diddle,
> The cat and the fiddle,
> We got paid today, and gave it to Riddle!

The University of Miami campus was a conglomeration of different classes of people. Of course there was us; we always marched to and from classes. There were two different contingents of Navy students attending the school too. One, the "V-5's". We didn't see much of them. I think it was some sort of intensive program. The other was the "V-12's". We saw a lot of them. I think that they were actually in the Navy but it was a sort of student program and they didn't march around or do much of anything except hold hands with the co-eds (our view of them; I guess we were envious.) They did wear Navy uniforms, though. And, finally, the civilian students, predominantly girls.

Before doing any flying, there was a good bit of navigation to be learned in the classrooms. First, and basic to all the rest was learning to do "dead reckoning" and plot it on maps. The maps, for us in the latitudes in which we would be navigating were usually Mercator projections for over the ocean and over land the Lambert projection which was used for most aerial charts over land. The instruction included the theory used for making the two different projections and the relative advantages and disadvantages of each projection. Both projections dealt with the problem of picturing a round Earth on flat paper.

Dead reckoning involved drawing your intended course on your map without taking into effect the wind. Taking your speed into account, you could plot a position on this intended course for any time you chose. This was where you would be if there were no wind involved. However, airplanes are affected by the wind. If the wind came from your right, your actual position would be left of the intended course and vice versa for a wind from the left. If it were from behind you, you would be further along on your course and if from ahead of you, you would not be as far along on the course. This seemed very logical when it was first explained to us. Later we were disillusioned when we found out that the wind had a mind of its own. Before a flight a weather officer would give you his estimate of what wind speeds and directions you might expect. Unfortunately, that was just an estimate. Sometimes it would be accurate but at other times the weather would introduce changes and then you were on your own.

To do the map part we were taught to use the basic navigator tools. The Weems plotter—a combined plastic ruler and protractor. Dividers—the same instrument used by draftsmen to measure distances, in our case mileage on our map. And finally the navigator's old faithful—the E6B computer. Not really a computer in the sense we use the term in modern times. It was a circular slide rule on one side and on the other a rotatable plastic disc on which you could use a pencil to work vector problems to calculate a wind speed and direction. These three soon became essentials to a navigator. In fact, I have heard pilots needle a navigator by saying, "How come when I ask you the time you reach for your E6B?"

These were just the basic starting details, the foundation on which we built our job. In actual conditions it got to be more complicated but we don't want to get into a detailed discussion of navigation here. We soon got to the part that most people associated with navigators—Celestial Navigation. It would also be tedious to go into details about Celestial Navigation here. I learned to do Celestial then; although I understood the theory in only a very basic way. The theory involved spherical trigonometry and back at 'Southern I had changed majors twice because of my problems with any math higher than college algebra! At the working level, using Celestial Navigation involved three skill areas. First, how to identify and find a group of several stars. Second, how to use a sextant to measure the star's altitude (in degrees) above the horizon. Third, how to convert a star's observed altitude into a "line of position", a problem of simple arithmetic and simple draftsmanship on your map. To get a "celestial fix", you had to take readings on three stars.

In theory, celestial navigation works out as a beautiful system. In actuality, at many times it bordered on being impractical. It was moderately important on slow but long-range planes, especially if crossing the Atlantic or Pacific. But on modern jets it is far too slow.

The classroom instruction was from experienced Pan American Navigators. Pan American Airways had been the pioneers in over— water flights at a time when other airlines stuck to over-land routes. Their pioneering flights had been in flying boats, slow lumbering craft which were larger inside than the usual DC-3's used by overland airlines. With no modern navigation aids available, the Pan American crews had been leaders in aerial navigation. Unlike modern public school teachers, the Pan American classroom instructors we had did not teach at the speed of the slowest learners in the class. It was a case of get it now or else. Remember, you are trained as a B-17 gunner already and if you don't pick it up here in class right away, there are plenty of openings for B-17 gunners in Europe! The training was not to be all classroom of course. After learning a few of the classroom basics, we soon were ready for training flights. Even so, classroom instruction did continue at the same time.

The planes for our flight training were very much a surprise for us. What little flying we had done already in gunnery school had been in B-17s. The B-17 at that time was a modern plane; it flew at an indicated airspeed of about 160 miles per hour and could climb to 30,000 feet. Pan American Airways did not have any B-17s to use or anything else of a comparable vintage. We found that we would be flying in the old flying boats that Pan American had used to develop overseas flights. They had two types of the craft. One type, which we flew mostly, was a two engine Consolidated Commodore. The other was a four engine craft made by Sikorsky. Both craft had a "parasol wing". With a parasol wing, the wing does not merge with the fuselage, rather it is perched several feet higher than the fuselage (boat in this case) on struts. The engines are attached to struts between the level of the wing and the fuselage. The fuselage itself was a big aluminum boat which originally in passenger carrying days had seats. For navigation training most of the seats had been removed and replaced by tables, one for each navigator trainee.

The planes always had a distinctive smell inside. Being a boat, I guess part of it was the inevitable bilge smell. Add to that the smell common to most military planes of that time, a combination of waterproofed canvas smell and hydraulic oil smell. And, since it was a boat, just a trace of barf-bag smell. You soon got used to it.

The flight instructor told us that there was a strict protocol involved in boarding the plane. You (meaning cadets and possibly flight instructors too) did not board until the plane captain did, unless he gave you permission to board. The plane was always tied up to a dock and you boarded from dry land. After everyone was on board, a launch would pull the aircraft out to a clear area where the pilot would start the engines. Then, the long taxi out to where the captain would start his take off. When he was at the proper place, the plane captain would check his engines, then turn into the wind. A take off in a flying boat is a real experience. Speed builds up more slowly than if you have wheels, then even when you had flying speed the pilot had to break the "suction" of the water against the speeding hull. Bounce, bounce, bounce. Finally you were airborne. I don't remember what airspeed was cruising speed for the flying boats; it was less than a hundred miles per per hour. I believe we usually had ten student navigators on each flight. The instructor would give us a destination—usually either the Bahamas or one of the other islands in that area and you would first plot your course, then calculate the compass heading for the pilot to fly to maintain that course. With ten students, I don't know whose heading the pilot would fly; possibly one he had personally computed.

Flights were sometimes day flights, sometimes night flights. The night flights were primarily so you could practice celestial navigation. We found out that these planes were not designed for the convenience of student navigators doing celestial navigation. There was no astrodome, the small bubble on later planes where the navigator could use his sextant. In the boats there was a sliding hatch at one place in the ceiling. You slid the hatch open and tried to use your sextant with nothing between you and the star except for the slipstream. That is, if you could see the stars you wanted. Before opening the hatch, you would have selected what three stars you wanted to use. When you tried to find them, invariably you would find that one of them would be obscured by the big parasol wing overhead. Or a patch of clouds. So, you would make another quick star selection.

Most of the flights would be out to the Bahamas or other islands in their area. We did make a couple of flights down to Havana—without landing there of course. The weather was always beautiful and coming back you could see the lights of Miami long before reaching the Pan American terminal at Dinner Key.

There was one flight that I always remember and I'm sure most of the other cadets on it must remember it too. We usually flew on week days, each flight lasting about five hours. There always was a flight lunch of sandwiches, a big thermos of coffee and thermoses of water. One flight had to be scheduled on Sunday morning and they told us that since it was Sunday there would be no flight lunch. We were all accustomed to eating three meals a day and the prospect of missing a meal caused us a little alarm. No need to worry, one observant guy volunteered. There's a nice delicatessen in Coral Gables. Let's take up a collection and one of us can go and get sandwiches for all ten of us. The plan for delicatessen sandwiches sounded to us like a good one and we put it into effect. One of the guys went to the deli and bought the sandwiches. I think that they must have been pastrami and there probably were some kosher pickles also. No thought had been given to getting anything to drink; since none of us had a car it would have made a rather large load with drinks for ten. No matter, we could drink water from the plane thermoses. At chow time on the flight, we all ate our pastrami sandwiches. They were delicious.

A bit dry, with no beverage. Later the misery began. Deli sandwiches, especially with kosher pickles, need a beverage. A big one. Either with the sandwich or not too long afterward because pastrami, and kosher pickles especially, can generate a terrific thirst. We found that the plane thermoses, usually filled with drinking water, were every bit as dry as we all were now. The Pan American ground crew had not filled them. This was not enough of an emergency to cut short the flight but by the time we landed we had ten very, very thirsty student navigators on board.

The training, both classroom and flying continued. I was disappointed in that my friend, Ed Yablonski was eliminated from training about half way through. Being a trained gunner, he immediately went to a B-17 combat training base and before I graduated, he was flying missions as a tail gunner on B-17s, flying out of Italy. He survived the war and we still try to amaze each other with war stories.

Our scheduled graduation date was June 30, 1944. On June 6, we were ordered out for an unexpected formation. They marched the whole lot of us, as well as all the Army permanent staff to a small tennis stadium. There someone, probably our Commanding Officer, announced to us that the invasion of France had started and was in progress. Then he introduced a minister who led us in a prayer for the success of the invasion. It was a very solemn occasion, even in the outdoor setting and we were all very quiet going back to our interrupted activity.

Every or at least many military groups, especially during training days, has an individual who never seems able to get things right. Our's was a cadet named Seering. We called him Junior Seering and everyone liked him, even as we liked telling and retelling stories about his misadventures. One story involved the barber shop and our regular Saturday Morning Inspection. Our room was on the second floor of the Santander and there was a barber shop on the third floor. One Friday night Junior, in anticipation of the next day's inspection, went up to the barber shop and asked for "the works" from the barber, hoping to impress the inspecting officer. The next day at the inspection, he received a gig for needing a haircut! He was perturbed and I didn't blame him. Another story involved Saturday morning inspection also. At the inspection you were supposed to have everything in order; about your person as well as your area in your room. This was in anticipation of "Open Post", your permission to go to town Saturday night for fun. At this particular inspection, Junior was standing at attention by his cot. The inspecting officer looked him up and down critically, then said, "Mr. Seering. Your uniform is dirty. Is that the cleanest one you have?"

"No, Sir," Junior replied. "I'm saving my clean one to wear when I go on Open Post." Junior did not go in to Miami that night.

At our graduation we all anticipated receiving our Navigator Wings and a commission as a second lieutenant. Because the Army was turning out so many more second lieutenants they decided on a program to reduce the number without at the same time reducing the number of pilots, bombardiers, and navigators. A decision was made in Washington that in future graduations only part of each class would become second lieutenants. The others would become "Flight Officers". Flight Officers were a type of Warrant Officer, equivalent to the lowest grade of the four levels of Warrant Officer. However, when a flight officer was promoted, he was not advanced to the next higher Warrant Officer level. He was promoted to Second Lieutenant! Instead of wearing the gold bar of a second lieutenant, the Flight Officer's rank insignia was a blue enameled bar. Being selected to be a Flight Officer became known as "getting the blue pickle!". There was a further indignity to it. At that time personnel overseas received a financial benefit known as "Overseas Pay." For enlisted personnel, it was twenty percent of base pay; for officers it was ten percent. A Flight Officer received the enlisted differential, although the base pay for both ranks was the same. So when a Flight Officer overseas received a promotion, he became a second lieutenant, same base pay but only ten percent overseas pay whereas he had been getting twenty percent before. A promotion which brought a pay cut.

When they announced a few days before graduation who would

be flight officers I had a pleasant surprise. Cadets who had enlisted for the cadet program before a certain date were "grandfathered in" as second lieutenants. I was grandfathered in and did not go through the selection process.

Several weeks before graduation we were given a little more permission to leave the quarters area; specifically we could go in to Coral Gables but not to Miami. This was to let us shop for officer's uniforms. Our selection would be made at the two tailor shops in Coral Gables. The tailor would take your measurements and order the uniforms. Shortly before graduation you would pick them up to wear to graduation. It was a pleasure to deal with a tailor who actually wanted your uniforms to fit, compared to the supply personnel at Keesler who threw the uniforms on the counter for you to hope they would fit. Approximately.

Graduation day finally arrived. The ceremony was held in a movie theater auditorium in Coral Gables. There was not a great deal of oratory involved. But it did take a little time because there were two parts involved. In one part, you received your aeronautical rating as a navigator. In the other, you received your commission as a Second Lieutenant or warrant as a Flight Officer.

As we came out of the theater, we realized first of all that now we didn't have to march as a group. We could straggle as a group back to the Santander, not worrying about keeping in step.

There was an old Army custom that when a new officer received his first salute from an enlisted man, he must give the enlisted man a dollar. We found several groups of the Navy V-12's on the street, it being common knowledge to them that they could pick up a few bucks spending money by saluting the new looeys. Our group made a conscious effort to avoid the V-12's and find an Army enlisted man. We were successful, finding a couple of GI's who were stationed with the Army hospital now functioning in the big local Biltmore Hotel. The GI's dutifully saluted and were very much surprised when we each gave a dollar to one or the other of them.

Back at the Santander we picked up our possessions (new uniforms!), our orders ordering us to our next base assignment and orders giving permission to go on thirty days leave. Unfortunately for some of us—including me—we learned that our orders would be delayed and we would have to stay in the area until our orders arrived. There was no place to stay in Coral Gables now, since we couldn't stay in the Santander any more. I took a bus into Miami and found a hotel room.

MIAMI INTERLUDE

Miami, Florida

The Miami Interlude started out as the beginning of what looked to be a dull, dismal week-end. The cadets I had been closest friends to had all gone, taking off for their thirty day leave. Usually when we had a free evening, we would go off in small groups. My friend Ed Yablonski was now in Italy, flying combat. Most of my room-mates were gone also and I was alone and felt very much alone. It was a happy time in a way, being newly commissioned and newly rated as an aircrew member. But there was no one to celebrate with. There had been no trouble in getting a hotel room. In Miami, as well as Miami Beach most of the hotels either had been taken over by the government to use for troops, or, if they were still open commercially were mostly hoping for business.

I felt like the occasion called for a celebration, even if there were no one to celebrate with. I stopped in a liquor store, planning to get a bottle of whisky. There I had a surprise. Although my friends and I were accustomed to being able to order drinks in a bar, we found that for customers in a liquor store, whisky (bourbon) was in short supply. Not rationed; rather the proprietor would sell it to you only if you had been a major customer or if you were ready to buy a big order of stuff that did not ordinarily sell well. I was not interested in a big purchase; only something to celebrate a special occasion with. He suggested a bottle of brandy and reluctantly I agreed. Whenever I had had a drink in a bar or night club it was always with a mixer of some kind. So, I looked about for something to use as a mixer. I had never tasted brandy and I felt I would need something to go with it. I passed a little sidewalk stand that sold fruit juices and decided to buy a container of fresh pineapple juice.

Back at the hotel room I tried a mixture of brandy and fresh pineapple juice. Today I like pineapple juice moderately well, although it's not a favorite. And I enjoy an occasional snifter of brandy. But, I found out that together the combination has nothing to recommend it. Absolutely nothing! Especially when you make an evening of it. But that didn't stop my solitary celebration; and the next day I suffered the after effects of my bad judgment. A head ache all day; a major headache!

Later on, I remembered the Miami Interlude for two events, one minor and the other major. The minor one was the brandy and pineapple error. That was the bad one. The other one, the major one was a happier event. Finding Estelle!

One of the popular attractions in downtown Miami was the Mayflower. The Mayflower was a waffle house, a moderately large one. Most of us cadets were familiar with it, usually in stopping there for a late evening snack before heading back to Coral Gables. I had been there several times and enjoyed their waffles. The afternoon after the brandy fiasco I stopped by for something to eat. There were several other former cadets, now lieutenants, there in the same boat I was in—waiting for their orders, just like I was. I knew them only slightly but we started talking as we waited for our waffle orders. The waitress serving us was Estelle. She was very slender, with dark hair and sparkling eyes. We all were trying to impress her. One of the guys, a fellow named Russo tried to impress the rest of us, saying he had a date to meet her when she got off from work. She went along with the banter but did not agree that she had a date with him. She said, "I have a date with Lt. Thompson." That was the first I had heard of that but I thought she was pretty and I wasn't about to turn down a date with a pretty girl.

Estelle and I started talking as two individuals now rather than as participants in a group conversation. I asked her when our date would be and she said right after she gets off from work; I could pick her up then. I picked her up at the Mayflower about two hours later and we found that we had a strong interest in each other. We saw quite a bit of each other in the time I waited for my orders to the new base. The details would be more appropriate for a romantic tale rather than a military reminiscence so I'll pass over them here. The only military aspect of it was when we spent some time in Biscayne Park, overlooking Biscayne Bay. The ground was damp from a brief shower and I pulled a Walter Raleigh stunt, spreading my brand new officer's raincoat down for us to sit on. I didn't notice when I did it that there was a smudge of grease on the ground, left by a power mower. I never was able to get that grease spot off the raincoat!

We felt that our acquaintance would be over when I picked up my orders for a new base, since we had no idea where it would be. Estelle went with me when I went out to the Santander in Coral Gables to get my orders. The orders were a real surprise. They ordered me to a nearby Florida base, Boca Raton Army Air Base. Not a next-door site but Boca Raton was just a fairly short distance up the coast; not too far from being next door. But first, there would be the leave. We said good-bye to each other, hoping that it would only be a temporary separation.

BOCA RATON AAB

Boca Raton, Florida

The leave time passed quickly. Most of my friends from Cullman were away in one of the services. The only exception was Asa Fuller, now a new lieutenant in the Army Corps of Engineers. He was home on leave also. His brother, Forney Fuller was a lieutenant (non-flying) in the Army Air Corps and not home. My buddy, Maclin Morrison was somewhere in the Army. Glenn Rounds was still in Army Air Corps Officer Candidate School at Miami Beach. I had gotten together with Glenn for dinner once before I graduated. We were at a restaurant on Miami Beach and Glenn couldn't really relax. When I asked him why, he said that there were several of his upper-classmen watching him and his table manners and since he had committed the grave sin of resting his wrist on the edge of the table he would have to turn himself in for that! I was amazed and told him that our own training was more interested in how well you could navigate rather than how precise your table manners were.

During the leave I went to Birmingham for a couple of days, hoping to meet up with some friends at 'Southern. Since it was July the college was not in a regular session and the campus was deserted. The only contact that I had had with anyone from 'Southern was earlier with Cornelia Banks while I was still a Cadet at Coral Gables. I had become friends with her when she was editor of the school newspaper and I worked on her staff. She married Bob Lively who was a Navy Officer at a Navy school in Miami. I attended their wedding at Miami Beach and later she invited me over for dinner at their apartment.

On the trip back from leave, I rode the train all the way past Boca Raton to Miami. I believe that Boca Raton was too small to be included as a regular stop in the train's schedule. This was no hardship; a little longer to ride but getting off at Miami gave me a chance to see Estelle again. The stay at Boca Raton AAB would be for only one month but before that month was over, Estelle and I decided to get married. Wartime romances and marriages have the reputation for being short-lived. Ours was an exception; it lasted almost fifty years and ended only with her death.

Within a short time after reporting for duty at Boca Raton, I learned what my ultimate aircraft assignment would be. I had been assuming all along that it would be either in a B-17 or a B-24 and had hoped it would be in a B-17. This was not to be.

During the month at Boca Raton I would be in school being trained on the APQ-13 Radar, specifically learning how to bomb by radar. Me? A navigator? Bombing by radar?

Several years later I learned that I had been investigated by the FBI who had sent an agent to Cullman to interview people I knew to determine if I was a trustworthy American citizen. Radar was a secret piece of equipment at that time and they didn't want any Axis sympathizers learning about it. A good precaution, I guess, though if I did want to blab to the enemy I probably wouldn't have known how to go about doing it.

Another discovery at the time was of more immediate interest to me. I would not be going into a B-17 crew or a B-24 crew. It would be a B-29 crew! So what's a B-29? I had never even heard of that plane.

Where the B-17 and the B-24 had only one navigator, we learned that the B-29 had two navigators, both trained on the APQ-13 Radar. One navigator would function as the navigator in the front part of the plane while the other navigator would function as a radar operator in the radar room in the back section of the plane. The navigator up front did have a radar scope and could see what the radar was showing, providing the radar operator had the set turned on. I ended up as the navigator up front on our B-29 crew.

Just like it had been in both gunnery school and then in navigation school the training was part classroom, learning how to operate the radar set. The other part was flying, learning how to operate the set while in the air. The school did not have any B-29s; the flying was in either B-17s or B-24s. All but one of my flights were in B-17s. The one B-24 flight was mildly uncomfortable. It was the only time I ever flew in one and I found that although it was a rather large plane, it didn't have much room for excess crew members. During the time I was not actively using the radar set, I had to sit somewhere. That somewhere turned out to be the original Bombardier's station in the nose. You had a beautiful view there. But they had taken all the machine guns out and hadn't done a very good job sealing up the holes where the guns had projected out. This was summertime, we were flying locally in Florida and there were frequent little rain showers. Whenever the pilot flew through a rain shower, rain would come pouring in through the former gun-ports and I ended up somewhat wet. Not a real hardship, of course, but it was enough to cool any enthusiasm I might have had before for B-24s.

During the war, wives were not authorized to accompany military personnel. Authorized in this sense of the word meant that if the couple chose to be together, the wife's expenses were not paid by the government. After we were first married, we stayed in a nice little hotel in Del Ray Beach, a little community a few miles north of Boca Raton. A very comfortable and cheery room but expensive for a new second lieutenant, especially since there were no cooking privileges included. Estelle became an expert at finding places to stay and she found a nice one room apartment which a couple had made to rent to military families.

The day before pay day our money ran out at the same time the month ran out. We ended up with just enough to eat at a quiet little inexpensive restaurant. As we came out after the meal, we had only one quarter between the two of us. No problem, really, since we had just eaten, we had bread and coffee in our apartment and the bus ride to the base was free on the government-owned bus. We had a friendly debate on how to spend that last quarter.

Should we buy ice cream cones, since we had not had any dessert? Or should we buy a pack of cigarettes, since we both smoked? (Yes, in 1944 you could get a pack of cigarettes for a quarter!) Decisions, decisions. Estelle said, "I'll toss the coin. Heads it's cones, tails it's cigarettes." She tossed the coin up in the air, missed catching it and we watched it roll underneath a car parked right by us. At least we had a good laugh together for our quarter.

At the end of the radar training we learned where our next base would be—Lincoln, Nebraska. This would be a brand new part of the country for both of us. I had never been north of Tennessee or west of Mississippi (except New Orleans!). And Estelle, who was born in New Jersey, had never been as far west as Nebraska.

ON TO NEBRASKA!

The trip to Lincoln was a long, tiring one. For a change, it was not on a troop train. I was traveling with my wife, Estelle, this time. But it was all by coach. I don't remember the routing. It was from Florida (probably Fort Lauderdale) to Chicago, the much longer leg of the two-leg trip. We left in late afternoon and most of the trip was during the night. It was tiring for me but I was in good physical shape (else the Army wouldn't have had me!) But it was much more tiring for Estelle. She had gone to Florida to recuperate originally from a condition which started with weight loss and was corrected by a thyroid operation. Where her normal weight was around 125 pounds, when we married she was my tiny 98 pound bride. But, not a word of complaint from her during the whole trip to Chicago.

We did have a rest in Chicago after the long over-night ride from Florida, a room in a down-town hotel. After resting in the hotel, we went for a walk in down-town Chicago. It was a warm, beautiful sunny September day and we enjoyed being outside and moving. As we were walking, Estelle suddenly stopped, a look of panic on her face. (Pretended panic?) I asked her "What's wrong?"

She said, "It's after Labor Day."

"That's okay," I said. "We're in the Army."

"But look!" she said, pointing down.

"At what?" I asked.

"My shoes!" They looked okay to me, a pair of white leather shoes.

"We have to go to a shoe store!"

"Here? Can't we wait until we get to Lincoln?"

"No! Let's find a shoe store here."

Since I grew up with no sisters I was completely ignorant of women's fashion rules. She explained to me that a self-respecting young woman did not wear white shoes after Labor Day. We found a shoe store without much trouble and she yielded the proper shoe-ration coupon and I provided the money. Shoes, during the war, were rationed!

Our train for the trip to Lincoln, Nebraska left in the late afternoon. Where the train from Florida had been tired old passenger coaches this one would be one of the most modern ones running, the Burlington Zephyr. A train it was a pleasure to ride in. It was still by coach but the seats were individual reclining seats. The coaches were shining stainless steel and air conditioned.

The train reached Lincoln around two-thirty AM and we went into the huge, nearly deserted station. Our number one need was a hotel room for at least the rest of the night. I found the phone number for what I assumed was the leading hotel and asked for a room reservation. "Sorry. We're completely full," the clerk replied.

"Full?" I answered. "Can you give me the name of another good hotel?"

"I could," she said. "But it wouldn't do you any good. We're all full tonight."

"Why?"

"It's the Nebraska State Fair. Everybody's in town for the Fair. Sorry I can't help you."

Not quite ready to give up, we tried a couple more numbers but what the clerk had told us appeared to be true. We spent the rest of the night (what was left of it!) stretched out on the wooden benches of the waiting room. It was quiet but the benches were hard, especially so after the soft seats of the Burlington Zephyr train we had just left.

Next morning we decided to have a nice breakfast before trying to find a place to stay. We bought a local newspaper to read while eating. Estelle seemed to have a built-in instinct for finding places to stay. In the paper she found an ad for a small efficiency and she suggested we go look at it before trying to get a hotel room.

When I first saw the place which was advertised, I was a little dubious. It was a two story, square, unimpressive looking building.

Not dilapidated or down and out, just plain and unadorned by any architectural eye-catchers. Inside, on the upper floor a central hall ran the length of the building. There were rooms opening onto the hall for its length. The owner, a Mrs. Rankin, showed us the one room efficiency which had been advertised. A tiny room with a double bed, a couple of chairs, and a small two burner gas stove (no oven!). The bath was a community affair, actually two affairs (one for women, one for men) at the end of the hall. Although I was not too impressed, Estelle whispered to me, "Let's take it."

Actually Estelle's instincts had been sound in this case. The room was tiny; there's no getting away from that. But we were only scheduled to stay in Lincoln for a short time and the place was convenient to the GI bus which went to the Air Base. Mr. and Mrs. Rankin, the owners, were an older couple, semi-retired. Mr. Rankin had been a printer and he still operated his print shop occasionally to do small orders. The shop was on the lower level of the building. Estelle and Mrs. Rankin became friends during the daytimes when I was at the Base. Mrs. Rankin made casseroles a couple of times for us to have as our evening meal. I learned that Southerners do not have a monopoly on hospitality and that Mid-Westerners are also active in that league.

I found that the Air Base, at least as far as we were concerned, was a collection point for assembling air crews. Pilots, Co-pilots, Bombardiers, Navigators, Engineers, Radio Operators, and Gunners—they were all collected here to be sent, in the proper numbers for each job, to training bases to be trained as B-29 combat crews. Our only duty was to report to the base each morning to let it be known that we were not AWOL. For the officers there were no other duties. Probably the gunners in the lower grades did catch details such as KP. We were not assigned into actual crews at Lincoln; that would be a prerogative of the individual training bases.

During the time we were in Nebraska, I grew to like the state. Of course there were a good many things favorable to that impression. It was early fall and the weather was very pleasant. The people were all friendly. I was newly-married and Estelle and

I were happy with each other. Much, much later after I retired from the military and was working for the U.S. Civil Service Commission, I made two trips to Omaha in the spring and summer and had the same favorable impression there. I mentioned liking Nebraska on one of the later trips and the local resident I was talking to said (in effect), "It's nice here in the warm months. But come back in the winter time before you make any final decisions— the snow drifts were nine feet deep in our parking lot last Winter!" But on this trip we were out of Nebraska weeks before the winter hit.

And where did we go next? A place I'd never heard of— Pyote, Texas. We looked it up in an almanac before we left Lincoln and the almanac said that at the last census the population of Pyote was 201 people. It was located about 22 miles east of Pecos and about fifteen miles west of Monahans. The map showed a little community of Wink about eighteen or so miles to the north. To the south? Nothing but unpopulated Texas!

PYOTE AAB

Pyote, Texas

Pyote AAB was the official name of the base; actually it had an unofficial name with people familiar with the base. It was "Rattlesnake Bomber Base". I've heard that it lived up to the rattlesnake part of its name in the hot months of the year. While we were there it was late fall and winter and we did not suffer from its normal blistering heat and other joys of a semi-desert location, including the rattlesnakes. Except for the hangars on the flight line everything else was one story wooden buildings. The roads were paved, though, but there was no landscaping, other than the stationary weeds near some buildings and the blowing tumbleweeds when it was windy, a frequent condition.

Traveling from base to base with a wife gave you an additional problem not shared by the bachelors. Finding a place to stay. Our first place was in Pecos. It was in a small two or three story small-town hotel. Not air conditioned, of course, but that was no problem because the weather was now pleasant and an open window gave a room temperature that was not too bad. There was one problem. Our second floor room was located at the rear of the building overlooking an alley. On the other side of the alley was the rear part of a bowling alley. The pinsetters of course kept their doors and windows open for ventilation and we could hear strikes and spares and gutter balls as we fell asleep. Falling asleep had to be early because I had to be at our daily briefing at the base at five AM and the base was a forty-five minute bus ride from Pecos. That translated into getting up at about a quarter to four every morning.

After about a week or so of staying in Pecos, we decided to

move to Monahans, which was on the other side of the base. The early rising need was still with us but I believe the move gave us an additional fifteen minutes in the early morning.

Estelle found that sitting around a hotel all day waiting for me to come home was not a routine she wanted. She went out to the base to look for a job, because she found that if a woman (a wife in most cases) had a job, there was a dormitory where she could stay, including her husband if she were married. She was immediately lucky in getting a job with the Post Exchange. An unusual job. It was as a fill-in employee. Some days she didn't have to go in to work. That was no problem since her real need from the job was the room on base, not the wages. When she did go in to work, it was to a variety of jobs. One was in the coffee shop in one of the hangars on the flight line. Other times it was as a sales clerk in the main Post Exchange. And one time she filled in as manager of the base Guest House. We slept in the Guest House ourselves for the two weeks that assignment lasted. After I was assigned to a regular air crew she became a special favorite person to the gunners on our crew, especially to one named Vey and the tail gunner, Slingluff. They found that when she was on the register, they could make more trips through the candy line than they could have when they didn't know the clerk on the register. Later on they surprised her with a Plexiglas heart which they had made. They had gotten a piece of Plexiglas from the aircraft glass repair shop and carved it into a heart to be worn on a neck chain. They hand-carved it and shaped it with a file, then polished it to a high gloss with tooth powder (a popular dentifrice). They wanted to mount an officer's Air Corps insignia on it, the type and size we wore as a lapel ornament. Since they were enlisted men they didn't feel like arguing to persuade a PX clerk to sell an officer insignia to an enlisted man. So, they used a high pressure begging campaign on Estelle to give them one of mine. She wouldn't agree at first but I guess Vey and Slingluff used their best Pennsylvania sweet-talk on her, telling her that if she gave them the insignia she would be glad later on that she had done it. When they finished the heart, including mounting my insignia on it, they cornered her and had a little informal presentation ceremony. She was very touched by their gesture which involved a lot of hand work on their part.

The crew to which we were assigned was one of the better ones, at least in the relationship among us. They were, listed in their duty position in the plane:

The Bombardier, who of course sat right up in the nose of the plane, was Boyd Madsen. He was a first lieutenant and had been an instructor at one of the bombing school bases. He was from Salt Lake City.

The Aircraft Commander, who sat immediately behind the Bombardier on the left side of the plane was Elbert Smith. Elbert was a first lieutenant also. He had been flying bombing training planes at the same base with Boyd. A lot of flying and practice-bombing experience for each of them but of course it was not in B-29s. They both knew each other, I think, but were not close friends. El was from Chicago and had been a Chicago taxi driver when he went into the Army.

Across from him, on the right side, was the Co-pilot, Danny Hurlburt. Danny was a Second Lieutenant, right out of flight training. He was from Missouri.

Immediately behind Danny was the seat of the Flight Engineer, M/Sgt. Reid. The Flight Engineer on a B-29 was an extremely important position. The B-17s and B-24s had engineers also, I believe, but the one on the B-29 had a different type job. The B-29s were so much more complex mechanically than their ancestors that the engineer's job became more complex also. In the earlier planes, the pilot's instrument panel had all the instruments, basically "flight instruments" (involved in flying and navigating the plane) and "engine instruments", those instruments showing information on the engines and fuel flow. In the B-29 most of the engine instruments (except the most fundamental ones) were mounted in an instrument panel monitored by the Flight Engineer. Where fuel was not the predominant worry for bombers flying in Europe, for the B-29's with their much longer over-water flights. fuel consumption was usually one of the biggest worries of a flight crew. The engineer monitored the engine and fuel instruments continually and kept a running log of the engine power settings used; the time at each power setting and the estimated fuel consumed at each setting. Sgt. Reid was an aircraft mechanic from many years back and the pilot swore that Reid could listen to the sound of the engines and tell if there was a minor misfunction in one of them. He trusted Reid's ears more than he trusted the engine instruments.

Next position in our nose-to-tail description of positions was the Navigator. For this crew—yours truly. I had a little table to work on. The table was hinged diagonally so I could fold it up if anyone wanted to pass. This was necessary because the round bin holding the ammunition for the four machine guns in the top forward turret extended from the roof of the plane almost to the floor. It ended about fifteen inches from the floor level, where a smaller ammunition bin for the two machine guns in the lower forward turret projected up into the cabin. The lower right corner of the Navigator's table hooked onto the turret ammunition bin. For anyone to pass through, the Navigator had to unhook his table from the bin and fold it up. The anyone was usually someone who wanted to use the urinary relief can which was immediately behind me! Immediately in front of my desk was a rack of electrical equipment which was part of the plane's structure. Immediately behind the Navigator was another bank of electrical equipment.

Around the intrusive upper turret on the right side of the cabin was the position for the Radio Operator, Sgt. Tyson. The plane had VHF voice radios for the pilots for short range communications. Tyson handled the long range communications, both sending and receiving; his communications being sent with dot/dash code equipment. He was also the crew member trained with first aid to treat any crew member wounded.

Immediately behind the radio and navigator positions was a wall, dividing us from the forward bomb-bay. The crew quarters for the plane were pressurized, a new development used on the B-29s but not earlier planes. At the lower side of the wall was a round door opening into the forward bomb bay. It had a little round window in it for the radio operator to use on the bomb run to tell the bombardier and pilot if all of the bombs had released properly from their racks in the forward bay. It was also one of the bail-out alternatives for the crew in the front part of the plane.

Immediately above the door to the bomb bay was another opening, the start of "the tunnel". Because the B-29 was built to pressurize during flight, you couldn't walk through the two bomb bays. The tunnel was your route from the front of the plane to the back. It was just big enough so that you could crawl on your hands and knees through it, without wearing a parachute of course. At the forward end of the tunnel, there was the opening for the astrodome. When the navigator wanted to use his sextant, he had to climb up into the tunnel, then turn around so that he was sitting with his feet dangling down into the forward cabin and his head projecting up into the astrodome where he could use his sextant. The tunnel was about eighteen to twenty feet long and crossed the length of both bomb bays.

In spite of the large size of the plane, there was very limited clear space for the crew inside. In the front portion described above, there was only one spot of relatively clear space. When you entered the plane through the ladder in the nose wheel well, this space was the opening up through the floor of the plane into the forward cabin. When everyone was aboard, there was a hinged trap-door to the well which would then be closed, forming a bit of floor space, roughly about four by four feet square. This was our only clear area up front.

At the rear end of the plane as you exited from the tunnel, immediately in front of you was the pedestal seat for the top gunner. Also on either side of the plane near the top gunner's seat was a "blister". The blister was a Plexiglas dome which bulged out the side of the plane and in each one a side gunner's gun-sight was located. These were the side gunner's work stations. In addition to manning the guns, the side gunners had a very important additional duty. From their positions they could see the rear of the two engines on their side of the plane. The side-gunner's important additional duty was to tell the pilot immediately if anything unusual seemed to be happening with the engines on their side, things like smoke, or flames, or a stream of oil. The two side gunners were Sgt. Vey and Sgt. Slider.

I don't remember the name of the upper gunner—he was very quiet and usually let the other gunners do all the talking. He was the very youngest member of our crew. I do remember one remark he made about his gunner's seat, right after we flew our first combat mission. He said it was his church pew. When you asked him why, he said it was because he did so much praying there.

Immediately behind the three gunners, a wall closed off a little room where the radar operator's APQ-13 set was. The wall let the room be dark so the details on the radar scope were more easily discernable. The Radar Man was Lt. McMinis. He was a second lieutenant, like I was, and had navigation training, like I had. The back door of the radar room marked the end of the pressurized area. Next was a section of the plane which was not pressurized and behind that in the very tail of the plane was a small pressurized compartment, just big enough for one man, the Tail Gunner, who was Sgt. Slingluff.

Getting into and out of the plane was a little unusual. The nose wheel of the plane was located right by the Flight Engineer's station. On the ground of course the nose wheel would be down and there were steps, like a small ladder which you could climb to get in the forward part of the plane. When the plane was airborne and the nose wheel retracted you couldn't bail out through that way due to the size of the nose wheel. Emergency procedures, if you had to bail out, called for the pilot to lower the nose wheel so you could bail out through the nose wheel well. Of course if the plane's hydraulic system had ceased functioning you couldn't bail out that way because the nose wheel would not come down. We didn't like to think of that. The next alternative was to bail out through the bomb bay and that involved having the bomb doors open. The bomb doors were activated by compressed air and hopefully they could open, even if the hydraulic system was not operational. If the bomb doors couldn't be opened, the alternative here was to hope that there would be enough time to crawl through the tunnel (sans parachute), buckle the chute onto your chute harness and bail out through the rear door. If that was impossible, the only alternative left was to fold your hands and start to say, "Our Father, Who art in Heaven...."

Entering the plane was a different proposition for those members whose duty stations were behind the tunnel. Behind the radar room, in the unpressurized section of the plane was a side door. This was their entry route. Due to the shape of the fuselage, when the plane was sitting on the ground, the entry door was around fifteen or so feet above ground. Each plane had a wooden ladder to use in the climb into the plane. Last man in would pull the ladder up into the plane.

Having spent six weeks in Gunnery School getting to be on a first name basis with the machine gun, I was very much interested in the defensive machine guns. Where in gunnery school we had actually held the grips of the guns themselves when firing them, in the B-29 the guns were "untouched by human hands" when being used in combat. The B-29 had a remote firing system. The guns were in turrets and the gunners had gunsights which were linked to the turrets electrically. The top front turret had four machine guns in it. The other three turrets (upper rear, lower front, and lower rear) each had two machine guns. The tail gunner had two machine guns also which were separate from the central fire control system. The central fire control system had a primitive analog computer which calculated the amount of "lead" to give the guns when firing. After my weeks in gunnery school, I learned that my only job with the guns was to set three sets of figures into the computer—our altitude, our airspeed, and the temperature. Each turret was under the primary control of a specific gunner but control could be passed from one gunner to another, necessary to continue firing at a fighter as he passed the plane.

One of the earliest training missions was one designed to test the Navigator's mettle. They called it the "get lost mission" and we flew it in a B-17. It was a night mission and I had to go away from the navigator station for about an hour and a half while the pilot flew somewhere unknown to me. At the end of my isolation (in the rear of the plane) I was to go forward to the Navigator Station, use my sextant to take a star fix to learn where I was and then give the pilot a compass heading toward home base. In plotting a celestial fix, you plot your position relative to an assumed position and the closer the assumed position is to your true position, the more accurate the celestial fix is. I guess I fudged a little on my flight. When I went to the back part of the plane, I kept watching the stars and could guess what our approximate course was. When Smitty called me to come up and find where we were, I assumed that we were over New Mexico. We were and my celestial fix looked pretty good to me and I gave Smitty his compass heading to go back to Pyote.

We flew one training mission which was miserably uncomfortable for the crew. It was a bombing training mission. By now the season was early winter and our practice bombing was from 20,000 feet. All of us were wearing only minimal cold weather clothing, counting on the plane's heater to keep us reasonably warm. It didn't!. Sgt. Reid kept manipulating the heater controls but nothing he could do helped to get the heaters going. We were just getting unheated air, coming into the plane at the temperature it naturally was at 20,000 feet. The plane's pressurization system was working so we didn't have to use oxygen masks. Since it was a practice bombing mission, the Bombardier could only release one bomb on each run and we had to make a lot of runs. The bombs were 100 pound practice bombs—Blue Devils. These practice bombs were made of light steel and were filled with sand, plus a small charge of black powder to give a flash of light at night or a puff of smoke in the day time. When we finally dropped the last of our required bombs, Smitty immediately brought us down to a lower altitude and as soon as we landed everyone headed for the hot coffee.

The B-29 aircraft were a relatively new design and used the largest engines available at the time and even these were just barely powerful enough to lift off the ground the loads necessary in the war. The biggest problem was that the engines sometimes at the worst possible time would overheat. Usually just one of the engines but at a take off it was critical that all four engine's performance be up to snuff. Pyote was located at an altitude of over two thousand feet. This meant that the air was thinner than at sea level and thus the wings had less lift. Because of the constant possibility of an engine overheating, as soon as the plane lifted off the runway, the pilot stopped climbing and flew at an altitude of about five hundred feet off the ground for five or ten minutes to give the engines a rest from the high power setting necessary for a take off. A real opportunity for sight-seeing, only there wasn't all that much to see except desolate West Texas countryside.

Because the planes, and especially the engines were such a new design there were problems cropping up every day and these kept the ground crews busy. One night after Estelle had gotten off from a stint in the coffee shop in a hangar, she very seriously said to me: "Dear, when you are in one of those planes I want you to be especially careful."

"Why?" I asked her. "Why especially careful?"

"Be careful of all those bugs."

"Bugs? I haven't seen any bugs."

"But all day when I was in the coffee shop, I heard those mechanics and they kept saying that the planes had a lot of bugs in them. I hate bugs!"

I'm not sure that she believed me when I explained that the mechanics were not talking about little six-legged creatures. But I'm also not sure that she wasn't just teasing me.

When Christmas approached, we could see that it would be a little on the drab side. It was my second Christmas away from home but it was her first Christmas away. At that time we were staying in the small bedroom in the employee dormitory. Somewhere she managed to locate a spindly little artificial tree, about eighteen inches tall. We set that up on the chest in the room and it seemed to make things a little more Christmasy. We both could eat in the Officer's Field Ration Mess for a nominal charge and of course the Mess put on the usual big holiday feed on Christmas Day. And there was the Officer's Club where we could do a little celebrating. Best of all, it was our first Christmas together and we were happy just being together.

Pyote—the town—was so small that there was not much in

the way of stores. A small grocery store, a drug store, and a little movie theater. Probably a liquor store also but I'm not sure on that. On one of her explorations to Pyote Estelle struck up a friendship with a Mrs. Price. Mrs. Price owned several pieces of property in Pyote and she had about three small "apartments" which she rented to couples. One of them was vacant and Estelle wanted us to move into it. I was happy in the Dormitory but she felt restless because now that she was married she wanted to be able to cook for the two of us. We decided to move into it and found that the one we moved into was the smallest one. Actually it was more in the "shack" class and you had to go to a community bath and toilet outside. But, it had a stove.

After moving into Mrs. Price's apartment, we found the surroundings somewhat different. It was the last building before the West Texas desert began. At night we could hear coyotes howling, a new sound to both of us. There were several gaunt cattle wandering around. Occasionally one particular cow would forage through our outdoor garbage container, hoping to find something remotely edible. And there was a scrawny little dog wandering around, more terrier-looking than anything else but no particular type of terrier.

Estelle's family were all accustomed to more meat in their meals than our own family had been. She had never done much of her family's cooking, since that was considered her mother's province. She wanted to surprise me with a meat loaf, so she went to the little Pyote grocery and surrendered some meat ration coupons for some ground beef. When I came home at supper time, I could smell that something good had been cooking but nothing as good as the smell showed up on the table. When I questioned Estelle, she said, "I wanted to surprise you with a meat loaf. Mrs. Price told me how to fix it. I made it and put it in the oven until it looked done. Then I took it out."

"And?" I prompted. "Why didn't we have it at supper?"

"When I took it out, the meat loaf looked good. But there was a lot of clear liquid in the pan. It didn't look right to be there so I threw it away."

I had watched my Mother fix meat loaf many times and I remembered that she always had to pour off the liquid fat that had accumulated in the bottom of the pan. I described that to Estelle and she said she wished that she knew that when she took the pan from the oven.

I asked her where she threw the meat loaf and she said that she put it on a paper for the little stray dog to eat. I remarked that it was probably the biggest meal that the dog had had since the war started.

That event doesn't mean that she was not a good cook. Her family was a large one and most of the older members worked, including her mother. Estelle had not had any opportunities to learn but she was a fast learner. And her next meat loaf was delicious!

The last training mission for us was to be a long distance flight to practice distance flying. A standard flight; from Pyote to Houston, then diagonally across the Gulf of Mexico to Havana, Cuba, then to a little island south of Cuba (Isle of Pines) where we were to drop a practice bomb, then retrace the whole route back to Pyote, all this without landing.

Because of the B-29s tendency to have engines overheat, most crews declared an emergency over Havana and landed there. While there the crew would do a little overseas shopping. These emergency landings were suspected by the training people but none of them ever did anything about it. For our crew, our pilot was good, our plane was good and we made the whole trip without landing in Cuba.

When I got back to our little room it was in the small hours of the morning. I expected to receive a warm kiss from Estelle to welcome me home. At first she was a little stand-offish and I was puzzled. Then she explained. Since she didn't expect me to be back that night, she had gone to the Pyote grocery and bought a favorite delicacy of hers—pickled herrings. I believe the Polish word for it is something like "Sledgies". She was afraid that the herrings had made her breath a little on the strong side, hence her initial coolness. It was good to be home again and I convinced her that I didn't mind the sledgie-breath one bit!

We finished our crew training at Pyote but for several weeks there were no orders to move out, Apparently there was a strike somewhere in the B-29 chain of manufacturing and the flow of new planes had slowed. Since we were supposed to ferry a new plane overseas, we were kept at Pyote till the flow of new planes began again.

HERINGTON AAB

Herington, Kansas

The trip from Pyote to the next base was to be made by troop train and this meant that Estelle and I would not travel together as we had from Florida to Nebraska. Also, we were not told which of two alternative bases we would be going to. Estelle went with me to the place where the troop train was loading and we spent a couple of hours there together. I was worried about this situation because I felt that I should be the one telling Estelle where to go and how we would meet there. She assured me that she had made the acquaintance of the wife of the officer in charge of the move and knew where we would be but she said that she had promised not to tell me where it was. I found later that this was all just a brave line of happy-talk on her part. She knew which two bases might be our destination but she didn't know which one it would be. Even that was more than I knew.

This troop train ride would be a little different from any of the earlier ones. At least I knew my fellow crew members very well this time and several others more casually. Our aircraft commander, Smitty, was close friends with another aircraft commander, Dave Kellogg. Smitty and Dave had several interests in common. First, flying. Both loved piloting airplanes and they liked to rib each other about which was the best pilot. Second, bourbon. Kellogg had a third passion which he liked to pursue whenever he could—women. To fortify themselves for the long train ride they made sure that they had taken enough bourbon with them for the trip. I don't know if the Army had any regulations about taking bottles on a troop train; it probably was a no-no even if the regulations didn't spell it out. As far as I knew, they were the only two planning to binge their way to our destination.

Troop trains did not keep the fast schedule that most passenger trains did. We left Pyote around mid-afternoon and by dark we were rolling along, somewhere in either North Texas or Oklahoma. By that time Smitty and Kellogg were in rare high spirits. The coaches we were in were not especially old nor again, were they especially modern. I would guess they were a vintage of around 1930 or so. For the time that would not have been considered especially old. Smitty and Kellogg wanted something more exciting to do than just sitting on a seat and hangar flying about their own flying skill. They disappeared toward the vestibule separating our car from the next one and we didn't see them for a while. They were gone about thirty or forty minutes and when they came back they were both looking flushed and windblown. It wasn't long before they told us what they had been doing. Apparently in the vestibule one of them had dared the other to open the outside door and climb up on the roof of the car. They both did this and stood up on the coach roof as the train sped along, probably around forty-five miles an hour. The rest of us, all of us being cold sober, were amazed that they both would pull such a hare-brained and dangerous stunt. I wondered a little then and even more now what would have happened to our two crews if we had showed up at the staging base with almost full crews, minus only an aircraft commander in each case.

We made a stop in Kansas City where the train lingered in the station for two or three hours. I guess we must have switched to another railroad company and had to change locomotives and crews. Of course we didn't see much except the area around our track while we were there. Finally, we were on our way again.

Down the line several hours later, we were shunted over to a side track to wait, probably for another train to pass. There was another side track immediately adjacent to ours. Most of us had alighted and were walking up and down to stretch our legs. Another troop train pulled onto the other siding. It had Army troops too, though these were apparently ground troops. When the ground troops saw the air crew people from our train, they immediately started shouting to each other: "Hey, guys. Looky here! Airplane Drivers. Lots of Airplane Drivers!" We pretended that they weren't there. I have always wondered where they were headed—toward the Pacific Theater like us? Or would it be Europe for them?

We arrived in Herington in late afternoon and the train was shunted onto the side track going onto the base. It was a small base, the most prominent features being the aircraft hangars. On small bases the hangars tended to dominate the base visually, since they had to be taller than the usual one story wooden buildings. That was true here too.

After sitting in a train coach so long, I was ready to stretch out and give my leg muscles a break and after an evening meal I turned into bed early. About two AM I was awakened by the Charge of Quarters of the VOQ. "You have a phone call in the Billeting Office," he told me.

Who would be calling me here, I wondered? Who even knew I was here! Half-awake, I followed the CQ back to the Billeting Office. The phone call was from Estelle. "How did you know I was here?" I asked. And, "Where are you?"

"I'm in the train station in Kansas City," she answered. "I found out that you would be going to one of two possible bases. The woman said it probably would be to Herington but it could be the other base. Were you asleep?"

"Yes. But I'm glad to hear you. Will you take a train here tomorrow morning?"

"There's one leaving in a few minutes and I'll try to get on that one. If I'm not able to get that one, I'll take the one tomorrow morning. I love you."

"Meet me in the Officer's Club when you get here."

The next morning we didn't have any sort of duty scheduled, so I sat around in the Club after breakfast, waiting. At that time of day, there wasn't much going on and there were few people in the Club, other than employees. Most of the guys I had traveled with from Pyote were still sleeping.

Around ten AM I decided to go outside and walk around a bit

in the vicinity of the Club. As soon as I walked out of the door I saw a tiny, slender, familiar-looking figure approaching me. It was Estelle, of course. We were back together again! At least we would be together for the duration of our stay at this base. We had lunch together, then after finding that I wouldn't have any scheduled duties until the next morning, we took the bus into town to look for a place for us to stay.

During the war many home owners rented parts of their homes to service people. Sometimes it was just a bedroom with no kitchen privileges. In other cases it could be a bedroom with kitchen privileges. Though it varied in each case, kitchen privileges usually meant access to a kitchen where you could do light cooking; breakfast or a light evening meal in most cases. The place we found did not provide kitchen privileges but it was what easily could have been the family's guest room. Very clean, quiet, and very comfortable. We were happy to find it, knowing that our stay would be only for a week or so.

Herington AAB was a staging area for B-29 crews going overseas to the Pacific. At Pyote where we had trained for months, most of our personal flying equipment was "loaners" which we used while training and then turned in before leaving the base. Here we would be issued new flying equipment which we would take with us when we left the base. Including a new B-29 aircraft! Of course we couldn't keep the plane but the personal stuff we could. A new B-15 flying jacket, with a fur collar (synthetic), mohair fleece lining, knit cuffs, and an outside shell of sage-green synthetic sateen. There were trousers of the same material. A shoulder holster and a 45 caliber automatic pistol. Since the only time we probably would wear the pistol would be when flying a mission, a holster on the belt would be impractical. The gun would fall out when the parachute opened if we had to bail out. Hence the shoulder holster. Made us feel like newly-ordained gangsters. Sage-green flight suits, one of the most comfortable outer garments I ever wore but they always looked like you had slept in it. For McMinis and I, full sets of navigation equipment. Plotters, dividers, an E6-B calculator, brief case, and a brand new A-14 sextant. The sextant was heads and shoulders ahead of the old A-10 sextants. With the old one you had to count off two minutes while using it and make sure that you had a good piece of lead in the mechanism that marked the little plastic recording disc. The new sextant had a built in clockwork timer and averaging device. Celestial navigation could get tedious but the new sextant did a lot to ease the tedium. The big pain in the neck was the full set of books needed to solve the mathematical work in figuring a star fix. There were several different systems for doing this math. One skinny little book was the easiest to carry (I think it was called the "Ageton System"). But its small size was not enough to win it a place in our kit because the actual paperwork with it took several times as long to calculate and required many more steps where you could make an error. The system we would use went by its publication identity. I think it was called H.O. 214. It was a mass of numerical tables printed in a hardback book about five by ten inches and about an inch thick. Not a bad size but unfortunately each book only covered four degrees of latitude. They gave us complete sets. You didn't have to take the whole set on a mission to Japan. But since you would be flying generally north on each mission, you had to take enough books to cover the route from the Marianas Islands (in the tropics) to most of Japan. One other book, a copy of the Air Almanac. It covered the ephemeral information for the sun, moon, several planets, and the imagined point in the sky called "The First Point of Aries".

 We were to fly overseas in the new B-29. This system got the plane into the combat area without having to call on a professional ferry crew. It also gave us some more experience in making long over water flights under peaceful conditions before being thrown into combat. Before the overseas flight, we made two or three local flights to check the plane out. On one of them I had a major role to play; it was a "Compass-Swing" flight.

 In an ideal world compasses would point to north or show your course as a departure in degrees from North. In our real world this was not the case. First there was an error to correct for called Variation. This was an error caused by the fact that we measure from the North Pole but the compass points to the North Magnetic Pole which is located a good many miles south of the North Pole. This error is predictable and most maps we would be using would show the amount of variation for the different areas. Another error—the one we are involved with here—is one resulting from the fact that an aircraft has a lot of equipment in it which affects the compass operation. Magnetos in the engines for ignition and generators in the engines to power the plane's electrical system; a good many radios generating radio waves. Plus considerable amounts of iron, particularly in the engines. All of these cause the plane's compass to give erroneous readings. This error varies from plane to plane and within one plane can change when the ground crew pulls off one engine and replaces it with another one. This error would not be physically correctable. Rather, a table of corrections had to be computed to apply to the readings. For smaller planes the table of corrections would be calculated on the ground on a compass "rose" (a paved area with compass lines painted on it.) For a larger plane with a navigator station, the crew would fly a flight called a "compass swing". It would be done on a sunny day. The pilot would fly straight and level on a particular compass heading. The navigator, who was using the astrodome would use a "sun compass", an ingenious little gizmo, to determine what the true heading was. The difference between the pilot's heading and the navigator's sun compass reading was the amount of deviation and would be recorded for the deviation table. This process would be repeated for different headings all the way around the compass face. Actually it was a bit more complicated because the Navigator had to compute the celestial data for the sun to enter into his sun compass and he had to keep changing the celestial data in the sun compass as time passed. Actually a "swing" with a sun compass was probably more accurate than a ground "swing" on a compass rose, since it would be a measurement made when the plane was actually flying. The staff in the flight operations section told us that in Kansas the farm field lines were laid out exactly North and South and East and West and that we could swing the compass with the bomb sight. I think the Bombardier's reaction was a few moments of silence, then a disinterested "Huh???" We actually did our swing with the sun compass.

With our plane "checked out" to our satisfaction and all of our new equipment issued to us, we were at the point where it was time to go. I'm not sure but I believed we stayed a little longer because the next day was Good Friday, then it would be Easter later. They let us stay for the religious holiday. I remember one event. There was an outdoor loudspeaker around the BOQ/Club area and there was some beautiful music playing over it. They told us that it was the Good Friday music from Wagner's Opera, *Parsifal*. I guess the Chaplain was a music lover and was playing the music because of the day.

The day for us to leave arrived and it was a sad occasion for those of us who had wives at the base. Beside Estelle, Danny Hurlburt's wife was with him, as well as Mc Minis's wife. After final kisses and embraces, Smitty herded us all into our new plane.

Our destination for this leg of the flight was Travis AAB in California, the big aerial departure point for Pacific points. At least it was for the Army. I'm sure that the Navy had their own big departure base somewhere in California.

While browsing around the Base PX, at the jewelry counter, I saw a beautiful pearl Rosary. Although we had not been attending Church since getting married, Estelle prayed with her Rosary frequently. At the time she was a Catholic and I was a Protestant. I thought it would be a nice gift for her, so I bought it and somehow managed to get it wrapped and mailed to her. I learned later that she was both surprised and pleased by my gift. She used the gift as her only Rosary for many years until her death, two wars and forty nine years later.

The stay at Travis was brief and now it was time for the departure to Hawaii. As I plotted the course line on my Mercator chart I realized what a big adventure even the first leg of the flight would be. California, on my map, looked so big and solid. Hawaii, our destination, looked so tiny. So much water, about twenty two hundred nautical miles, as I remember it. Could I find it? Does this celestial navigation really work? The crew in flight operations had to include their own scare story. "Be sure and put the Magnetic Variation in right when you are figuring your Compass Heading. There was a Dutch Crew flying a B-25 who put their variation in the wrong way and the last we ever heard of them was as they disappeared somewhere up near Dutch Harbor Alaska." I tried to pass it off as professional banter. But I checked my math several times when figuring out the compass heading for the pilot! You should remember that this was 1944 and only ten years earlier flights to Hawaii by any one other than Pan American Airways in their modern flying boats were something of a stunt.

The weather was good and our flight was uneventful and we arrived at Hickam AAB safely.

KWAJALEIN ATOLL

The next stop after Hawaii was Kwajalein Atoll. The flight to Kwajalein was not as intimidating as the flight to Hawaii. Where the flight to Hawaii had been mostly at night, the flight to Kwajalein was in daylight hours. These were just my first views of long overwater flights. Later, night flights became easier since navigational aids were usually more abundant at night. At night you had stars (assuming good weather!) and the night time range of Loran was much better than its daytime range. But unless your destination is a big city with bright peacetime lights blazing it's more comforting to be looking for a small island destination in daylight. Kwajalein was a small island. And, at that time, it was the gateway to the war zone. Although Pearl Harbor and Hickam were the first places hit, Honolulu itself had not been hit. But Kwajalein had been fought over.

Kwajalein still was showing one very visible memory of those times. Much building had taken place since Americans secured it. But that one memory was especially visible, a large pile of scrap aluminum, bits and pieces—big pieces of what had been aircraft. The individual aircraft had lost their identity and nationality, at least to a casual observer. It was all piled into a big mound, waiting for disposition. I assume that it was loaded on an empty ship heading back to the States to be melted down and reused. Maybe airplanes again. More likely pots and pans. It was gone the next time I passed through the island, right after the war.

After landing most of us had occasion to visit the nearest latrine. It was there that I first saw that phenomenon of World War II, that graffiti which appeared miraculously in latrines all over the Pacific and even later back in the states. There it was, written on the wall to inform all who saw it: "Kilroy was here!" It doesn't matter who Kilroy was. What mattered was that he was there!

We learned a more sobering fact very soon. We would be taking off the next day for Guam. But we learned that our plane's machine guns would have to be loaded. Ever since we left Kansas the ammunition bins in the turrets had been empty. That would change now. Our planned route would pass fairly close to Truk Atoll. The Atoll had been converted by the Japanese into one of their major bastions and supply points. Our Navy had hit the base with a big carrier bombing raid and as a result, Truk itself was not the base it had been. But the Japanese still held it; it had an airfield and it could be a trouble spot for us. I guess the biggest potential danger, though, would have been if a Japanese aircraft carrier suddenly showed up in the area at the same time that we did.

Smitty and the other officers on the crew disappeared somewhere. I barely noticed that they were gone; for myself I didn't feel like leaving the area around our plane. Sgt. Reid was probably busy checking the condition of those parts of the airplane other than guns. The four gunners were busy loading and checking the guns. I don't know where Tyson was; probably helping the gunners. It became late afternoon. I had felt a longing to be helping with the guns. But I couldn't have been any help, really. The guns themselves I knew and understood. But they were mounted into turrets and I had never even seen the inside of a B-29 turret's mechanics. Besides, the gunners probably would have resented having a nosy second lieutenant trying to tell them what to do when he knew nothing about the subject. They were all good guys and I trusted them with no mental reservations. They finished and soon they were gone also. I sat and watched the plane and the Pacific close beyond it. The sun was nearing its setting point and soon it would be getting dark and the sparkle would be gone from the waves. It was a peaceful moment and I wanted it to last a long time. But it ended too soon; the sun sets quickly in the tropics. I watched our plane as it began to get dark. I thought it was such a beautiful creation and I was proud to be a member of its crew.

GUAM 1

The Lay of the Land

The flight from Kwajalein to Guam was smooth and uneventful. No sign of enemy aircraft. For that matter, there was no sign of American aircraft either. We had the sky to ourselves, at least within the range of our vision. Bright sunshine all the way and unlimited visibility. But we were glad to see Guam when it finally came into sight.

It was early afternoon when we landed at North Field, later renamed Anderson AB. We followed the FOLLOW ME jeep which led us to what would become our own revetment. A FOLLOW ME jeep was a regular Army jeep with a big sign mounted on its back, the sign saying FOLLOW ME. Its purpose was to lead a plane unfamiliar with an airfield to its assigned parking spot. On the field each B-29 had its own revetment, in most cases a circular parking spot with a small shack close to it. The small shack was for the ground crew's comfort and convenience; a shelter during a rain storm, a shady spot from the tropical sun and a place where the crew chief could secure his tools. In effect it was the work station for a particular ground crew. It was also the spot where the crew chief and his crew would wait hopefully for the return of their plane from a combat mission. A crew chief would be assigned to each plane permanently and in most cases a special relationship grew up between the aircraft commander and the crew chief responsible for his plane. Crew chiefs took their responsibility very seriously and the aircraft commander respected this feeling. Each revetment was close to the long taxiway so that a plane would only have to roll a few feet before turning onto the taxiway. There was minimum spacing between revetments which simplified traffic when the planes made a mass take off.

When we were parked and Smitty shut down the engines, the ground crew immediately gave us some startling news which they had just learned. It was news that President Roosevelt had died. The news was a big shock. In addition to being the war time president, President Roosevelt was our Commander-in-Chief. And he had been president since most of us had become aware of national news.

We were given a quarters assignment immediately on reporting in. The quarters were Quonset huts, the tropical version. I guess that the big difference between the tropical version and the colder-weather version was that our version had screened ends rather than solid ends with a canvas curtain which could be rolled down over the screen in stormy weather. Of course there was no stove in our Quonset. I had heard the description of a Quonset as looking like a big round oatmeal box which had been cut in half lengthwise and placed on its side. Our personal furnishing was a folding canvas cot and two wool GI blankets. No chairs or cabinets or tables. Most of us would find a wooden box or two to set by the cot to keep our possessions on. After enduring several training films on malaria, I expected to be sleeping under a mosquito net. But mosquitos were no problem, probably as a result of vigorous aerial spraying of the area with DDT. Consequently, no bothersome nets and few problems with bugs.

Right away Smitty went to a meeting with the Squadron and Group Commanders and some of their staff (probably the Operations Officers). When he came back he said that they had planned to split our crew up and use us as individual replacements for vacant positions in existing crews. Smitty argued that we had had a better than average training record and cited the fact that we had made the long flight from Pyote to Cuba and returned without landing in Cuba as most crews were doing. The commanders agreed to let us stay together as a crew.

Before the airfield had been made, the whole area had been covered with a jungle. We called it jungle although it was probably more like a thick forest and did not have the dense undergrowth of a conventional jungle. Bulldozers had pushed all the trees down and pushed them over to the edge of the area which had been cleared, leaving long windrow lines about ten feet high of tree trunks. It was disconcerting the first night when we noticed as it was getting dark, that there was a guard perched up on the windrow, armed with a carbine. Our Quonset mates who had already been on Guam told us that the sentries were there because there were still Japanese stragglers in the jungle.

With the canvas cot and the two wool blankets there had been no sheets or pillow. I folded one blanket length-wise so that the folded blanket was as wide as the canvas cot and used it as a mattress, folding one end back about fourteen inches so that it made a pillow of sorts. I slept every night with my pistol under the pillow part of my blanket. I used the other blanket as a cover.

The fellow on the cot next to mine was Lt. Godsey, a co-pilot on another crew. His cot was about fifteen inches from mine. We slept as the Army usually required with our heads on opposite ends. One night, probably around two or three AM I was awakened from a sound sleep by something pounding on my thigh and a sort of squealing sound. I immediately reached under my blanket pillow for my pistol and started to look around for something to fire at, a confusing job in the darkness. Fortunately somebody else managed to get a light turned on. It turned out that Godsey was having a nightmare and was kicking vigorously in his sleep. He said that in his dream he was in a bar and a gang of guys started beating him up and he was fighting back. I told him he came mighty close to being shot by me because I felt somebody attacking me and I knew that for me it was not a dream. I thought at the time that it was a Japanese straggler making a one-man banzai charge.

Our living amenities were all of the rough-hewn variety. Toilet bowls were not bowls by any stretch of the imagination. They were old fashioned privies, the pit having been blasted out of the underlying coral rock. We had a large, impressive shower and sink facility with about eight or ten sinks and an equivalent number of shower heads. The walls were planks up to about arm height, then screen wire from there on up to the ceiling. There was no hot water. And, sad to say, there was usually no cold water either!

In the humid tropics a daily bath or shower is almost a necessity, at least for one raised in our culture. Some ingenious individual had come up with a solution for the usual lack of water in the shower room. Remembering that a Quonset was shaped like a half of an oatmeal box, the residents in most of the Quonsets had scrounged lengths of steel and nailed a little gutter along the side of the Quonset, slanting it toward one end. At the end stood a couple of open-end steel drums for the gutter to drain into. There usually were several rain showers during the day and night and these kept the drums filled. Next to the drums was a wooden box and on the boxes a couple of steel helmets. To take your shower, you undressed, went out to the drums, took a helmet full of water and poured it over your head and body. Then, gave yourself a good soaping and finished off with several helmets full of water. Modesty? It was an all male environment and no one ever gave a thought to modesty.

Getting clean clothes was a little more complicated. There was no laundry service or machines. You washed your clothes in a smaller drum with water from the big drums, then hung your clothes on a make-shift line. At one period I had an extended problem with one batch of laundry. I washed it and hung it on my line. Before it dried, I had to fly on a combat mission. The missions lasted a long time and the little showers came fairly frequently. When I returned from the mission, expecting to find my washing dry on the line, it was wet from a shower or showers while I was gone. Before they dried I had to go on another mission and came back to a line of wet clothes again. It would have been impossible to bring them indoors when I had to fly because there was no place to put them. The soil on that part of Guam was a red clay, like real Georgia clay. With the scant washing I was able to give them my white boxer shorts acquired a semi-permanent auburn cast. When I came home, Estelle used to grumble about it every time she did laundry.

The privies were the source of several stories. They were blasted down into solid coral rock. The structure was of rough wooden construction and most were either six-holers or eight-holers (using Chick Sales terminology). To prevent the growth of flies, someone would spray fuel oil down into the pit every day or so. One individual, one of those individuals who likes to read and smoke when doing his duty was sitting on one of the seats and, finishing his cigarette, dropped it through the next adjacent seat. The result was an explosion, not a disastrous one but enough to teach the individual a lesson about smoking in GI privies.

For drinking water, everyone had their own canteen. You could either fill it from the traditional Army Lister Bag of water, or fill it at the mess hall. The Lister Bag was made of canvas, rubberized on the inside and hung in a convenient shady spot. It was fine if you didn't mind your drinking water having a rubber and chlorine taste. The mess hall water was a little tastier and was pretty good when you were thirsty.

The problem with water was because Guam had no lakes or streams, at least any of real consequence, and no underground aquifers to draw on. The problem was vastly compounded because our air base was manned by several thousand Army personnel. South of us by about three miles was a huge Marine camp with a whole division of Marines housed there. Further on down there was another Army airfield (smaller than ours), and the port with extensive port workers. Plus, the civilian population of Guam. Some of the water which did arrive at our base had a slight fuel-oil taste to it. You had to be a little on the thirsty side to feel like drinking it.

The food in the mess hall was fairly good. The biggest complaint was that lamb stew appeared on the menu more often than any of us would have chosen. There were stories in the states even after the war about GI's in Europe complaining about being served Spam so frequently. I don't remember that we ever had Spam in our mess hall. With us it was the too-frequent lamb stew. I think the reason for that was that our Quartermaster was getting a lot of lamb (mutton?) from Australia which was closer to us than the states. Lamb stew can be rather tasty in the winter in a colder climate. But we were in the tropics and the stew was a little too rich for our appetites. At breakfast the eggs were always scrambled eggs, made with reconstituted powdered eggs. Except for flight crews who had just returned from a combat mission—for that meal it was always a real treat to have real eggs for that first meal after landing from a long tiring flight.

For many of the areas in the Pacific war, a big problem in areas which had been secured from the Japanese Army was the danger from Japanese stragglers. These were remnants of the Japanese Army who were hiding out and trying to keep the war going in their own little limited way. In most cases they had been thoroughly indoctrinated by their Japanese training that it was the ultimate disgrace to become a prisoner of the enemy. For some reason, the Japanese stragglers on Guam didn't see things the way the banzai enthusiasts on other islands did. One of them achieved a bit of fame on his own. In quite a few squadron areas, a softball diamond would be set up for off-duty troops to play on. In this case, the diamond was fairly near one of the many windrows of bulldozed trees. This guy would come out of the jungle and sit up on the windrow, watching the softball game. When a player would hit a homer, he would jump up and down and cheer, along with the player's team mates. If anyone headed over toward the straggler, he would disappear into the jungle.

There was another straggler incident which was even more unique. A Major was sitting in one of the privies, doing his duty and reading a book. He looked up and stared at a Japanese straggler who was walking toward him, his hands raised. The man wanted to be made a prisoner. This, of course was contrary to all the stories about Japanese not wanting to become prisoners of war. When the interrogators questioned the Japanese, he said that he did not want to be shot when he was surrendering, as his superiors had warned him would happen. He said that he figured that no one would shoot him while their pants were down. Very true but the Major couldn't have shot him in any case because the only time any of us walked around with a gun was when we were getting ready to fly on a mission.

One night our crew was the only crew in our Quonset which

had not been scheduled to go on a mission. Where there were normally about twelve or so people lounging around the Quonset; this night there was only about four or five of us. The lights put out as much illumination as a candle, so it was too dark to read or play cards. Nobody had a radio and we were all lying around, half awake. To help keep crews awake on the long missions, there were "wake up" pills available to you if you felt the need. One of the crews scheduled on the mission that night had to abort the mission right after take off. One of the crew members had apparently taken several wake-ups right before take off. When his plane came back, he was hyperactive from his pills, couldn't read or do anything he wanted to and in an effort to get sleepy had imbibed of the creature in the bottle. It made him belligerent. He started down the line of Quonsets, looking for action. He would stick his head in the door and ask in a loud voice, "Anybody in here want to fight?" One of the fellows in our quarters replied that we were not interested in a fight, so he went on to the next Quonset in the line. We never heard if anyone took him up on his invitation. Probably no.

We had a theater of sorts. An outdoor one with a professional sized screen. There were no formal seats. For seating there was a huge number of boxes, roughly the size and shape of a coffin on their sides in concentric half-circles. The boxes had been shipping containers for bombs. The movie equipment was professional grade thirty-five millimeter film equipment and you had a movie of acceptable quality. The big annoyance was the weather. You learned to always take a raincoat and helmet to a movie because without much warning it would suddenly be raining. At the first pitter-patter of drops, everybody stood up to don their raincoat and helmet. A few minutes later the shower would be over and then you had to take the coat off because it was too hot with no rain falling. I remember one scene in one movie. I don't remember the name of the movie but it was a war-time movie and took place in New York City. The hero was a second lieutenant and escorted his lovely date into his apartment. The living room had a "step-down" entrance into a large, very large and luxurious living room. Suddenly a loud voice from among us piped up, "That's his place? On a second lieutenant's pay?" Probably one of our own second lieutenants speaking and we all had the best laugh of the whole movie at that part.

The basic level in the Air Corps (and also later in the Air Force) was usually the Squadron. At this field on Guam, the lowest level you identified with was the next level up, the Group. We were assigned to the 19-th Bomb Group and found out that it had a prominent history in the current war. It had been at Clark AAB in the Philippines when the war started. They were equipped with B-17s and as the Japanese moved in, they had to retreat down through the islands to the south, fighting as they retreated and finally ended up in Australia from where they continued to fight. Eventually they were brought back to the states and later were equipped with the new B-29. After Guam was recaptured from the Japanese, the 19-th was one of the Groups moved to Guam. We were assigned to the 30-th Squadron, one of the three flying squadrons in the 19-th.

Somehow I learned that Noah Sweat ("Soggy" Sweat), one of my room-mates at Coral Gables was on Guam also. He was in the 29-th Bomb Group, I believe. I took a walk to their Group area and had a chat with Soggy. He had already been on Guam somewhat longer and had flown several missions. He gave me a technical navigation tip which he had picked up and which I found useful a couple of times on my own later missions.

I understand that the crews flying in Europe usually flew daily missions. We did not. Our missions usually were at least thirteen hours long, sometimes a little longer. And that was just the time in the air. The take-off was usually in mid or late afternoon for a mission hitting Japan at night. For a mission hitting Japan in the daytime, take off was usually the night before. Thus, a single mission would take place on parts of two days. This does not include the briefing and preparation time before the flight and the de-briefing after return to the base. And after the return to the base, long hours of hard work for the ground personnel to get the plane ready for the next mission. It would have been physically impossible for us to have flown daily missions.

GUAM 2

Typical Mission Scenario

Of course every mission was different from the ones before it and the ones after it. But the general scenario was usually basically similar. When not flying, usually we didn't have any duties other than keeping up with the bulletin board for the mission notice. The notice's two main items of concern to you were the time of the briefing and what crews were scheduled to fly on the mission; more to the point—was your crew scheduled? A normal mission scheduled probably about twelve crews per squadron or 36 for the Group. A maximum effort mission would schedule every plane in commission for flying. The time of the briefing depended on whether it was planned to hit the target area at night or during daylight. For a night mission, the briefing would be around mid or late afternoon with take off scheduled right after evening chow. With about six or six and a half hours of flying to reach Japan, a seven PM take off would put you over Japan around one or two in the morning. For a daylight mission you would take off around ten PM or eleven PM to arrive shortly after daybreak. The actual time we used on our watches was Greenwich time.

The briefing area was a big barn-like wooden building. Inside were seats for the crews and up front a small stage. Our center of attention as we assembled before the briefing started was the big wall map at the rear of the stage. It covered the ocean from the Marianas, up past Iwo Jima to Japan. For Japan it showed only three of the main islands, Honshu, Shikoku, and Kyushu. Honshu was where the largest cities were located—Tokyo, Osaka, Yokohama, and Kobe. There were a couple of larger cities on Kyushu—Fukuoka and Nagasaki. The fourth main island was not in view. It was Hokkaido and not included for two reasons: there weren't many targets on it and more importantly (to us) it was beyond our B-29 range. Even some of the targets on the northern part of Honshu stretched our range and to reach them the planes could have bombs in only one of the bomb bays; the other bomb bay had to be used for a big removable bomb bay fuel tank.

The reason for the interest in the map was because the route for the mission would be outlined on the map, in colored yarn. The route would be the same for all missions as far as Iwo Jima. At Iwo the route would then vary, depending on what part of Japan was the target for the mission being briefed.

At the scheduled time for the briefing, someone would shout, "Attention." and we would all rise and stand at attention until the command, "At ease," or "As you were." Then we all took our seats again and the briefing would begin. The first briefer would tell us what the target for the mission was, and for the larger targets some background on the intended target. He would be followed by several other briefers, each giving information about their own special area of concern. One would tell what enemy opposition might be expected, either flak or fighters. Another one would brief us on what sort of bombs we would be carrying. A weatherman would explain the predicted weather. One briefer who was given special attention would be the one who gave the location and description of the rescue facilities. This was a vital interest, since when you left Japan there would be at least three hours of over-water flying before any land—that land being Iwo Jima. The first rescue facility would be the submarine. The Navy would put one of their submarines on station ten miles off the Japanese coast. If a plane were damaged over Japan or developed serious mechanical problems, the pilot would try to reach the sub's assigned station where the crew could bail out. I don't know what the overall tally for such rescues was but the sub did pick up two crew members who bailed out of one of our 19-th Group planes (the Navigator and the Tail Gunner). There certainly would be other saves for other Groups. About fifty or a hundred miles farther was a Dumbo on station. Named after the little elephant in the Disney movie, the Dumbo was a B-29 with a lifeboat fastened under the fuselage beneath the bomb bays. The lifeboat could be dropped by parachute where a plane ditched. Those were the two rescue facilities of most immediate concern to us. On some missions there might be another Dumbo closer to Iwo Jima. But no more rescue facilities south of Iwo. At Iwo the pilot would make a decision whether he should land there or continue on to home base—Guam in our case, or Saipan or Tinian for other B-29s. Iwo Jima usually became a very busy place after a mission. A few planes landing might have battle damage or a wounded crewman; others mechanical problems. Probably the majority would be planes where the crew didn't feel that they had enough fuel to make it home safely. We would take off with a normal fuel load of six thousand gallons and when we got home again, the engineer would estimate that we might still have two hundred gallons. The B-29 was a thirsty critter and there was usually some discussion, the engineer saying that when the plane went into a landing attitude, there was a question as to whether all of that two hundred gallons would be available to the engines. No one ever settled that question for us.

After the main briefing for everyone, the group would break up into smaller groups for information of interest to the various job specialties. For me, it would be the Navigator briefing. The group navigator would give us the latest information on weather—cloud cover and wind speed and direction for the weather en route and at the target. I had long since learned that these were only estimates. And one very important bit of information to Navigators—the Time Hack. Time accurate to the second was vital for celestial navigation.

The Navigator was responsible for navigating the plane to the Initial Point of the bomb run if it were a night mission and planes were bombing individually. If it were a daylight mission the Navigator was responsible for reaching the assembly point for the formation. Once in formation, the Navigator in the lead plane was responsible for the element, though of course you did have to keep up with where you currently were!

The Bombardier took over for the bomb run from the Initial Point to the target. When he spotted the target, he would center the telescope in the bomb-sight on the target and from that point the pilot did not fly the plane. The bomb sight telescope was linked to the plane's autopilot. With the Bombardier guiding the telescope, the bomb-sight flew the plane until the bombs released automatically at the proper point. The release point was determined mechanically by the internal mechanism of the bomb sight. After the bombs fell, the Navigator was responsible for navigating the plane back to home base. This was the situation for the old bombing cliche, "Up until the bombs release, you're working for Uncle Sam. After release, you're working for yourself!"

The Bombardier would be given as much information as was available to locate the target, especially if the target were a smaller one, such as an individual factory.

I don't know what was covered at the Pilot's special briefing. But I'm sure some of it involved timing of the engine start and procedures for taxiing. Take offs were an involved procedure. The objective was to get about a hundred and twenty or thirty planes airborne as close to the same time as possible. The field had two parallel runways, about twenty five yards apart. Your plane took off one minute after the plane ahead of you on your runway took off. The same applied to the other runway so that there was a plane taking off on one or the other of the runways every thirty seconds.

After the briefing, crews reported to their own aircraft sitting on its revetment. Ground crews would have been at work many hours before this, checking engines and electrical equipment, loading bombs and machine gun ammunition, pumping in the six thousand gallons of aviation gasoline. Even the Mess halls got into the act—they provided a sandwich lunch and canned juices for the long flight. The crew chief would have his crew standing by, helping the flight crew in any way needed. After preflighting the plane, the flight crew would board and sit, waiting for the time to start engines. Timing was important here. If you started the engines ahead of time, you would be burning fuel while waiting and eleven or twelve hours later you might be wishing for every gallon burned and wasted by starting too soon.

The group take offs were one of the most impressive things I ever witnessed or participated in. There would be a line of B-29s, well over a hundred, nose-to-tail, each with four engines idling. To give an idea of the noise just when idling: right after the war car manufacturers started making muscle cars. A car with an engine cylinder displacement of four or five hundred cubic inches was considered a muscle car. Each engine of the B-29 had thirty three hundred and fifty cubic inches of cylinder displacement. There were four engines on each plane and the total cylinder displacement for each plane would be thirteen thousand and four hundred cubic inches—as much as twenty seven muscle cars. Each plane's engines would be idling when standing still, or revved up to make the plane move and keep up with the line. A lot of deep-throated noise.

Although taxiing toward the take off was a thrilling display of power, for me the take off was the scariest part of most missions. We were loaded to the maximum possible; the B-29 was underpowered for take offs and the engines sometimes would overheat. The runways were about two miles long and slightly "sway backed". The sway back was a little bit of help in helping the plane overcome its inertia and build up speed. At the lift-off end of the runway, the over-run continued two or three hundred yards, then suddenly you had a bonus of five hundred feet of altitude. The field was built near a cliff of about five hundred feet height and if you made it past the cliffs, you were high enough so that if you had an engine problem then, the Bombardier could salvo the whole bomb load into the sea and magically make the plane twenty thousand pounds lighter. I loved that massive, gray-black cliff!

One of the more noticeable differences between the B-29 missions and those flown in Europe by B-17s and B-24s was formation flying. In Europe it was necessary to join up formations soon and fly most of the mission in formation for mutual protection from German fighters. For the B-29s it was a different matter.

Formation flying uses more fuel than our cruise-control flying did, since the following planes' pilots were constantly jockeying the throttles to keep their place in the formation position. For the B-29 crews, minimizing the fuel burned was vital. On night strikes, there would be no formation at all during the whole mission. For daylight missions crews would fly independently to a formation assembly point right by the Japanese coast and assemble into formations there.

After the take off, there was the three to three and a half hour flight to Iwo Jima. Going north, Iwo was just a check point. After crossing the island, the Navigator would give the Pilot a Compass Heading for either the target area (night strike) or the assembly point (day strike). This would usually be another three to three and a half hours of flying. After the business in Japan was completed, the flight home began. If you had no battle damage or mechanical problem(s) and if it looked like you had enough fuel to get home, the flight back to Guam retraced the flight going north. Otherwise, you hoped you could reach Iwo Jima and make a safe landing there.

Assuming that your plane was still in good condition, there remained one more tricky task. At take off time, everything had been precise and done according to the clock. At landing time, there would be over a hundred planes arriving at the base at one time, each crew member hoping that there was enough fuel to get the plane down safely on the ground. I don't know how the pilots managed it but somehow everybody was always able to fit into a landing slot approaching one of the runways and land.

The ground crew assigned to your plane was always happy that their plane was back, especially so if there had been no battle damage to deal with. The Aircraft Commander and the crew chief would confer, the AC telling of any malfunctions that had cropped up on the flight. Then, it was off to the de-briefing session.

De-briefing was in the briefing room. There was a large porch in front of the main briefing room. The Red Cross would have two or three workers there (female!! The only women we ever saw) and they would be giving out coffee and doughnuts. Also, a medic would be handing out to you your combat ration if you chose to take it. The combat ration was a shot of bourbon. This was before your crew was debriefed. It was usually a noisy, boisterous crowd waiting to be debriefed. Everyone was tired and tense, with the tension slowly leaving (for most of us) thanks to the coffee, the bourbon, and the unaccustomed feminine presence.

Debriefing was by Intelligence people and the purpose of the bourbon was to get you to relax and be readier to talk and give them any information you had which might be of interest to them. Without the bourbon, you usually were dead-tired, tense and not too ready to talk to anybody except the other crews who had shared the experience.

One final chore remained, and this was a voluntary one. Breakfast! Real fried eggs out of a shell instead of the usual scrambled eggs made with powdered eggs.

The workload for the crew varied, depending on what your position was. The Flight Engineer, who kept up the Cruise Control Log and monitored the engine instruments worked every minute of the flight. So did the Navigator and Radio Man. The Bombardier had nothing to do except during the time over Japan. The two Pilots took turns flying the plane but that essentially was minding George, the autopilot, and watching the flight instruments for anything unusual. Two gunners would be on watch at all times, each sitting in one of the side blisters and watching the rear of the engines. But with four gunners on board, they could take turns watching, The Radar Man would usually switch on the radar set when we approached Iwo Jima, switch it off as we left the island and then turn it back on as the plane approached Japan. But from about thirty minutes before we made landfall at Japan, through the bomb run and until about thirty minutes after we departed the Japanese coast, everyone was at their station and in contact over the interphone with everyone else on the crew.

Being young and in good physical condition you usually shook off the fatigue of a mission without any real problems. But, when missions were going out every other day, after several days or a week the fatigue started building up. I remember coming back from one mission and finally reaching my cot in the Quonset about two-thirty or three in the afternoon. The cot looked so inviting I couldn't resist the urge to stretch out for a few minutes. Still wearing my flight coveralls and big clunky GI shoes, I lay down, my feet still resting on the floor. I woke up the next morning, feet still on the floor and my body in the same position it was when I lay down.

GUAM 3

First Missions

The first combat mission our crew flew was actually a combat mission, even though we did not get credit for flying "a Mission". They did count the flying hours as "combat flight hours". The distinction is mostly one of counting air time logged and giving credit for major missions.

In the early months of the war, the Japanese had taken control of all the islands in the Marianas group. The most southern and also largest island was Guam which was an American possession before the war. Guam was one of the stopping points for Pan American Airways new flying boats air route across the Pacific. The flying boats used on this service were much larger and newer than the old parasol-wing antiques we flew in at Coral Gables.

Next island, going generally north, was the island of Rota, a fairly small island. Still going generally north were the larger islands of Tinian and Saipan. There were other larger islands in the Marianas group farther north but they did not figure in the wartime flying picture.

Although it was a small island, the Japanese had built an airfield on Rota and established a garrison there, probably a small one. Our top military command did not see Rota as being enough of a prize to warrant a landing and fight to secure the island. So, the island was "neutralized", meaning continuing small bombing raids, enough to make Rota ineffective as a threat. The neutralizing solution as far as our commanders were concerned was to make Rota a training target. When a new crew arrived on Guam, they would fly their first mission against Rota, aiming their bombs principally at the runway to keep it unusable for further Japanese flying. As I remember it, we dropped a full load of five hundred pound bombs on the target. With frequent similar missions by other crews on other days, the runway on Rota was probably pretty well chewed up. We didn't encounter any anti-aircraft fire and of course there were no fighters to worry about.

I assume that the troops at Rota could detect any major B-29 raid leaving Guam for Japan and that they would radio this information back to Japan. But since all of our missions headed for Iwo Jima first Rota could only tell the Japanese defense people that there was a mission on the way and it could be for any part of Honshu or Kyushu. They would have to wait until the planes passed Iwo Jima before they could narrow down a guess as to our target. That was Rota's small contribution to the defense of Japan and I wonder if it was really of much help.

About the time we, meaning our crew, were ready to fly our first mission, the battle for Okinawa was raging. The B-29 aircraft did not participate directly in that battle. But, I believe it did make what I hope was a major contribution to that operation. The troops fighting on Okinawa were being supported by a large armada of Navy combat vessels, supply vessels, hospital ships—all of the array of vessels supporting a major landing operation. The Japanese had gone into the Kamikaze tactic in a big way during this battle. To refresh your memory, the Kamikazes were loaded with an explosive and the Japanese pilot would crash purposely into an American target, usually a ship.

Kamikaze planes were usually smaller, single-engine planes and presumably were taking off from small airfields on the major southern Japanese Island of Kyushu. It was here that the B-29s came into the picture. The Kamikaze planes were small and could be hidden easily. But their landing fields could not be hidden so easily and the American photo-reconnaissance planes located the airfields involved. The assignment for the B-29 crews was to make these airfields unusable for Kamikaze takeoffs.

Since the Kamikaze planes were small planes, they did not require the long paved runways necessary for larger, heavier planes.

They could fly from grassy fields, such as we had at Carlstrom in Arcadia, Florida.

The missions against the Kamikaze airfields would be daylight missions, and this meant that we would be bombing the target from formation flights. For each targeted field, the attacking flights would be fairly small, about six to twelve planes. Even if the flight only had six planes it could do considerable damage to the target field, since each B-29 would carry forty five-hundred pound bombs. The fusing put on the bombs was interesting. Half of the bombs had instantaneous fuses and these bombs would explode as soon as they hit the ground. The other half of the bombs had delayed action fuses, the delay period ranging from a few minutes up to thirty-six hours. The field surfaces were all grass or dirt and could be repaired quickly by dumping dirt into the bomb crater and leveling it. That was the reason for the delayed action fuses—to keep the field unusable as long as possible.

The first mission went uneventfully until we were in the target area. The Initial Point for the Bombardier was about ten miles west of the target airfield. Our bomb run was on roughly the heading to go back to Iwo. As we approached the target, there was some anti-aircraft fire, not a great deal of it but enough to keep your attention focused on it. Before Boyd locked the bomb sight on the target, Smitty was pulling back and forth on the flight yoke, making the plane behave a little like a roller-coaster. But when Boyd locked the bombsight onto the target, Smitty flew a flat altitude. The anti-aircraft fire continued and we passed over the target. Apparently Boyd had done something wrong in setting up the plane's bombing circuitry and none of our bombs dropped. They still hung intact on the shackles in the bomb bay. Boyd rechecked his pre-bomb run routine and located the problem. Smitty broke away from the formation; made a hundred and eighty degree turn and we did the bomb run again. This time the bombs all dropped properly.

A few of our friends in other planes in the flight teased us for making the second bomb run. But for our crew, it seemed the natural thing to do. We didn't want to drop our bomb load into the sea and certainly didn't want to haul it back to Guam.

The second mission was another flight against the Kamikaze airfields on Kyushu. On this one, everything went smoothly and uneventfully.

The third mission was another one against the Kamikaze airfields. By now everything had started to become routine. A smooth flight into Kyushu, a routine lining up on the Initial Point and what started out as a routine bomb run with the usual moderate amount of anti-aircraft fire. Suddenly things were no longer routine. I don't remember whether it was just before we dropped our bombs or just after. I think it may have been just after. We were flying smoothly and level when there was suddenly a big bang inside the front area of the plane. The plane pitched up sharply and Smitty called out over the interphone: "Stand by to bail out!"

I looked up toward the pilot's area and it was partially obscured by grayish-white smoke. Then there was the calm voice of Danny, the copilot, saying, "Hold on Smitty! She's flying OK now". Danny had taken over control of the plane because Smitty had been wounded.

Fortunately our target was close to the coast and in a few minutes we were out in the relative safety of the open ocean. There had been no Japanese fighters and after several minutes flying over the open Pacific, we felt secure from anything else from the Japanese. Now we could take stock of our condition.

Our guess was that what had hit us was a small cannon shell, probably a 20 millimeter one. The roof of the plane, from above the pilots' seats sloped downward toward the nose of the plane. From the area immediately above the pilots' heads, the roof was panels of clear Plexiglas. The cannon shell had entered one of the Plexiglas panels in front of the copilots seat, angled down and hit the top of the pilot's rudder pedal where it had exploded. Smitty had taken a small piece of shell casing into his right leg, above and to the right of the knee. The Bombardier's seat was just ahead of the pilots rudder pedals. Boyd had been hit by the force of the blast and it threw him forward onto the bomb sight. Fortunately for him, he was wearing a flack jacket and steel helmet. His backpack parachute was on his back also. He was not wounded, though his parachute took a beating from the explosion. I think the shell must have had some phosphorous in it to give it more of an incendiary punch. Little flecks of burning material had been blasted into the chute and smoldered until he put them out.

We never could figure out where the shell had come from. Japanese fighter planes were armed with 20 millimeter cannon, I believe. But the trajectory of the shell seemed to rule out a fighter plane, unless the pilot nailed himself a terrifically lucky (for him!) shot and we hadn't seen any fighters. If it had been from Japanese ground defense guns, normally the path of the shell would come up from below the plane. My guess was that it had been from a ground defense gun which had missed anything while ascending and had hit us by mere chance on the way down. No matter which, the Japanese had scored one on us.

Sgt. Tyson, the radio man, was the person designated and trained to give emergency medical care to anyone wounded. He came forward and helped Smitty out of his seat and over to the only clear area up front, the door to the nose wheel well. There Smitty could stretch out and Tyson treated the wound. Since the wound was not really too serious, we could find amusement later in one aspect of it. Just before going into the target area initially, Tyson had eaten his flight lunch and washed it down with a good bit of canned tomato juice. It turned out that Tyson was one of those individuals who get very upset at the sight of blood. Although Smitty had not been bleeding very much, the sight of the blood had upset Tyson's stomach. He was able to contain his feelings until after he had done a good job of bandaging Smitty's leg. Then, it caught up to him and he upchucked. Very self-consciously he tried to clean the messed up area as well as he could with the limited materials he had. We all agreed later that the sight of the upchuck was bloodier looking than the actual blood had been.

With only one pilot able to function now, we faced a seven hour flight back to Guam. McMinis, the Radar Man came forward and sat in Smitty's Pilot seat for the whole flight home. The three or so hour flight to Iwo Jima gave Danny and Smitty time to make a decision about Smitty's condition. He did not seem to be losing any significant amount of blood and was reasonably comfortable stretched out on the nose wheel door. If we landed at Iwo Jima, he would get professional medical treatment at least three hours sooner than if we continued on to Guam without landing. Danny and Smitty decided that when we reached Iwo Jima if the plane and its fuel supply looked okay, it would be better to fly back to Guam without landing. For Smitty it would have been much better, since the medical facilities at Iwo Jima were probably in a tent while those at Guam would be in a wooden building.

The weather for the flight back could probably best be described as "usual Pacific calm," meaning good visibility, moderate winds and little if any turbulence. We reached Iwo Jima at the expected time and everything looked okay for the plane to go on. So, we went on, turning onto the course for Guam.

As we neared Guam, Danny made a comment over the interphone that gave us something to think about. He said, "I guess you guys don't know it but I've never been checked out on landing a B-29." That was a new thought for us. Being "checked out" meant formally demonstrating to a designated check pilot that you could be expected to perform the operation professionally well. We all respected Danny's flying ability, especially his cool reaction when Smitty was wounded, so we didn't give it a whole lot of worry. Maybe a little but not a whole lot. There was nothing else to do.

When we reached the airfield's traffic pattern Danny was able to get us into a landing slot with not too much trouble. A job for the Navigator was firing the signal gun, the "Very Pistol." Right behind my seat there was a hole in the ceiling of the plane designed to accept the muzzle of the signal pistol. The signal pistol fired a rocket signal flare and combat procedures called for a plane's crew to fire a red star flare just before touching down. The flare alerted the waiting ambulances that there was a wounded person on the plane and one of the ambulances would tag along behind that plane, following it to the revetment.

During the long flight back home, Smitty had not complained about pain. I don't know if the wound was not painful or if Tyson had given him a shot of morphine. The wound itself turned out to be only a flesh wound and had not hit any of the bones in the leg or knee. He was in the hospital two or three weeks and then returned to duty status.

Hit a Brace, Mister!

Bombs Away!

Estelle Thompson

Wartime Wedding Picture

Christmas Party, Japanese PX Warehouse Crew

Relaxing at the Frolic Danceland, Miami

Delta Sigma Phi Hobo Party—Last College Fling!

B-29 Flight Formation Approaching Japan

Troy Thompson Jr.

GUAM 4

New Crew

With Smitty in the hospital, his crew was no longer a complete crew. Now we had become ten crew members to be used as replacements for vacancies in other crews. I believe I was the first of our original crew to be reassigned to another crew. I replaced the Navigator on Capt. O.G. Estes' crew. I don't know why he needed a replacement since his Navigator had not been wounded. Gossip among the crew was that it was a serious personality clash between Estes and the Navigator. I never did try to pry into the matter and found, as we worked together, that I seemed to fit into the crew harmoniously.

Next to be reassigned from Smitty's crew was Boyd Madsen, the Bombardier. I guess that Boyd would have been a highly desired replacement, since he had been a bombing instructor in Bombing School. Boyd was also reassigned to Estes' crew so I would continue flying with at least one member of our original crew.

Since the change in crews did not involve changing my quarters assignment I never did get to know them as well as I did the first crew—Smitty's crew. One of Estes' Gunners apparently was a student of history before going into the Army and he liked to call me "Magellan", after the Spanish sea captain.

I never did fly any more missions against the Kamikaze airfields and I don't know if any more were flown by other crews. With Estes crew we would be flying what had become traditional targets for B-29s—factories, and then mostly fire raids against cities.

Our crew had arrived on Guam in the latter half of April. The month before, March, the Group's planes took part in the most devastating raid of the war against Japan, "the" March fire raid. Several factors coincided to make it even more devastating to the Japanese than the Atomic Bomb raid against Hiroshima. The Atomic Bomb had a more decisive emotional impact on the Japanese but the March fire raid against Tokyo caused more destruction and loss of Japanese life.

This impact was due to a combination of factors rather than a single planning factor. Tokyo is located along the west bank of Tokyo Bay (Tokyo Wan in the National Geographic Atlas) and the Tokyo metropolitan area covered a lot of real estate. The raid was one of the early fire raids and the target area was the eastern part of Tokyo, near the waterfront on the Bay. The factor which made the fire raid so much more devastating was one which couldn't have figured in the planning. Mother Nature, at the time of the raid, brought a winter storm with very strong winds from the East; probably the winds were around sixty miles an hour. These strong winds blew the flames over against other predominantly wooden buildings outside the target area and created what must have been an impossible job for the firemen. The Japanese government controlled news so rigidly that they would not let the population know of any of their military defeats, such as the naval battle of Midway. This raid could not be hidden, though, since a big portion of the civilian population had been involved.

"Tal" Alred, the Radar Man on Estes' crew, told me about some of the raids on Tokyo in March. The Japanese had not developed radar controlled anti-aircraft guns as effectively as the Germans had. Their optically controlled anti-aircraft cannon was fairly good—if they could see the planes involved. In the Tokyo area they had a large number of anti-aircraft guns and searchlights. On a night mission, though, they couldn't do much damage, since the sky was full of individual American planes which they could not see without radar. The cannon would fire aimlessly and the searchlights would search frantically. When one searchlight would happen to lock onto a B-29, every other searchlight in the Tokyo area would also lock onto that hapless plane and all the antiaircraft cannon would also concentrate on that one plane. Big trouble for the B-29 crew involved!

To make the planes harder to see at night headquarters (above our Group Headquarters) came up with a new idea. Since the Japanese defenses did things strictly by eyesight, why not make the planes harder to see? To put this idea into effect orders came down to paint the underside of all the planes black, including the underside of the long wings. It sounded like a good idea to a person sitting behind a desk and not going out on missions. The pilots were very unhappy with the idea after it was put into effect. Before the change, the planes were all the same aluminum finish that Boeing made them. There were identifying numbers and the US white star insignia, plus nose-art pictures on the fuselage. But they were mostly aluminum finish. The pilots complained that the paint added "about two hundred pounds of weight" and cut the airspeed for a particular throttle setting by about ten miles per hour. Both of these were undesirable, considering that fuel conservation was always one of a crew's biggest worries. To make the change more galling, the new paint job originated in the night missions over Tokyo. But on day missions the black underside was much more visible to the Japanese gunners on the ground and shortly after, most of the night missions were against smaller cities which did not have the searchlights and antiaircraft cannon which Tokyo had.

We had one minor experience which would have been unusual except at the time we did not realize that it was unusual. A technical modification to the aircrafts' radio communication systems came out. Our crew was ordered to make a one day flight to the big base on Tinian Island for the pilots and the radio operator to have a short indoctrination and training period. Although this was not a combat mission and was a fairly short trip, the whole crew had to make the trip. For those of us not involved in the radio equipment, there was nothing to do except wait. Most of us just stretched out on the concrete ramp, under the shade of the big wing and snoozed. Boyd was not involved in the radio training and he decided to go visiting, trying to locate any of his former bombing students. He came back with an unusual story. He said that there was a very secret area and he had talked with one of his former students about it. The student said that the area had a very unusual, very secret item. Some sort of thing that was big, would be carried on a B-29, and the temperature for it had to be controlled very carefully. This meant nothing to us at that time, just as the incident with the Oak Ridge female workers had meant nothing to us back in Knoxville. It was only later that we learned anything about the atomic bomb.

GUAM 5

A Hodgepodge

While the memory of the first three missions falls into place in an orderly way, putting events with mission number and target; on later missions the mission number, the target and the memorable events don't connect as readily. It soon became something of a treadmill; go out, get scared sometimes; get bored more times; and as the number of missions grew, get more and more tired with my canvas cot and blanket-mattress becoming a more and more important goal to look forward to. Smitty was a good pilot and he loved to fly. I found that Estes was also a very good pilot and I had the feeling that, if the facts of a combat situation gave us anything of a chance of returning, O.G. would get us back. A comforting feeling.

I had expected to see more Japanese fighter planes coming up to tangle with us. But I can remember only two missions where there were any. On one, our assembly point was just a few miles off the Japanese coast. That day they did send some fighters up. None attacked us, meaning our own plane. But during the time the planes were assembling into an organized diamond formation it was attacked. Several large planes, flying in a big circle at about sixteen thousand feet, trying to join into a formation are in a vulnerable defensive position. I didn't see it happen when one of the planes was hit. But the plane crashed into the ocean and, looking down, I could see the big plume of flames rising from the water. We wondered if anyone bailed out, and if they did, was it into a life as a POW?

On the other mission where we met fighters, there apparently were more fighters. At the Navigator position, I had one small window which looked out just ahead of engine number one and engine number two (the two left engines). The gunners had much better visibility and they were calling out sightings. I did see one fighter who did a chandelle up past my window. He did a quick wing-over and was gone from my view. There was another fighter which was more threatening but I couldn't see that one from my seat. Boyd, at his Bombardier seat in the nose could take control of the front turrets, upper and lower, and fire at anything attacking from head-on. After it had happened, Boyd said that a fighter had attacked us from the front, diving at us. With our own airspeed of around two hundred knots and the fighter's speed of probably around three hundred and fifty knots or more, the two planes would be closing at around six hundred knots. Boyd said that the fighter didn't look like he was firing; it looked more like he was trying to ram us. If so, he passed a few feet above our tailfin, a near miss. There had been little time to wonder about it and when he was gone, he was long gone.

At the time of most of our missions, we found the Japanese fighter opposition usually missing. I have wondered about it and I suspect that our good fortune was a gift of those men who I consider some of the unsung heroes of World War II—the Navy's submarine crews who were cutting off the Japanese oil supplies. With little oil coming through to them, the Japanese probably had very limited supplies of gasoline to train new air crews. And it does take gasoline to train pilots!

Oddly, some of the heaviest flak I saw was not over Tokyo but on a mission over Kobe. It was disconcerting watching the big black puffs of smoke, right at our altitude and marching along right at our speed but off to one side, at least the puffs I could see. But whether there was flak or no flak—it varied from mission to mission—it seemed to happen mostly on the big city raids. Compared to the experience of the B-17 and B-24 crews flying from England and Italy I guess we were especially lucky. I certainly don't feel that we were deprived of anything we would want.

The raids against Germany had been mostly at altitudes of

twenty-five thousand feet, I believe. The designers of the B-29 designed a plane that could also bomb at those altitudes, even up to thirty thousand feet. But when it came to putting the plane into use against Japan, the commanders found that bombing from that altitude against Japan was not a good tactic. First problem was the jet stream. I'm not sure but I believe its existence was discovered in the early raids against Japan. But it created a serious bombing problem. Assuming that at the time of a mission the wind in the stream was blowing at two hundred miles an hour—how do you plan to hit your target? With the wind behind you, you zip along so fast that the Bombardier doesn't have enough time to track the target through the bomb sight. With the wind coming straight at you it reduces the ground speed so much that the plane becomes a big, slow sitting duck for enemy fighters or antiaircraft gunners. And if it blows to your side, to maintain the bombing course the plane has to "crab" so much that it seriously affects bombing accuracy.

The other big problem was fuel. Hauling ten tons of bombs up to twenty five or thirty thousand feet burns up a whole lot of extra fuel. And fuel was always the critical problem for the B-29s.

The answer to the two problems seemed to be the only obvious one. Don't go that high! So, before our crew arrived on Guam, the top command (Twentieth Air Force) decided to fly missions at sixteen thousand feet or less. For night missions it became even lower.

Not long after joining O.G.'s crew, the missions started becoming mostly night fire-bomb missions with occasional daylight missions. This meant that the types of bombs began to vary. Day missions were almost always five hundred pound high explosive bombs—forty of the five hundred pounders. They were shaped something like a watermelon, roughly about two feet long and about fourteen or so inches in diameter. Of the total weight, most of it was not explosive but the heavy steel casing. Before loading the bomb onto the shackles on the bomb racks, the armorers would screw the tail fin assembly onto the bomb, then screw in a nose fuse and a tail fuse. On the outside of each fuse was a small, multiblade propeller. As the bomb fell through the air, the wind would spin the propeller, unscrewing it until it fell off. When it fell off, the bomb was fully armed and any impact would cause the fuse to detonate, then the booster charge would blow and finally the high explosive inside the casing, all this practically instantaneously. As a safety measure, each fuse would have a safety wire—a length of plain wire holding the fuse propeller in place so it couldn't spin itself off. The other end of the safety wire would be fastened to either the bomb shackle or rack. When released over the target, the safety wire would stay in the plane and the bomb would arm itself and detonate. If the plane had a mechanical emergency over friendly territory, the Bombardier could "Salvo" the whole load and the safety wire would stay in the fuse so that the bombs didn't explode when they hit.

The armorers had a strenuous, dangerous job. The danger was not of an explosion. The danger was that the heavy bombs had to be hoisted with a little winch from their low, nearly flat dolly up inside the bomb bay. Once up inside the bomb bay, the bomb had to be maneuvered so that the two lugs on the bomb casing moved into the shackle, a removable gizmo which held the bomb until the bomb sight triggered the release. The shackle in turn was mounted onto the bomb racks, an integral part of the plane. The task became harder as more and more bombs were loaded. When the job was finished, you could see that a full load was a full load. The bombs for the fire raids came in more different varieties. Most common was a gray jellied gasoline bomb of about a hundred pounds each. These were assembled into clusters, then each cluster would be hung on a shackle.

There was one peculiar type fire bomb which we used only once, I believe. It was basically clusters of small fire bombs, each probably weighing about ten or fifteen pounds. These were packaged into packages roughly the size of the five hundred pound explosive bomb. Each package was hung on the shackles as a larger bomb would be. The unusual feature was that there was an explosive charge of primer cord in the center. It was set so that a few seconds after it fell from the plane, the primer cord would explode and scatter the smaller bombs. On the one mission when we used that type bomb, we were one of the later planes into the target area. It was a dark night and as we approached we could see that not only was the city below burning but the sky was filled with flashes of light, like a fireworks display. At first we thought that the Japanese must have massed all the anti-aircraft cannons they had at that one city. Then, the Bombardier told us that the fireworks was only the primer cord bursting from the planes' bombs ahead of us to scatter the small bombs over a larger area.

For the first few planes approaching the target on a fire raid, the mission had smooth air. As the first planes approached, the blacked-out city blended into the blackness of the surrounding fields. To find the city itself, the radar set was able to pick up the buildings and distinguish the building areas from the open fields. The radar was needed for only the first few planes. After the first few planes had bombed, then the city became visible in the darkness from thirty to fifty miles away and no radar was necessary. When a whole city, especially one of predominantly wooden buildings, starts to burn, it creates a tremendous amount of heat, which of course rises. The rising column of hot air becomes a strong wind blowing vertically, creating extremely bumpy air for the planes. On one mission, we were one of the last planes over the target and the rising column of air must have been rising at gale force. We hit it and it was like a blast, throwing the whole plane up violently. We had not dropped our bombs and I guess that the bombs and shackles must have pivoted up so that rather than hanging down, they were hanging up briefly. Then we hit another blast, this one a downdraft, and the plane dropped, the bombs in the bomb bay pivoting down now and slamming their ten ton weight against the shackles and racks. The jolt was like hitting something solid, very solid. The lights went out in the plane and all of our loose items were scattered everywhere. The lights came back on in a few seconds and Dempsey, the Radio Man, and I started looking for our loose items. Most of us crew members wore chest parachutes. With a chest chute, you wear the harness but not the chute itself—if you have to bail out you snap the chute onto two big clips on the harness over your chest. My chute ended up over under Dempsey's table; my dividers, plotter, and pencils were scattered all over, along with my map and log. I had been wearing a steel flak-helmet and the impact threw me up against the ceiling, mostly against the oxygen regulator valve. Without the helmet it could have caused a gash in my scalp but thanks to the helmet I wasn't hurt a bit. I didn't know any plane could stand up to that rough treatment but the plane itself was okay—many, many thanks to the Boeing company and its designers and assemblers.

We had another one of those rough rides on another mission. Not nearly as bad but for Dempsey it was a disagreeable experience. Right behind my desk and next to the round door to the front bomb bay was the relief can. The can was about eighteen inches high and fastened to the plane's frame with a metal strap. At the top of the can was a removable top and from it extended a rubber tube and a small plastic funnel. The relief can was for the crew to use when they needed to urinate. By the time we were in the target area, it had been visited several times by various crew members. On the bomb run, Dempsey was at his assigned post, peering through the small window in the bomb bay door to tell the Bombardier and Pilot if all the bombs had cleared the racks. We hit another one of the strong updrafts and it pitched the plane up. Normally the relief can would be secured by its metal strap anchor. This time it was not secured properly, came loose, the top came off and poor Dempsey was drenched, since the can was probably about half full. We all felt sorry for Dempsey, a quiet serious individual. O.G. was concerned that he would be cold but we were at only about eight thousand feet altitude and it was July.

As the raids continued, the towns selected became smaller and smaller. Headquarters (20-th Air Force) adopted a new tactic. Each time a mission took off, Headquarters would broadcast a warning to the Japanese. The warning would name five or six towns and tell them that from that group, we would be bombing two or three but not the others. For us, it was an unusual feeling, approaching a city which had been warned that you were coming.

At times I have had humanitarian regrets over the bombings,

especially the fire bombings. I know that there were many people killed and most would have been civilians. The sight from the air was spectacular but not in a pleasant way as it would be for a celebrative fireworks display. Here were homes being burned, many of them and people burned to death. Several years later when I was on duty with the American occupation of Japan, I was associated with Japanese who were in the fire-struck areas. One in particular, Masae, a pretty young woman who was our housekeeper and cared for my children. If I had known Masae before the war, I don't know if I could have gone through with the fire raids. I have never been troubled with "flashbacks". But at bed-time I never want any kind of red light, such as a clock or radio with red indicator lights—I dread the possibility of waking up and seeing the fires again.

But there had been precedents in the war in Europe. The Germans did their utmost to break the Dutch and the British with their bombings of Rotterdam, London and Coventry and other cities. And, the British and we had done it to the Germans later, especially at Dresden and Hamburg. I'm sure that the Japanese would have bombed our cities mercilessly if they had the geography and resources to do it.

On one daylight mission to a target on the western part of Honshu, it was a clear day and I could see what appeared to be a larger town in the interior. I looked at my map and saw that it was Kyoto and it did look like it was larger than some of the smaller cities we had been bombing. I wondered why there was no mission scheduled for Kyoto. It was later that I learned that the town was historic and a religious center for the Japanese with many beautiful temples and shrines. It never was bombed, presumably for this reason. Thank goodness.

GUAM 6

Places Other Than Japan

Aside from each crews' home base, the next most vital place to them and closest to their affections was Iwo Jima. It had been attacked, fought over, and secured at a high cost in lives near the beginning of the bombing campaign against Japan. Fighting had been fierce and brutal and the first time we had to land there, there was still the lingering smell of death in the air. The soil was gritty volcanic ash. Most, if not all, of the bodies had been disposed of properly but with countless bombs and artillery shells landing among entrenched troops, sometimes there wasn't much left to bury. The first time we landed there, probably late April or early May, one of our gunners went walking about, looking for souvenirs. The Japanese Army did not use leather shoes like our GI clodhoppers, rather their footwear was a tennis sneaker, one with a formed toe where the occupant's big toe fit. The gunner found one of these sneakers, partly buried in the dirt and decided he wanted it for his souvenir. When he tried to pull it up, he found that the foot of its previous owner was still in the shoe. The gunner was emotionally shaken by his find, though I'm sure that worse experiences than that were common among the Marines fighting there earlier.

I believe that our crew made at least two landings there. On one of them our plane's fuel consumption had been much higher than predicted on the trip from Guam to Japan and then back to Iwo Jima. O.G. decided that we probably would not have had enough fuel to get back to Guam, so we landed. It turned out, later, that the plane had a malfunction which did not show up readily to the crew. The engines were huge, radial affairs (meaning that the cylinders were in a circle around the crankshaft rather than in a line). There was a device on the engine to facilitate starting a cold engine, the primer pump. Before starting the engine with the starter, the pilot would give the engine several squirts with the primer pump. On our plane the pump mechanism stuck and one engine was priming itself during the whole flight. Didn't hurt the engine but it used up too much fuel. All we needed was some more gasoline which was available at Iwo. We landed, refueled, and were ready to take off for home. Only, we couldn't. So many planes had made emergency landings and parking space was so limited we were locked into the middle of a lot of other B-29s, We had to spend the night there. That in itself was a little more primitive than back at Guam but we didn't really suffer from it. The Mess was not a mess-hall, rather, it was a mess-tent. Bed was another canvas cot—like mine back on Guam but it was in a tent also. For any of us who felt put upon there was the sobering thought that if we didn't have Iwo, we might be floating on our survival rafts, hoping to be picked up. That is, if we survived ditching the plane in the Pacific. But, with Iwo as an emergency landing field, next day we would be flying back to Guam with plenty of gas and our plane would be available for more missions after the engine repair.

The other landing at Iwo Jima happened with a little more drama, at least drama to our crew. We were on a daylight mission in the Tokyo area. I was looking out my little side window at the two left engines and the little I could see of the ground. Suddenly, the number two engine developed a big problem. Between the circle of cylinders and before the propeller hub was a cone of metal, sloping from the cylinders to the hub. Suddenly the cone was covered with black, bubbling oil. The cone covered a gear system between the crankshaft and the propeller hub and something failed drastically in the gears and they punched out through the cone. I called out a warning to the pilot over the interphone and he immediately feathered the engine. So, we finished our bomb run on three engines and limped back to Iwo Jima. No further disasters on that trip.

We had no more dramatic incidents affecting our crew on Iwo Jima. But when you had landed there and were waiting for the action to slow down, sometimes there was suspense, sometimes even drama as you watched the other planes approaching the island to land.

In one incident, a B-29 approached the island at unusually low altitude from the general direction of Japan. It appeared to be flying reasonably normally. But, before reaching the island, parachutes started appearing below the plane. We counted the parachutes as they opened. There were ten of them. A normal B-29 crew was eleven men and no more chutes appeared. The plane continued on its same course, generally south and we never saw it turn. It was probably being controlled by the autopilot. Who was the eleventh man who had not jumped? I suspected that it was the Aircraft Commander and that he was probably dead. But we never learned why the co-pilot had not tried to land the plane, as Danny had done when Smitty was wounded. Speculation could probably give several scenarios but I'll never know.

In another incident, another B-29 approached the island from the general direction of Japan. This one had obvious mechanical problems. Two engines were feathered, both on the same side and the pilot had both engines running at far above the power setting used to take off, probably at the seldom used setting called War Emergency. A B-29 would fly okay with one engine feathered. With two engines feathered, it was another matter. First of all, it would be difficult if not impossible for the plane to maintain its altitude and it would probably slowly lose altitude. This is assuming that both dead engines were not on the same side. If the two dead engines were on the same side of the plane it would be impossible or nearly impossible to make a turn. The situation was either hopeless or very close to being hopeless. Just guessing, I would estimate that the plane's altitude was not much more than eight hundred feet. Too low to even think about turning with two dead engines on the same side. The poor hapless pilot continued on a straight course, disappearing over the distant southeast horizon. Another unfinished tale for us to wonder about. Ideally we hoped that the plane had been able to ditch and be picked up by a crash boat from Iwo Jima. But probably that was just a hope.

To increase the effect of the strikes against Japan, after Iwo Jima had been secured and some emergency flight facilities put into place, the Air Corps based a fighter wing on the island. They were P-51s (Yes, I know that later they were referred to as F-51s but this was 1945 and they were still called P-51s!). The tactic used was to have a B-29 with a Navigator on board fly toward the target area in Japan. The P-51's would fly formation with the B-29, using the big plane to find the way to the target area. The B-29 Mother-Ship would fly circles just off the coastline while the P-51s made their attack. When the fighters were through in the target area, they would again rendezvous with the B-29 to be guided back to Iwo Jima. This could be another reason why we encountered so few Japanese fighter planes on our missions.

Truk

As we flew past the Japanese stronghold island of Truk when we were approaching Guam from the States, we had been especially alert, both for anything approaching us from Truk and also for unsuspected Japanese carrier planes. Apparently the Navy's carrier plane raid on Truk had devastated the place but they still had an airfield capable potentially of future problems. We learned that Truk was being kept in a neutralized condition by continuing small air raids, just as was happening to Rota. We were scheduled to fly one of these small raids. A very small raid, just our plane. It was a daylight flight and our bombs were the usual five hundred pounders. At our briefing, the briefer who described possible defenses, said, "There are no known fighters there. There are one or two large anti-aircraft guns but they are old and the barrels are nearly worn out. You won't have any problem."

The flight to Truk was in beautiful weather, beautiful as the weather in that part of the Pacific frequently is. Brilliant sunshine sparkling on the quiet waves below. Little white, puffy clouds. Visibility from here to way, way out. No way for us to hide and of course they could spot us easily. The anti-aircraft gun or guns opened up before we reached the island, coming fairly close to us but not close enough to do any damage. Boyd made his bomb run routinely and we left for home.

The whole flight took a bit over six hours, as I remember. About half of the thirteen plus hours our regular missions to Japan took. Our flying time counted as combat time on our cumulative record of flying hours. But we did not get credit for a combat mission.

Search and Rescue

In the briefings for our regular missions against Japan, the briefer would tell us to report our ditching position if we were forced to ditch our plane. But they cautioned us strongly "Do not report your ditching position in the clear. Report it in code!" Reporting in the clear meant giving the actual geographical coordinates of the spot. There was a system for coding the position's coordinates. The reason was that although we (the US) controlled the ocean for practical purposes, there was always the possibility of a fast Japanese warship, like a destroyer, being in the area and the precaution was one of guarding against being picked up by the enemy.

One B-29 crew whose plane was approaching an emergency ditching for some reason broadcast their intention to ditch and gave the expected impact point in the clear. It became the object of a search mission. Our crew and two others were chosen to do a three plane search of the area where the plane reported they would ditch

We flew to the suspect area at a reasonable altitude, probably around eight thousand feet. We carried no bombs, only in the forward bomb bay we had one of the huge dropable bomb bay fuel tanks. With no bombs, plus the big auxiliary tank, we were set to fly for a long time.

When we reached the estimated plane's ditching position, all three of our planes dropped down to a very low altitude, from five hundred to no more than a thousand feet. We flew a very loose, broad vee formation, our plane flying in the lead. In each plane, one person would scan the sea below continually from the Bombardier's seat. Two more, one in each gunner's blister, would also scan the sea to their side. We would fly for about fifty miles, then the formation would make a wide turn to pick up a new course parallel to the first course back in the opposite direction for fifty miles. We repeated this procedure until the formation had scanned a square about fifty miles on a side. Unfortunately, we found nothing. It was tedious and grueling on the whole crew. Watching the surface continuously without looking up is tiring. For the pilots, flying that long at such a low altitude meant staying on the controls almost continuously without much relief from George, the autopilot. And for me, it meant using the driftmeter every few minutes. The driftmeter was a type of telescope looking down. With it you could tell how much the plane was drifting due to the wind.

In the whole search we saw nothing but water, water, and more water. No boats, no debris, nothing. The whole flight, including the trip to and from the search area lasted roughly about twenty hours.

We wondered what happened to the plane. I guess that there were only three alternatives. One, the plane did not survive its ditching and plane and crew sank immediately. Two, the ditching was successful and a Japanese destroyer or submarine picked them up. Three, we missed them on our search. None of the three was a happy alternative.

We learned later of another ditching which had a happier ending. The B-29 was on its way home, bombs gone and the fuel almost gone. The pilot radioed that they were ditching and they ditched successfully. The crew all made their way out of the floating plane successfully and inflated their one man life-raft dinghies, usually attached to their parachute harness. The Navy sent a fast ship which picked them all up successfully. Usually when a plane ditches, even in a successful ditching, the plane sinks very soon. The crew and their Navy rescuers assumed this plane would sink in short order and they left the scene. But with no bombs and with practically empty fuel tanks, this particular plane turned out to be amazingly buoyant. Next day a reconnaissance plane spotted the ditched plane, still floating. Another day later a Navy warship showed up and sank the B-29 with its cannon. This was to prevent the Japanese from showing up in a submarine, boarding the plane and taking any classified equipment. The briefers later warned us to not expect this with every ditching. They said that usually you could expect the plane to sink very soon.

GUAM 7

Two Wars End

The end of the war in Europe came as something of a surprise to us. We had no newspapers, magazines, or radio broadcasts. No radio because this was back in the days when radios tended to be bulky and none of us in our Quonset had one. There was an Armed Forces radio station and when flying on a mission we could listen to it on the plane's radio compass. But their news coverage was skimpy, especially about the war in Europe. I remember that the Armed Forces radio station would frequently play selections from the musical "Oklahoma". Sometimes when we were returning from a fire raid I would find it ironic listening to one song from that musical, "Oh What a Beautiful Morning". It was a beautiful morning for all of us because we were all alive and well. But for the unfortunate Japanese in the town we had bombed it was far from a beautiful morning.

I guess the news about VE must have broken after darkness. We had returned from a raid earlier in the day and most of us were asleep. It was probably around eight or nine PM when we suddenly started hearing a lot of cannon firing in the distance. Somebody, half asleep like most of us, said, "It's coming from the Marine Camp" (two or so miles south of us). We wondered what was happening and then somebody who was walking down the line of Quonsets stuck his head in our door and said, "The war's over in Europe. The Germans surrendered."

Quite frankly, none of us in our Quonset got up to celebrate. We were glad it was over in Europe but it was still going on in the Pacific; we were exhausted and knew that if we didn't get some sleep right then there would be no time for sleep later because later we would be going out again.

Missions did continue for us, just as they had before with no discernable lull in our effort, at least through the end of July and the first few days of August. But then suddenly we were not being scheduled for a mission. I learned later after the war that the first Atomic Bomb fell on Hiroshima on August 6, then three days later the second one on Nagasaki. Way down south of Japan on Guam where we were, none of us lower level people knew what was happening. This all occurred while we were in the lull in our regular missions. Peace didn't come to us with dramatic suddenness; rather we just stopped going out on missions for several days while we waited and wondered. Then we were told the fighting was over. Instead of the dramatic suddenness we expected it was just a routine feeling that came over a period of several days, a feeling that it was all over. No fireworks, no big hurrahs. It must have been far more fun celebrating it back in the States!

Later there was a Group announcement that there would be a Show of Force mission. The planes would fly up to Japan and fly over the major cities at low altitude, showing the Japanese population how many American aircraft were on hand. This would include B-29s from Guam, Tinian, and Saipan; more bombers from new fields on Okinawa, fighters from Iwo Jima and Okinawa, and probably a multitude of Navy planes from carriers.

Our crew was not scheduled for this mission, except for our Engineer Corky who went. He had been a Sergeant and had just been made a Flight Officer. He wanted to be on the flight, his first as a Flight Officer, to qualify for Flight Pay for the month.

A few hours after the Group took off on the mission, a rumor flashed through the Quonset area that a B-29 had crashed right on the field, just off the runway. Naturally a lot of us rushed over to the scene of the crash. It was a terrible sight, big and small pieces of aluminum scattered around and lingering wisps of smoke.

When I returned to the quarters area, there was an even bigger shock. The crew was one of the crews from our own Quonset. Everyone in the front part of the plane was either killed instantly, or in one or two cases died very shortly afterward in the hospital. These were guys I had lived with for about five months. Ed, the quiet Aircraft Commander. Godsey, the copilot who had slept next to my cot and scared me so with his midnight nightmare. Chuck, the Navigator. And Little Joe, the Bombardier. And our own Engineer, Corky, who had died making his first and last flight as a Flight Officer. Their Radar Man had not been on the flight and of course he was still alive and well.

I always think of the irony of the crash. There were fifteen or sixteen men in our Quonset. During hostilities, two had been wounded—Smitty who had a light wound and returned to flying missions, and Dave Baird, Bombardier on Lt. Gungle's crew. Baird had a rather serious wound in one of his arms and was sent home. But no casualties from hostilities during the whole time. Then suddenly, during the first few days of peace so many gone. Most of the remainder of us from the Quonset were pallbearers at a brief military burial service. They were buried in plain wooden boxes in a cemetery on Guam.

There was another shock of a sort also. I believe that the plane they were in was our usual plane, *The City of Lexington*. O.G. was from Lexington, Kentucky, and named the plane after his home town. It had been a good plane with only the one time when one engine failed. The rest of the missions everything needed always worked. I didn't hear much about the cause of the crash. Apparently they had had engine trouble, and came back to land. The plane was not lined up right with the runway to land and the pilot decided to abort the landing and go around again for another approach. The plane must have stalled at low altitude and couldn't recover.

Earlier I learned that there had been top level discussions about what would constitute a normal combat tour for air crews. Two alternatives were considered. In one proposal, the tour would be fifty missions; you would fly twenty five missions, then be given R&R (Rest and Recuperation) in Australia for a week or two, then return for the remaining twenty five missions. The other alternative was a tour of thirty five missions and then you would go back to the States. The decision was for the thirty five mission tour. At the time missions stopped going out, my mission count was twenty seven missions.

After several days of inactivity, we learned that a decision had been made about disposition of the various B-29 Groups. Our 19th Bomb Group would remain on Guam permanently. (It was still based on Guam in 1950 and was involved in the Korean War, flying its missions from Okinawa.) Crew members with a high mission count would be transferred to a B-29 Group on either Saipan or Tinian which would transfer an equivalent number of crew members with low mission count to Guam as our replacements. I never learned what the magic cut-off number was but I was in the high-mission-count group and was transferred to Saipan. I lost track of all the guys from our Quonset. Although I was casual friends with some of them, I wasn't really a "buddy" as I had been with Ed Yablonski in Gunnery School.

At Saipan I moved into a Quonset which was almost empty, with only one crew living in it. A couple of the guys in it were somewhat memorable. One, I think he was called Bernie, was fond of his whisky. One night he felt like doing some sociable drinking. He would say, "Well, guess I'll have me a little pick-me-up. Who wants to join me?" No one would accept his invitation. Earlier someone had found a Japanese skull and had put it on the top of a cabinet and Bernie would walk over to the cabinet, look up at the skull and say, "Care for a drink with me, Tojo?" (The real Tojo, you may remember, was a Japanese Army Officer who became the de facto ruler of Japan.) Of course there was no response from the skull. Bernie would have his pick-me-up and the rest of us would continue our reading. Later there would be more invitations from Bernie, none of which were accepted. Before the evening was over, Bernie had "tied one on." The next day several of us from the Quonset were scheduled to fly a compass-swing in a B-29. Bernie was the copilot.

After a B-29 has been sitting idle for several hours, the crew would have to go through a propeller rotation with all four engines. With a radial aircraft engine where the cylinders are in a circle around the crankshaft, several of the cylinders at the bottom of the engine are upside down or nearly upside down. If there is significant oil leakage inside the engine and the plane sits idle, the result could be one or more of the bottom cylinders might be filled with engine oil. A cylinder could take the compression of the fuel-air mixture but since liquid oil is not compressible the engine's starter could cause the filled cylinder to be broken off. To make sure that there was no trapped oil, the crew had to manually turn the propeller through three complete revolutions. A strenuous job. The propellers had four blades and the engine with the prop hub was about six or so feet above you. In the routine, two men would push the bottom blade around and up as high as they could reach while the next two men took the next prop blade when it came in reach and so on until twelve blade-pushes had taken place for that engine. Then, on to the next engine. The whole crew was expected to help, both officers and enlisted. Bernie, who had felt little pain while having his pick-me-ups the night before, was feeling all the accumulated pain he had not previously felt. He was helping the pilot pre-flight (i.e., inspect the plane's exterior) and every time he looked up you could see that he was feeling much pain in his head. I felt sorry for the poor guy.

The other man from the Quonset who was memorable was Danny Wong. Danny was Chinese-American; grew up in New York City and was one hundred percent New Yorker in his speech. This was 1945 and before President Truman desegregated the military it would be hard to say which service, either Army or Navy was the most segregated. One day several of us were discussing segregation and somebody asked Danny if he had had any trouble in the Army, since he was not Caucasian. He said he had had no trouble with the Army. He had gone to the Navigation School in Louisiana. He said that when he graduated he went to the train station to go on his graduation leave. During those times the trains, at least those traveling in the South had White Coaches and Colored Coaches (the Colored Coaches were usually up front, toward the engine). At the track area there was a gate and a train conductor directing the passengers. "White passengers this way," he pointed.

"Colored passengers that way," he pointed to the opposite direction. Danny said that when he neared the conductor, the conductor addressed him personally, "Colored passengers THAT way." Danny didn't even slow down; he just said over his shoulder "So who's colored?" in his New York accent. He continued walking, leaving a rather puzzled conductor who couldn't decide where Asians fit into the system. This to me is another example of the inanity of the old segregation laws and system. I had grown up in all-white Cullman, Alabama, and when I started to College in Birmingham I was first exposed to the Jim Crow system at its sternest.

When I first arrived on Saipan, it was around mid-afternoon. The guys in the Quonset showed me to our mess hall when it was time for evening chow. It was late afternoon and the sun was nearing the horizon. As I sat down with my tray at a table, I noticed that some of the diners who were seated were holding slices of bread up toward the sun and squinting. I asked one of the men I was with why they were doing that. He said that the mess had gotten some flour with weevils in it. The cooks had to go ahead and bake bread with it and the men were looking for the weevils so they could pick them out. For once I was glad that I was not in the habit of eating sliced bread along with my meal.

For the high level planners, I guess the big question now was how to get as many men back to the States as soon as possible. When going overseas initially, our crew was ferrying a new plane and we did not have to endure the long ride across much of the Pacific in a crowded troop ship. Going back, we would also be ferrying a plane.

A B-29 could carry a lot of weight in the form of bombs. The high level planners decided that with all that weight carrying ability going back in all those planes and with so many non-flying troops as anxious to go home as we were it would be a shame to waste the weight carrying capacity. So, the plan evolved for each plane to carry in addition to its eleven man crew, an additional eleven non-flying people. It was a workable plan, in spite of the fact that there were only enough seats for the crew.

The non-flying people had to sit on the floor all the way back across the Pacific. A very long flight with stop-overs at Kwajalein and Hawaii. I remember that there was one man who always sat on the floor immediately behind my chair. He was a Corporal, an older man—probably in his mid-thirties—and he said he had been a cook. Since there was no window he could look out of, he spent most of his time watching the radio operator and me.

The B-29 we ferried over to Guam was brand new, almost fresh out of the factory. The one going back was something of a tired bird. Aircraft, at least most of them, can be kept in good condition more or less indefinitely, provided they are given periodic detailed maintenance. This bird had been flying many trips from Saipan to Japan with probably only minimum maintenance. I found out that the Loran set had died and that meant I had to do more basic navigation, sun sights when the sun was in a helpful alignment and more readings on the driftmeter than usual.

Fortunately the plane's engines were in better shape than the Loran was and we had no problems, other than crew and passenger fatigue. We landed at Travis AAB in California, our starting point when we went over. I was anxious to see Estelle after the long months we had been separated and wondered how long it would take to cross the country to New Jersey.

The Army had devised a good plan to help those of us wanting to get across the country to the East Coast as soon as possible. A little specialized airlift. The planes were C-47s, that little troop-carrier version of the DC-3 that had been made in such large numbers. Much faster than traveling by train, though for us ex-B29 crew members the much shorter range of the C-47s and the more frequent stops for fuel seemed a little amusing. We were, or at least I was, going home for thirty days leave. Soon I would be back together again with my Estelle.

We were a mixed group of returnees. Some of us, like myself, were coming back from the Marianas Islands and our skin was normal looking, maybe a bit more tanned from the tropic sun. Others apparently had been stationed in areas of the Pacific subject to malaria. You could tell them by the color of their skin. They had been taking Atabrine regularly, the war-time synthetic substitute for Quinine. I guess Atabrine was probably effective but it caused the skin of the person taking it to turn yellow. I imagine that their appearance came as a little shock to their families when they met.

We finally landed at McGuire AAB in New Jersey. At a check-in desk we were told we would be free to go but come back Monday morning for a copy of our leave orders. In very short order I was on a train bound for Newark. Estelle was living at home with her parents in one of the Newark suburbs and I would be with her soon.

The "soon" turned out to be not quite as soon as I would have liked. A seedy taxi driver wandered around Hudson County a bit, padding his fare before finally delivering me to the Banaski home. This took up an hour or so, a benefit to the driver but not to me. By this time it was around eight-thirty PM, a foggy October night. When I knocked at the door, it was Estelle's mother who answered. I asked, "Is Estelle here? I'm Troy. Her husband." After our marriage in Florida there had been no chance to meet any of her family.

Mom pulled me inside and gave me a hug. Then she said, "She's over at her girl friend's house." Then she called Theresa, one of Estelle's younger sisters. "Go call Stella. She's at Mary Zalewski's." Theresa was a pretty teen-ager and she disappeared to make the call. Then Mom herded me into the kitchen and asked if I would have a cup of hot tea. Without waiting for my answer, she started fixing it.

Estelle's family were Polish-Americans and soon I grew to love Mom as much as my own Mother. I immediately felt welcome. We sat together at the small kitchen table, getting acquainted. It was about forty-five minutes before Estelle got home. Her friend lived about a twenty minute bus ride away and Estelle was lucky in not having to wait long for a bus. Since this is a collection of military-flying reminiscences and not a romance novel, I'll omit any description of my reunion with Estelle and leave it to the reader's imagination. Let's just say that we were in love and very happy to be back together again.

CIVILIAN INTERLUDE

The leave was for 30 days. We planned to spend half of it with Estelle's family in New Jersey, then go to Cullman to spend the second half with my family. While in Cullman, I was notified by the Army that my leave was being extended. I don't know if the Army did this as a humanitarian gesture or if it was because the Army was being swamped with individuals being returned from overseas for discharge. It was nice having so much leave, although I'm sure that Estelle wished that we had been told of the extension earlier so we could have spent more of the leave with her family.

We were in Cullman for both Thanksgiving and Christmas. One aspect of the Thanksgiving dinner was a little uncomfortable for me. The house was an old fashioned Southern home with no central heating. The heating was by coal burning grates in most of the rooms. For the big Thanksgiving Dinner, Daddy insisted that I wear my wool uniform blouse and tie in honor of the occasion. I ended up sitting in one of the table seats nearest the grate which had a roaring soft coal fire in it. I was uncomfortably hotter for that meal than I had been at any time when I was on Guam in the Tropics. But, it was a happy occasion and we were thankful that we were all together. At Christmas the weather outside had grown colder and dinner then was not as formal as it had been for Thanksgiving Day.

My leave would be over on New Year's Day and the day after I was supposed to sign in at March AAB in California. Right after the war trains were the major transportation system but the airlines were starting to grow. We had airline tickets for California. It would be the first time Estelle had flown, and although I had been flying a lot it had been all in Army planes. It would be my first Civilian Airline flight. The first portion's routing was Delta Airlines from

Birmingham to Jackson, Mississippi; then to Shreveport, Louisiana; then to Dallas. Texas. At Dallas, we were to change to American Airlines. But, American had trouble with equipment availability and they had to cancel our flight and reschedule us for the next day. They provided us a hotel room for the night. But, the hotel was one of the small downtown hotels specializing in long term guests; a very small lobby at street level and stairs to the upstairs rooms. No major hotel rooms were available because they were all booked up. The reason? It was two days before New Years Day and Dallas, as well as most of Texas was eagerly looking forward to the first post-war Cotton Bowl football game.

The next day (the day before New Years!) American was able to put us on a plane. The ride was a little on the bumpy side and we had to make a couple of stops (El Paso and Tucson, I think). Estelle was having more and more trouble with nausea, especially on landings and she had to keep a barf bag in hand most of the time. Curiously, the Stewardess asked, "Are you sure it's all air sickness?" It turned out later that it was part air sickness and part morning sickness. We weren't sure that early if she was expecting a child but learned later that part of it was morning sickness. But, either way, it was a miserable feeling for her.

It was early evening when we landed at the Los Angeles airport. We decided that we had had enough traveling for one day and the thing we wanted most was a nice hotel room and a comfortable bed. The USO had a service desk in the airport and one of their many services was helping service people get hotel reservations. They were very nice to us but they could give us no help with a reservation. It was New Years Eve, the first one after the war. The best they could offer was sharing a room with another couple. Estelle's answer was, "No way!"

We sat in the terminal for a few minutes, deciding what to do next. We decided that riding a bus probably would not be too much more tiring than sitting in the airline terminal all night. Neither of us was familiar with the geography of Southern California. We knew that March AAB, my new station, was located at Riverside. We went to the bus terminal and boarded a bus for

Riverside, arriving some time around eleven PM. We called Mission Inn, the big hotel in Riverside to make a reservation.

The clerk at the Mission Inn said, "Sorry. We're absolutely full. You might call back in the morning and see if anyone has checked out." Sound familiar? This was a replay of our arrival in Lincoln, Nebraska while the state fair was running. We kissed each other at midnight to welcome in the New Year and sat out the rest of the night in the bus station.

When the early morning papers were delivered to the station, Estelle suggested that since we couldn't call the Mission Inn until later it might be a good idea to look at the ads in the paper to see if there were any rooms advertised. It was a good suggestion. There was one advertised at a location convenient to down-town Riverside. We took a taxi to look at it and found that it was just what we needed. It was a nice room in a comfortable, clean looking house. The owner was an older widower, a Mr. Hofstetter. He told us that kitchen privileges were included; we would take turns using the kitchen with another young couple. The other couple was about our age and the husband was a lieutenant, like I was. He was a pilot. The first thing we did was pile into the bed to make up for the sleep we had missed sitting in the bus terminal.

While March AAB was my duty station, there was absolutely no job for me there. Just report in every morning for a roll call and see if they had any task to assign me. There never was. We did have to participate in the regular Saturday Morning Parades. The lieutenants usually were given a flight-sized group of enlisted personnel to put through about forty-five minutes of close-order drill, then assemble into squadron-size groups for the parade.

In the Army enlisted troops wore what we called an overseas cap and the cap was trimmed with a colored braid. The color of the braid depended on the person's branch of service. For Air Corps (which we were) the braid was orange and blue. For Infantry it was sky blue; for Cavalry it was yellow and for Artillery it was red. On this one Saturday, my flight was all black men. (Remember this was while the Army was still segregated.) Every man had an overseas cap with Air Corps colored braid. Everyone, that is, except one very tall, very athletic looking man who was wearing an overseas cap with bright red Artillery braid. I do mean bright! I don't know if he had really been in Artillery or if he had bought a cap with Artillery braid on it as a hopeful gamble. The hopeful gamble that if he stood out so conspicuously, maybe the officer in charge would let him leave to preserve the uniformity of appearance of the flight. Not wanting to give in to his ruse, if he had one, I had him move over to an inside file where he didn't stand out so conspicuously. To myself, I admired his ingenuity, if it had been a trick. But if I had to participate in the parade I felt he should too.

Other than the Saturday parades, I don't think I ever had any other duties. I did fly once or twice, flights to qualify for flight pay. But there was no navigation involved for me. Just passenger time, sitting in a bucket seat.

I didn't dislike the Service, in fact I enjoyed some of the flying. But the war had interrupted my college career and I wanted to get my fourth year of college and the diploma. For that reason, I was anxious to be discharged. After several weeks of waiting at March AAB, the order to be discharged came. I had assumed that it would be done at March. But I found that I would have to go to Fort MacArthur in Long Beach, California.

Fort MacArthur was a very small base, right on the waterfront of Long Beach. It was a Coast Artillery base and the Army was using it after the war as a specialized center to process discharges from the Army. The discharge took only a couple of days of paperwork.

During the course of the discharge, I did make what turned out to be an important decision; important if I wanted to have any future association with the Army. I learned that I had been serving in AUS status (Army of the US). AUS was just a war time status and when I was fully discharged, I would be out. Completely out! The processor asked if I wanted to apply for a Reserve Commission in the same rank (First Lieutenant). I hadn't heard anything about all that but it sounded like it was a pretty good deal, so I said yes.

Since we expected the discharge business at Fort MacArthur would take only a day or two, Estelle continued staying in our room in Mr. Hofstetter's house. As soon as I returned, we immediately packed up and took a train for New Jersey. The train was all Santa Fe Railroad to Chicago (I believe) and at Chicago we boarded a Pennsylvania Railroad train to New Jersey. A long trip and a tiring one but there were no bad moments on it.

BACK TO COLLEGE

I guess I had not done any meaningful planning about returning to college, other than that I wanted to get my diploma and assumed that I could just enter any local college in New Jersey and be a college graduate one year later. When I tried to apply to several local colleges in New Jersey, I found that getting into college after the War was not the simple thing it was before the war. What complicated things so much was that during the war Congress had passed the GI Bill which had, among other things, a generous program for helping students finance their college education.

I was not the only ex-serviceman with hopes of entering college. I went to several colleges in the Newark vicinity to talk about entering school there for a final year of college. An advisor at one of the schools said that I would have to join the throngs waiting to get into any of the local schools and wait it out. He advised me that my best bet for getting into school was to go back to Birmingham-Southern again. As a former student who had been called into service I would certainly be able to get into the next semester. A letter from 'Southern, answering my query, assured me that I would be welcome to join the next semester. Also, that if I were married, 'Southern had built some housing for married students.

There would be a wait of several months for the start of the next fall's session. Since Estelle and I had found a small two room apartment, we waited out the time in New Jersey.

To have some income to live on, I went to work in a box factory for the duration of the waiting period. The box factory made corrugated cardboard boxes. The work was moderately strenuous, like most factory work is. The most demanding part of it was not heavy lifting. It was learning how to handle the partially finished boxes. The partly finished boxes would come out of the slitter machine onto a pile and my usual job was picking up the partially finished boxes and stacking them onto a dolly. The tricky part was handling a pack of partially finished boxes without slicing your hands with paper cuts. With a little practice you could put in a day's work and finish with only two or three cuts for that day. But getting that practice meant days of learning where you would get six or eight cuts in a day.

Estelle's pregnancy was, fortunately, a normal one and she had only the usual discomforts but no serious complications. Our son, Stanley Troy, decided to make his appearance in the wee small hours of the morning. We had no car so we went by taxi to Margaret Hague Maternity Hospital in Jersey City, about a thirty minute trip. After staying with Estelle several hours, the people at the hospital convinced me to go home and get some sleep; they would call me when the baby was born. He was born just a few hours after I reached home. Stanley's Christening was about a week after Estelle came home. Not being familiar with Polish customs, I expected that we would just go to the Church for the Christening and then come home and maybe have a slice of cake with Estelle's immediate family. It was actually a lot more festive than that. I don't remember much of the details but it did involve a big ham, a keg of beer, lots of potato salad, some kielbasa and the big whipped cream cake which I had expected. Plus, a lot of family and close relatives and friends, almost more than our tiny apartment could hold.

When Estelle and I discussed it afterward, I told her that I didn't expect it to be so festive. She said that it was a very small celebration; that I would see a big celebration when I went to my first Polish Wedding. She said that there were still big celebrations but in earlier days they were even more so. She told me about the biggest wedding celebration she attended several years earlier. After the Church ceremony, the wedding party began and went on for days. They did some really serious partying! The bride and groom stayed around a day or two and partied with the guests, then went on their honeymoon. When they returned from the honeymoon the celebration was still going on and the newlyweds picked up on the partying again. I'm not sure whether she was telling me the truth or whether she was stretching it as an elaborate tease on her part.

At Birmingham-Southern we moved into the married student quarters which had been built on an undeveloped, wooded part of the campus. The quarters were newly-built one story frame structures. In appearance they reminded you of some of the smaller war-time military bases but that didn't matter to most of us. We were all recently ex-military and thankful for a comfortable place to live. The number one advantage was that it was on campus and classes were within easy walking distance. And, not to be overlooked, they were affordable!

What would I major in? That had been a problem in my first three years, where I was a Chemistry major in my first year, a Geology major the next year, and an English major in that third year just before the Army called me. Looking over my earned credits to date and the requirements for a degree, I decided that Economics would let me finish in the three quarters of the academic year. So, it was Economics for me.

I believe that one of the big surprises to the people who were influential in bringing the GI bill into being was the excellent academic record of most of the students. In my own case, my grades in the last year after the war were a whole lot better than the ones for the years before the war.

The academic year passed quickly and I was able to graduate the following spring. Graduation day was clear and sunny and the exercises were held outdoors in the old football stadium, a concrete relic from the days when 'Southern fielded a football team. Mama and Daddy were there and Estelle had Stanley, our one-year-old youngster; all waiting in the concrete stands for the procession of graduates to appear. Estelle told me later that Stanley was frightened at first when he saw the long line of black-gowned graduates filing across from the far side of the field.

Estelle and I had decided to return to New Jersey after graduation, since the job market there seemed a little better than

Birmingham and certainly better than in Cullman for a recent Economics graduate.

It turned out that jobs were more plentiful in New Jersey and I found a job within a couple of weeks in the RCA Plant. This was in the days when radio sets depended on vacuum tubes instead of transistors and in the early days of television where television sets also involved lots of vacuum tubes. The RCA Plant manufactured vacuum tubes and I would be working in the Accounts Receivable section of the tube and parts sales operation. I also joined up with the local Army Air Reserve center.

I found that, physically, the RCA Plant was a nice place to work, but the work itself turned out to be a clerical treadmill, with most emphasis on volume production. Very soon I was longing for my flying days and service life generally.

ACTIVE DUTY AGAIN

I guess you could say that Joseph Stalin came to my aid, though certainly not out of any goodness of heart. He started the Berlin Blockade. At the Reserve Center I learned that there was a limited recall program for former Navigators. I immediately applied for recall and was happy when I found that I had been accepted and would be ordered back onto active duty.

When the orders came, they directed me to report to Hamilton AAB in San Rafael, California, for processing to go overseas. Estelle and I had somewhat mixed feelings. While we were both glad to be going back into active duty; we didn't look forward to being separated.

Reporting to Hamilton involved another cross-country trip, alone, and it would be by train. Everyone should experience a cross country trip by train. But only one. You don't get it over with as quickly as on a plane. And you don't set your own pace as in a car, where you can stop and dawdle or push yourself. The train sets the pace.

At Hamilton I learned that I would be going on duty as a Navigator with the US Air Force, not the US Army Air Corps. I didn't even know that USAF was now a separate and independent service. I'm not sure but I think the base was still being called Hamilton AAB. Things were a little confusing while the Army and the Air Force were separating themselves. Personally, I had been happy that I was in the Army and was ready to continue unchanged. But, Washington didn't consult me.

The stay at Hamilton was only a few days, then we were taken by troop-bus across the bridges to Oakland Army Terminal, a port facility, and loaded onto the US Army Transport, the General Greely. The General Greely was a small troop transport, built during the war around the hull of a Liberty Ship. As soon as our bus load of Lieutenants and a few Captains came on board, the Greely started to move. A very slow trip because it was tugs pushing the Greely across the Bay to Fort Mason in San Francisco. Meanwhile, several of us Lieutenants were detailed to oversee a small group of enlisted men as they transferred a large pile of life jackets to a new location. We spent the night on the ship, although we could leave and do a little exploring in San Francisco.

The next day the rest of the passengers boarded the Greely. We were surprised to see that these passengers were all women and a few children. They were all dependents of service men, going overseas to join their husbands. The whole passenger list was a mixed lot. A good many dependents, about an equal number of junior officers—mostly Lieutenants—and about fifty very junior enlisted personnel.

We found that the Greely would be stopping first in Hawaii, then it would proceed on to Guam. I still didn't know where I was being sent and began to suspect that it would be Guam again.

At Hawaii, the enlisted men debarked. Enlisted troop quarters, at least for the lowest grades, on a troop ship were accommodations much like a sardine can. Fortunately for these men, there was only a small group of them and they could spread out. The ship had a dormitory-like section with double-deck bunks and they put us Lieutenants there. The state rooms, originally officer's quarters, were assigned to the dependents.

The ship, of course, was not air conditioned. The dormitory had no port holes and rather dim lighting. None of us spent much time there, other than during the sleeping hours. For a change, I ended up in a lower bunk, right next to the hull. I could hear the ship's wake splashing against the steel wall of the hull and did not find it comforting or soothing—I would have made a lousy sailor. The lack of air conditioning was not too uncomfortable during the trip to Hawaii. But when we left Hawaii, we were going south-west into the Tropics and the air would get a little heavy in the dormitory, especially when we were trying to sleep.

The daylight part of the trip from Hawaii was beautiful with brilliant sunshine every day and a calm sea. We could watch flying fish darting from the water. There were deck chairs and you could set one up on the open deck and read, either in the sun or in a shady spot with a comfortable breeze making up for the uncomfortable sleeping quarters. I finished *Forever Amber* and some parts of Walt Whitman's *Leaves of Grass*. I had brought the Whitman book with me; the other book was part of the ship's collection of paper backs.

The nightly movie on deck was unusual. There was a moderately large screen and I think the film was sixteen millimeter rather than theater-size thirty five millimeter. The Greely was not a wide ship and the whole complement of passengers could not be seated facing the screen. No problem! The screen was translucent and the picture looked just about as good from the back side of the screen. Of course there was one problem. Any text appearing on the screen would be backward if you were watching from the back side of the screen. But we were not watching movies with sub-titles and you soon forgot that you were watching backward things.

The whole trip from Hawaii to Guam was uneventful. Bright sunny days when nothing significant happened. Dark nights in the dormitory which would have been much more bearable with air conditioning. The day before we reached Guam, a B-29 buzzed the ship several times. A person's name was painted on the side of the plane in huge black letters and when she saw it, one of the women passengers started shouting and dancing around—it was her name and presumably the pilot was her husband.

The Greely's stop at Guam must have been entirely without any significant sights or happenings, since I remember absolutely nothing about it. I ended up in transient quarters at the Air Depot; small buildings with a screened strip around the building. There were wooden shutters over the screening; they were hinged at the top and normally kept propped open except during storm conditions when they would be closed. The quarters were short on decor but not really uncomfortable.

After a short stay in the quarters—maybe two or three days—I found that I would be traveling again. This time by air, a flight on a MATS C-54. At this point I started to get a generalized idea of at least the country I would be stationed in. It would be Japan.

In Japan, the top Air Force headquarters was FEAF (Far East Air Forces). It was located in Tokyo. Next level down (at least as it concerned me) was Fifth Air Force Headquarters, located in Nagoya. After landing in the Tokyo area, there was another flight to Nagoya where Fifth Air Force would decide where to send me next.

I didn't see much of my new country before reaching Nagoya. At Nagoya, I checked into the transient BOQ which was in a modern tall building. Unusual quarters for a BOQ. It had been three years since the war ended and I remembered bombing Nagoya during the war but the building didn't seem to have any bombing damage and didn't look all that new. I guess we missed it!

There was a PX barber shop in the building. Since my last haircut had been by a civilian barber in New Jersey, I decided that maybe I would make a better impression when I reported in if I had a military haircut.

The barber shop was staffed by Japanese barbers, most of whom spoke a little English (very little!). I, of course, did not know a single word of Japanese and I slumped down into a barber chair, saying only "Hair cut!" That was in the barber's working vocabulary and he started cutting. As the barber finished cutting, I guess I must have dozed off—not fully asleep but not too alert either. Suddenly I felt vigorous pounding on my shoulders and lower neck. It really startled me! After all, only three years before we had been dropping bombs on these guys and they were shooting cannon at us. I looked into the mirror and saw that my barber's face had a calm, blank look, and his hands were giving my shoulders and neck a vigorous, pounding massage. The massage was part of the PX haircut and later I learned to appreciate the relaxed feeling when it was over.

The stay in Nagoya lasted only two or three days, then I found that I would be sent to Tachikawa Air Force Base. After arriving at Tachikawa (by air) I learned that the base was located at the town of Tachikawa which was about twenty miles west of Tokyo.

It was about three in the afternoon when I checked into the

BOQ. I left my bag in my new room and went down the hall to the latrine for a comfort stop. While standing in front of the urinal, concentrating on the task of the moment, I heard a feminine voice, "Haro. How are you?"

Startled, I looked over my shoulder. Behind the row of urinals there was a wooden partition, about four feet tall and on the opposite side of the partition was a janitor's mop sink. A Japanese woman was standing on the other side by the sink, filling a mop bucket. She was not old, nor was she really very young, a little plain but still somewhat attractive. She smiled and said something which I didn't understand, then "You just get here?" She didn't seem to find it at all unusual that she had greeted me and we were talking at what is normally a rather private moment in an American's public life. I soon learned that Japanese society, at least the level we would meet with, had rather different views of nudity and other aspects of personal life.

The first official thing to happen was that I was taken in tow by a Lieutenant Colonel pilot who rushed me over to the flight line for an initial flight. He and a copilot flew us around in the local flying area for about an hour. I learned later that he did this to make me eligible to draw flight pay.

The flight was my introduction to the Curtis C-46 transport airplane, the type aircraft I would be flying in. I found that basically the C-46 was a good plane and had many good qualities. Unfortunately, crew and passenger comfort was not one of the good qualities. And later, the squadron pilots explained some of the plane's quirks, chiefly that for the pilots it handled like a heavy truck. I believe that it may have had hydraulic assistance on the ailerons but no assist on either the rudder or elevator. Its main sterling feature was that it was powered by what most of us believed to be the best radial aircraft engine ever built, the Pratt-Whitney R-2800. (The 2800 signified that each engine's cylinders displaced 2,800 cubic inches.)

As I understand it, the C-46 was built expressly for one particular purpose. That was to fly freight from India over the Himalayas Mountains ("the Hump") to the Chinese forces fighting the Japanese in China. Like the C-47 (DC3s in civilian service) it was a twin engine, low winged monoplane. But the engines were much more powerful and it could fly higher than the C-47. After the war ended in 1945, I believe that most of the C-46s were taken out of active use and parked somewhere for a couple of years; our squadron rumors saying that they had been parked in the Philippines. The plane had a big, rounded fuselage, not like the slimmer C-47 and the unofficial nickname for it was "The Pregnant Whale".

The Troop Carrier Wing to which I was being assigned was originally equipped with C-54s, a four-engine transport. When the Communists started the blockade of Berlin, the American top commanders decided to call in all the C-54 transports in the Air Force inventory and use them in the new Berlin Airlift. To provide airlift for the American Occupation in the Far East, the C-46s were put back into service. And, since the C-54s were flown over to Germany to join the airlift, I was a replacement Navigator to help man the C-46s in Japan.

Where my only duties on Guam during the war had been flying duties, I found that I would have a ground job at Tachikawa. Officer-in-charge of a small Post Exchange Warehouse. The function of the warehouse was to serve as a depot for the Air Force Post Exchanges (later renamed Base Exchanges). The PX supplies came in to the central Army Post Exchange Warehouse in Yokohama. Our operation would receive the merchandise and supplies for all the Air Force PX's and reissue them to the base stores.

The operation had about fifteen Japanese office workers, and fifteen to twenty warehouse workers. Also, a civilian manager, Fred Roach, and five GI's who acted as supervisors to the warehouse Japanese. Thankfully, Fred did most of the supervising, together with Mr. Takagi, the senior Japanese worker. Although I was technically in charge, in reality I flew on so many one and two day flights I couldn't really get too involved. Takagi's book-keeping was strictly old fashioned green-eyeshade accounting. He kept his accounts in a big ledger, written meticulously with a dip pen in permanent black ink.

Like any good office, we always had a pot of hot coffee sitting on the electric hot plate. I usually poured my own, or if one of the Japanese poured it for me, I watched them like a hawk. I had gotten in the habit during the war of drinking coffee or tea with no sugar in it—no sugar tasted better than the saccharine which restaurants provided during the war. If a Japanese poured my coffee, they would invariably put a lot of sugar in it, thinking they were doing me a favor. Some of them would take five or six spoons of sugar in their own cup.

Two of the clerks were women typists. Number one typist was Setsuko, a fairly good typist, considering that her native language probably found English as strange as we found Japanese script. I believe that the other typist's name was Mitsuko. The male clerks used the abacus for their calculations. We also had two Sundstrand ten-key adding machines. While working at RCA, I had used that type machine eight hours a day almost continuously. I used it by touch and thought that I was a pretty hot operator on a ten-key machine. I always have been fascinated by the abacus and one day during an office bull session about the abacus, I foolishly said that I thought that I could beat a clerk using an abacus if I used the ten key adding machine. Fred had been in Japan much longer than I had and was familiar with the abacus. He suggested that we have a little competition between me and one of the fastest clerks. I agreed. We set up two identical sets of figures with no written total on them and at a starting signal we each started to add. I beat the clerk by a few seconds. Two people were surprised by the results. Fred was surprised by my speed on the adding machine and I was surprised at how fast the abacus was in the hands of an experienced clerk. I'm sure that it was not a real contest though because the Japanese clerk must certainly have felt it would not be good office politics for him to beat the boss. He probably could have beaten me easily.

There was one member of the office staff who was rather unusual. He was an older man, slim, with excellent posture. He always wore what looked like it must have been a Japanese army uniform without any of the usual decorations a uniform normally has. His name was Kito-san; somehow it always seemed appropriate to add the honorific—san to his name because of his age and dignity. We always assumed he had been a senior military officer but somehow his past never seemed an appropriate item to be discussed. I never was sure of what Kito-san's duties were, since Takagi did all the detailed supervision. Takagi was the only Japanese employee with much ability in English and neither Fred nor I could really supervise the young male clerks, all of them being in their late teens or very early twenties.

I was able to talk with one of the junior clerks, a young man, probably in his early twenties. His name was Iwamoto. I guess he must have been involved in maintenance on Japanese planes during the war. He told me a little about the famous Japanese Zero plane. He said that the supercharger on the Zero's engine was subject to mechanical failure and their pilots were instructed to use it for no longer than ten minutes at a time. Iwamoto didn't say so but I would bet that that rule was ignored when a Zero was in a dogfight.

My squadron, the 22nd Troop Carrier Squadron, along with the other flying squadron in the Wing, the 6th Troop Carrier Squadron, jointly operated an airline between cities in Japan and Korea, or more accurately between USAF bases in those countries.

One flight, the shortest one, was a flight to Misawa Air Force Base. Misawa was up at the northern tip of the island of Honshu, the main Island. Another flight was one to Naha AFB at the southern tip of Okinawa. These were both one-stop flights and we would be back at Tachikawa the same day.

A somewhat longer flight included several stops. First, a stop at the Air Force Base at Nagoya. Then on to Itazuke AFB located on the northwest corner of Kyushu Island. Then on to Kimpo AFB, our base at Seoul, Korea. By that time it was time to quit for the day and we would RON there (Remain Over Night). In the summer, Kimpo always seemed hotter than the Japanese bases and in the winter much colder than the Japanese bases. Next day we would retrace the route and stops back home to Tachikawa.

The really prized flight—as far as the crews' likes were concerned—was the flight which stopped at Okinawa and then proceeded on to Clark AFB in the Philippines. I guess that that one was rationed between our squadron and the 6th Squadron because it was considered especially desirable. Usually when you were assigned that flight, you ended up with a shopping list or two from friends for fresh fruit, an item in short supply for personnel in Japan. With a little longer lay-over before going back to Japan, the crew would usually take a taxi into Angeles, the nearest village to Clark AFB. To get your fruit or produce, you could go to the big community farmer's market and bargain with the sellers. Or you could take the more practical route which we all did. You could go to one of the bars and the proprietor would send one or two of the bar girls to the market with your list. The bar girl knew local prices better than you; could bargain in Tagalog for a better price than you could and meanwhile, the several of you in your crew could sit in the bar and sip cool ones with several of the other bar girls.

At the time I was making these trips, the trips to Angeles always had to be daylight excursions. The Huks, who were Filipino communist revolutionaries would select a town and capture it at nightfall. They would hold the town at night but retreat when daylight came again, since by that time the Filipino Army would retake the town. This was not a regular occurrence but the threat was always there. Consequently, Angeles was "on-limits" to us in daylight hours but "off-limits" at night.

There were several bars to choose from. My favorite was one run by Mrs. White, a Filipina business woman. It was quiet and relaxing. Another one, a favorite of some of the other crews, was Wong's Garden. The owner was Chinese, as the name suggests and his place was a little more high spirited than Mrs. White's establishment. High spirited meaning rowdier but it was rowdy only occasionally.

There was another place of a different type. It was a two story place and the part of the place that was most memorable was an unusual stairway leading from the ground floor, where the entrance was, to the upstairs bar. The stairway was made of beautifully polished red mahogany. Several of us sat at the upstairs bar one afternoon, talking to the proprietor who was sitting on a stool with us. She was apparently either a European or American and watched her bar-tender constantly as she worked. The bar tender was an attractive Filipina woman. Not that unusual a situation, except that rather than keeping an eagle-eye on the amount of liquor the bar-tender poured into the drinks the proprietor was monitoring the amount of ice the bar tender used. She said that the liquor didn't cost that much (no American taxes on it!) but the ice was the expensive item for her. That was because electricity was so scarce in Angeles.

There were features of the trips to the Philippines that are memorable to me. Routing was from Tachikawa to Naha, Okinawa for refueling and picking up or discharging passengers. Then the flight to the Philippines. Clark Air Base was located some hundred or so (more or less) miles south of the north shore of Luzon. Our route for this hundred or so miles was down the east coast of Luzon. We would arrive at this part of the flight around midnight. The eastern shore of Luzon was mountainous for most of the way and almost invariably there would be strings of thunderstorms all along these mountains. Our intended route was about ten or twenty miles out over the ocean and the navigators used to joke that the thunderstorms were almost a reliable navigation aid. At the proper place, we would turn to a due west heading and fly inland to Clark Air Force Base. Usual arrival time at Clark would be around four AM. After breakfast at Charlie Corn's restaurant in the terminal we were always ready for some sleep. Charlie Corn was a Chinese entrepreneur who had negotiated contracts to operate terminal restaurants at several Air Force Bases in the Pacific. I usually chose his chow-mein for breakfast. At four AM it was more like a late-night snack than breakfast.

Clark had been an Army Air Base in the quiet days before World War II. It had a long, long grassy parade ground, at least a mile long. At one end was the Base Headquarters. Along one side was a long sidewalk, shaded by towering hardwood trees. The walk connected old fashioned tropical style officer's quarters, fairly large houses surrounded by huge screened porches. About half way down the parade ground was the Officer's Club, built in the old-fashioned way buildings in the tropics were built before air conditioning. At the end of the parade ground were a couple of houses whose sides faced the headquarters building. These were Visiting Officer's Quarters and we were each assigned a bed on the screened sleeping porch. By the time you were able to crawl into your cot, it was about five thirty. About the time you were dozing off, you would get a taste of an old Army custom. In front of the headquarters building at the other end of the parade ground was the usual flag pole, and near it a cannon. The base custom was to begin the day at six AM by firing the cannon. Although it was about a mile away, it was pointed toward the VOQ and you were trying to sleep on a screened porch. The blast always jarred you fully awake.

This would not be the end of the problems in getting to sleep. The building was built on stilts and there was room underneath to walk around. It was there that the Billeting Office had established a hand laundry to launder the BOQ and VOQ sheets. About seven or seven-thirty the laundresses would arrive for work. They all knew each other and found it necessary to have loud and friendly conversations with each other. Not exactly a soothing lullaby and eventually someone would shout out "Shut up for pity's sake!"

Our payload was usually passengers, although on occasion we carried freight, some of which could be unusual. Sometimes it was machinery. Once it was a load of reconstituted milk for the messhalls in Korea. At the beginning of the Korean War it was a load of Korean currency, a new issue to replace the old currency which was suddenly obsolete when the North Koreans captured the printing plates. Another trip we carried a load of human blood for the hospitals in Korea.

For the Navigator, one disagreeable part of the trip to Kimpo in summer was unloading the cargo. At the Japanese bases there was no problem with Japanese cargo-handlers being unsupervised inside our plane. We always felt that they were entirely honest. But in Korea, it was different and we, or at least the pilot did, felt that an American officer should be inside the plane while the cargo handlers were unloading to discourage theft. My own theory as to why this seemed to be necessary was due to Korea's recent history. Up until the end of World War II, Japan had occupied Korea and to an occupied people, the occupiers are fair game. At the workers' level, they probably saw us as just a different occupier, and by that reasoning, we were fair game also. Therefore the need for an officer to stay in the cargo compartment. And the officer, by default, was the Navigator, the pilots being occupied with the flight clearance in operations. This was only a minor problem in colder weather but not so in hot summer weather. The C-46 plane had no interior insulation in the cargo compartment and the outsides of the planes were all painted with dull olive drab paint. Soon after landing in the afternoon, the interior of the plane became a sauna. The Korean cargo handlers would have eaten their lunch shortly before and lunch was kimchee, a pickled vegetable dish, which in their version was always heavy on the garlic, very heavy. Oddly, I still like kimchee, at least if the garlic is light or not used.

OCCUPATION LIFE

Life during the Occupation can probably best be described as very pleasant. I'm no historian by any means but I feel that the American Occupation of Japan avoided many of the problems of European occupations of Germany, especially the one following WW I. The main burden on the Japanese was paying for the expenses of the occupying military forces, primarily ours but also to a smaller degree those of Australia. Some of their more visible costs were constructing and maintaining buildings on our bases and making the Japanese train system available free of charge to American individuals. For instance, if you had no car and wanted to make the twenty or so mile trip into downtown Tokyo, you just went to the Tachikawa railway station and waited for the next train going east. It usually had an Allied Forces car, identified by a wide white stripe along the side. No ticket needed and no cash fare; just get on and sit down. The car would be attached to a train of several coaches for Japanese.

I rode on one of the trains once during rush hour where there was no Allied car attached. It was the standard rush hour crowd where the conductors had to put their shoulders to the task of getting everyone aboard, pushing the last few in like a football lineman. The only part that bothered me was that I was jammed up against a woman who was carrying an infant of about six months age, strapped to her back with the usual silk sash. I seemed to be more concerned about the baby's welfare than any of the other passengers, including the mother.

The Allied cars on the trains in the summer were the scene for what was almost like a comic opera or play. It was a continuation of the process of breaking the US Air Force off from the US Army. We in the Air Force were still wearing cotton khaki Army uniforms with only the insignia changed. Where with the summer khakis Army officers wore metal rank insignia on one collar and metal branch of service insignia on the other collar; the Air Force uniform had metal rank insignia on both collars. No problem here; everybody recognized and accepted that. The problem was neck ties. General MacArthur, whose headquarters was in downtown Tokyo, insisted that with summer khakis, neckties would NOT be worn. For all services! The Military Police patrolling downtown Tokyo were all from the Army's First Cavalry Division and they took a special delight in writing up DR's (Delinquency Reports) on Air Force junior officers for wearing a necktie in downtown Tokyo. When you rode into "Air Force Territory", i.e. stops west of the Shinjuku stop, the top Air Force Commander was equally insistent that neckties WOULD be worn with summer khakis and Air Force Air Police would give you a DR for not wearing a tie. If you were going into Tokyo by train, you would leave Tachikawa properly attired with a neck tie and wear it until you pulled into the Shinjuku station, where you would untie the tie, carefully fold it and put it into your pocket. Going back to Tachikawa later, at Shinjuku you would take your carefully folded necktie out of your pocket and put it on. My earlier practice in tying a necktie while running (at Maxwell) was helpful here.

Shortly after arriving at Tachikawa Air Force Base, my non-driving days came to an end. When I soloed a Stearman training aircraft at Arcadia I became a person who had soloed a plane but not an automobile. At Tachikawa, I found that I would be detailed to be Officer of the Day (OD) when my turn for the detail came up, usually every three or four weeks. OD's were selected from Navigator junior officers and non-rated junior officers. (Pilots were not selected because they had a detail of their own to pull, Airdrome Officer.) The OD would be issued a jeep to use during his one-day tour of duty. When you drove the jeep, you were supposed to have a Government Drivers License. When I told the person briefing me that I didn't have a Government Driver's License, he told me to go to Air Police Headquarters and get one.

I knew that to go through with this, I would either have to

admit that I couldn't drive and go through an embarrassing instruction procedure or do some skillful lying and hope I could get away with it. Deceitful me, I chose the latter. They issued me the Government Drivers License with no problems.

That left me with only the problem of starting and driving the jeep—for the first time—in a convincing way. Daddy had given me one or two lessons in shifting gears, so I basically knew what to do when shifting, only I had never had any real practice at it. Fortunately for me, the jeep was a forgiving little creature when it came to gear shifting and I guess I must have looked half-way convincing. The only problem with jeeps is that with their short wheel-base you have a tendency to overcorrect when steering until you have some practice. But, I got away with it. After a time or two as OD, I found that another job I would be catching occasionally would be Squadron Duty Officer. The job itself was simple, just drive our squadron aircrews from Squadron Operations out to their plane on the flight line. I was probably less convincing in this because the vehicle I used was a three quarter ton weapons carrier. It had a truck transmission and somehow I never got the hang of shifting without a few noisy gear clashes.

Beside my problem of surreptitiously learning to drive on government jeeps and weapons carriers, there was another problem with driving in Japan which affected us all. In the US all of us drive on the right side of the road. Our cars and trucks are built on this premise. But, in Japan people drove on the left side of the road and our vehicles were all American-made with the steering wheel on the left side of the car. If you wanted to pass the car in front of you on a two-lane road you had to pull completely out into the oncoming lane to see if there was room enough ahead of the vehicle you were passing for you to get back into your own lane again. There were several types vehicles you almost had to pass. Such as one of the many Japanese trucks which had been converted to run on charcoal fumes. Usually the charcoal converter would produce only enough of the necessary fumes for low speed operation. Another obstacle would be a farmer with his honey-bucket wagon. Because of the fact that there was no sewer system in smaller towns, most houses collected the waste from their indoor toilets in a holding tank. Periodically the honey-bucket man would call and collect the accumulated sewage, poetically called "night-soil". Usually his vehicle was a two wheeled or four wheeled cart, pulled by an ox. The collector would take his accumulated load to his farm and put it into a small concrete tank at the edge of his field to use as fertilizer. Don't laugh—most of the fields were a beautiful shade of emerald green! Very effective, even though it was not a healthy system. I'm sure the medical people could list a number of arguments against the system beyond the purely esthetic fault we found with it.

I had arrived at Tachikawa in late summer or early fall of 1948. When Christmas season approached, somehow the proposal came up to have a Christmas party for our warehouse staff. I don't know if there had been one the previous year, though I doubt it. I think that Fred initiated the idea, since I didn't and Christmas was still something of a mystery to our Japanese employees. I guess someone ordered some snack type goodies from the BX Snack Bar. And a good many bottles of whisky—mostly Canadian Club—from the Officers Club's locker. The party was after lunch and was held in the warehouse, since there was not enough room in the office. I have learned in recent years that some Japanese have a physical peculiarity in that it only takes a very small amount of alcohol to make these individuals very drunk. This peculiarity affects only a small portion of the population; the majority of the others are affected like Americans. I did not know this fact at the time of our party. Our group had two or three of the people with this trait. After the party got under way and the crowd mellowed up a little, these two or three individuals stood out. I remember one of the younger office clerks who was walking around crying, looking for sympathy. If someone (American) would ask him what his problem was, he would say (very plaintively), "I can't go home. My Momma be pissed off with me!" He most certainly learned that phrase from our GIs and not from any school textbook! I guess he survived the experience, since he continued working with us. And we as an organization survived too, since the AP's didn't raid our party and the warehouse survived intact. I never did care for office parties but I can say that that one was one of the most interesting ones I ever attended. Not too much fun but very interesting.

Christmas day for me that year was very non-festive. The regularly scheduled flight for Kimpo came up on Christmas day. To schedule the crew for that flight, Squadron Ops chose married people whose dependents hadn't arrived in Japan yet. That way they avoided scheduling someone to be away from their family on Christmas. No one could argue with that motive and I felt, when I saw my name on the schedule, that I would be doing a fellow Navigator a good turn. The flight proceeded on schedule, with the regular stop first at Nagoya. The next leg to Itazuke was a longer one and we ate our GI flight lunches on that leg. The standard menu, always the same: a ham sandwich, a roast beef sandwich, a boiled egg, an apple, and a Hershey bar. Plus a big thermos of hot coffee. We landed at Itazuke and were delayed in leaving; since it was Christmas they had to scare up a crew of cargo handlers to unload us.

We got into Kimpo, Korea, later and found the messhalls had long since closed after the big traditional Christmas meal. When the pilot mentioned to the operations officer that we had only had a mid-day flight lunch and no other meal, the operations officer said that he thought there may be some sliced turkey and bread at the bar in the Officer's Club. There was, only it had been sitting on an open plate for several hours and both the turkey and bread were somewhat dried out. There were no other fixings, so our Christmas Dinner was a dried out turkey sandwich and a highball. Not even any egg nog!

Fred asked me several times if I had had sukiyaki in Japanese surroundings. I admitted that I had not had that pleasure and he said he would like to organize a sukiyaki party for me in a Japanese home. It sounded like a fun idea so I told him to go ahead. One of the young male clerks, Iwamoto, who lived with his parents, volunteered to have the party at his home. Fred invited Takagi, since he was the senior Japanese in the organization. And he invited Setsuko, the number one female typist. Sukiyaki is cooked at the table and Setsuko would be the cook. Iwamoto's home was several miles west of Tachikawa, up in the foothills away from the level Kanto plain.

The date of the party was probably about the first week of January. The climate in the Tokyo area was roughly about like Tidewater Virginia or North Carolina. Nothing like Minnesota, of course, but it did get cold and Iwamoto's house up in the hills was even colder. We all sat on the floor on rice-straw mats around a low, polished black table. There was a charcoal fire in a hibachi and the warmth felt good on your hands.

To get the party going, Setsuko started bringing in little trays which held tiny china saki-cups and a small ornate china saki jar. I had never tasted saki before and Fred assured me that it is good when hot but doesn't have much to recommend itself when cold. Each little saki cup held only about two good sips, any more and it would cool off before you finished the cup. The dispenser jar held enough for only about two rounds and so Setsuko kept busy going to the kitchen for refills. Of course Iwamoto was part of the party but the rest of his family disappeared after a very brief courtesy greeting. Fred told me that for a party of all Japanese, drinking the saki involved little ritual-games. Since I spoke no Japanese and Fred not much more than that we had to substitute more smiles than wit. The night was cold and Iwamoto brought in some heavy cotton comforters which we spread over our laps and Setsuko started cooking the sukiyaki. She cooked in a medium sized pan over the hibachi. I don't remember all of the ingredients but I think that they included thin strips of beef, sprouts, onion, tofu and a sauce. The cook, for us Setsuko, would cook and continuously serve us from the pan and add more ingredients. It was delicious. There was a salad to go with it, mostly bits of octopus in a mild slightly sweet vinegar sauce. That was good also. In between servings the tray of hot saki kept reappearing.

Around about ten-thirty, the party started to lag a little and we all suddenly realized that we were very cold. The sitting on the floor caught up with me and my legs were now cold and stiff. I guess Takagi and Setsuko were used to sitting on the floor but

American legs were not conditioned for it. As we stood up, Fred announced that he was staying with Iwamoto's family for the night. He said that his part-time driver, Jimmy, would drive us back to Tachikawa. I guess Jimmy, a young Japanese boy in his mid-teens, must have come to the house by train, since he couldn't have fit in the jeep with us. I told Fred that it was absolutely imperative for me to get back to the base soon because I was scheduled for a flight and my briefing was at five-thirty AM.

It was around twelve-thirty or one when we started the drive back to the base. Jimmy was driving and I had the only other reasonably comfortable seat, the front passenger seat. Takagi and Setsuko were crowded into the rear seat; not a comfortable one in an Army jeep. The jeep was no longer government property; Fred had bought it at a surplus sale.

I never understood why Fred had hired Jimmy as a driver. Probably because he was familiar with the roads; anyway he was a bright if inexperienced jeep driver. Something was wrong with the jeep, Jimmy muttered, and he was not sure how to deal with it. Neither was I; I only knew how to drive one and that was a recently acquired skill. The road back to our base passed near another American Air Base, Yokota AFB. Jimmy had a Japanese friend there who worked for an American family living on the base. Of course we passengers did not follow Jimmy to the door and after a short conference, he returned to us. I never did learn whether the jeep was really malfunctioning or if Jimmy was lost. Probably the latter, since we reached our base not too much later after the conference with his friend. Jimmy drove me to the BOQ area and I felt relieved because now my only problem was in getting up on time for the flight briefing which would be not too much later. But, that left Takagi and Setsuko with a problem. They were stranded in the small hours of a winter morning on a military base. I suggested that maybe they could find empty rooms in one of the BOQ's. I don't know what they eventually did; possibly Jimmy may have driven them home. I didn't pursue the question with Jimmy later, since I had learned that many Japanese could understand English very well when it was to their advantage but the language skill evaporated when understanding English was not to their advantage. Besides, I didn't want Jimmy to lose face.

The flight briefing was for a flight to the Philippines with a very early take off, around six thirty. It was a bright, clear winter morning when we took off and as we climbed south toward Oshima and its radio navigational station, we could see, off our right wing, Mt. Fuji wearing a blanket of new snow on the several thousand feet at its peak. It was a beautiful sight on a clear day but within hours the clear day would be obscured as thousands of Japanese house keepers started their charcoal fires to cook breakfast. We would be gone by that time and Fred would be catching an early morning train back to the base. For us, we would be flying in the clear sky over the Pacific Ocean toward the soft, pleasant warmth of the tropics.

At Tachikawa Base the flag rituals were strictly observed. In the morning at six AM, the OD would stand in front of Base Headquarters at parade rest, facing the flagpole. A few seconds before six two Air Police would come out of Headquarters toward the flagpole, one of them carrying the triangular-folded American Flag. They would free up the chain leading up to the top of the flag pole and attach the flag to the chain. Then they would stand, formally, waiting for the bugle call. At six AM the public address system would play "Reveille" as the Police raised the flag and the OD stood at attention. After Reveille, the bugler on the PA system played "To The Colors" and the OD and Air Police would salute, holding the salute until the last note of the bugle call.

While raising the flag was a small but formal ceremony, lowering the flag at the end of day, the Retreat Ceremony, was a somewhat larger ceremony. A squadron would be detailed to provide a color guard for Retreat, usually about thirty five to forty five men. For the non-flying squadrons, the detail would be Enlisted Personnel. For the two flying squadrons, our 22nd Troop Carrier Squadron and the other squadron, the 6th Troop Carrier Squadron, the detail would frequently be a detail of Junior Officers. We would assemble in our squadron area and march over to Base Headquarters, arriving in time to be standing in front of the flag pole at parade rest a few minutes before time for Retreat.

When the bugle call "Retreat" started playing over the PA system, the officer in charge of the detail would call the detail to "Attention". A few seconds later, the bugle call "To The Colors" would start and the Officer in Charge would order the detail to "Present Arms" and the whole detail would salute. At the end of the bugle call, the command "Order Arms" would come and we would march back to the squadron area. It might be remembered that the bugle call "To The Colors" is equivalent in protocol to the National Anthem.

Tachikawa AFB was a fairly small base and in the business part of the base, you could usually hear the bugle calls. All vehicular traffic would stop and the driver of each vehicle was expected to get out, face the flagpole, and salute. There were usually several Japanese "guards" walking around on the base. They probably didn't have any real authority except over the Japanese civilian employees. They wore a painted helmet liner and carried a small billy club. These guards would salute at the Retreat ceremony, just as the Americans did

FAMILY LIFE... AGAIN!

During my first days in the Army, I had been single. Most of the guys I was with were single also, although there were a few married ones too. Being single seemed the normal thing. But now, with the war over and with several years of personal history, I as well as most of my peers were married. And being together with your wife and child or children was now the normal thing; at least in our way of thinking. The military services agreed and on Occupation Duty you could have your family with you. In fact, the Army provided handsomely for your family's living facilities, thanks to the Japanese reparations responsibilities.

The thing you had to do to get things moving was to get on the list. You, as an individual, could not just write to your wife and tell her to get a ticket to Yokohama where you would meet her. When she came across the Pacific and how she came were controlled by the military services. Once you were on the list, you could see how things were moving. And, sometimes the list seemed to move very slowly. But it did move and eventually our turn came in April 1949.

Both of our ocean crossings were by ship. But the similarity stopped there. Mine had been on a small Liberty-ship type transport and the ocean part was mostly in the tropics with very pleasant sailing weather. Estelle's crossing would follow the northern route, much shorter but much rougher seas to endure. Her ship was the Army transport, the *Darby*.

Estelle and Stanley flew to San Francisco where they boarded the *Darby* at Fort Mason. After leaving Fort Mason, the ship proceeded up the coast and made a brief stop in Seattle. Then, out into the Pacific for the trip to Japan. They followed the great circle route. If you look at a large-area Mercator map of the Pacific, the great circle route looks like the long way to get to Japan. But, if you take a globe and stretch a piece of string across the globe from Seattle to Japan, the great circle route makes sense. It is significantly shorter. Unfortunately for the passengers making the crossing the ocean is colder, darker and much rougher.

Most of the passengers on the *Darby* were military dependents. The ship dated back to pre-war days, was larger and had much more pleasant amenities than our Greely had. Estelle said that there was a very nice dining room, staffed with male Filipino mess attendants. She and Stanley were the only two passengers who consistently showed up for all meals; the others were consistently sea sick most of the trip. Stanley was a little blond-haired lad of three and the mess attendants made a big fuss over him, since there were so few passengers for them to take care of.

Since I was a Navigator, I was very familiar with the Weather Office in Base Operations and knew casually most of the weather staff. The weather people plotted the reported positions of the *Darby* daily and daily I followed the route they were taking. At the closest, I believe they were within two hundred miles of the Aleutian Islands, a reminder of how far north their route took them.

A few weeks before Estelle's arrival, the Army PX headquarters provided our office a brand new Chevrolet. Once a month Takagi and either Fred or I had to go to the PX Headquarters in Yokohama to settle our office's account. Tachikawa was due west of Tokyo and Yokohama is due south of Tokyo. You had a choice of routes to Yokohama. Either go directly southeast to Yokohama; or take the much longer route to Tokyo then south to Yokohama. Of course we always took the direct route which went through farm lands most of the way. A nice drive, except that in the winter the ride in a Jeep was a chilly experience. The new Chevrolet sedan made the trip much more comfortable. We even had a driver and guess who it was. Jimmy, Fred's part-time jeep driver! I guess Fred pulled a deal to get Jimmy hired. But, he was a nice kid and at least we were familiar with him.

The arrival date for the *Darby* finally arrived and I had a docking time for the arrival in Yokohama. I counted on Jimmy driving me to the dock in the new PX sedan and tried to impress on him the importance (to me!) of his reporting to the office on time. Normally Jimmy was pretty reliable. On my D-day he happened to oversleep and showed up at the office at the last minute. As we drove the back route to Yokohama he tried to make up the lost time but speeding on the Japanese roads of those days was almost an impossibility. We arrived at the dock just before the ship was fully docked but I spotted Estelle and Stanley standing by the rail and we both waved for a few seconds. Then I noticed some of the guys waiting on the dock with me had corsages or bouquets of flowers. I found that there was a florist shop inside the roofed-over area of the dock and went inside to get a corsage. Estelle teased me later that when she saw me disappear, she knew I had forgotten to get flowers for her. Forgotten? I hadn't even realized that there would be a facility for buying flowers. The three of us had a glad and happy reunion. Stanley had grown a little since I left and Estelle was still the same beautiful woman I left in New Jersey. It was wonderful to be reunited.

I told Jimmy to go back to Tachikawa and I assume that he did go directly back. Fred and I never did compare notes later to see if he did and I guess its just as well that we gave him the benefit of the doubt.

When Estelle arrived, I had absolutely no idea of where we would be staying. But the military—probably the Army—had everything set up. The Army had persuaded the Japanese government to establish recreation areas for American military personnel. Things like a ski lodge and seaside vacation hotels. Each type would have a season where they would be in demand for Military people. During each facility's off-season the facility would be used to house dependents who were waiting for housing on their sponsor's base. Since Estelle arrived in April (off-season for skiing), we would be staying in a ski lodge. We soon found ourselves on a Japanese train bound for the Akakura, located at Nagano, some distance north of Tokyo.

You may remember that Nagano was the site for recent Winter Olympic Games. But in 1949 it was a small Japanese mountain town with one ski lodge, the Akakura. It was an overnight train ride but the Army had thoughtfully provided sleeper-car accommodations for us.

We arrived in Nagano somewhat early in the morning and found that there was government transportation waiting to take us to the lodge. The transportation would be in a Weasel, one couple to each Weasel. The Weasel was an open tracked vehicle, capable of making the climb up the mountain even in heavy snow. There was no snow when we arrived but the Army hadn't switched the taxi service to wheeled vehicles yet.

When we were climbing aboard, there was a problem for Estelle; at least she felt uncomfortable about it. She was wearing an attractive blue suit with a knee-length skirt. The driver's seat was lower than the passengers' seat and Estelle felt shy about sitting down, since the driver was looking back and up toward us as we climbed in. I can't say that I blame the driver and his interest, since Estelle did have an attractive pair of legs. But she had been in Japan for only a few hours and didn't know how to react. I got in, then leaned over and turned the driver's head toward the front, saying to him softly "*Dami, dami!*" I'm not sure what the expression translated to in English but I think it was something like "Naughty, naughty!" The driver smiled and nodded, then proceeded to start the engine while Estelle settled into her seat. Fortunately Stanley was not frightened by the experience of being in the Weasel and he enjoyed the trip up the mountainside.

The lodge was an attractive building which faced toward the valley below. There was no snow and no unexpected snow storms occurred while she was there. The dining room was operated as an Army field-ration mess. While not gourmet by any means, the food was usually pretty good, mostly like Midwest family fare.

With no snow and the location being on the bare slope of the mountain, there was not much to do other than the enjoyment of couples reunited after months of separation. The lodge was in a hot springs location and had large baths for guests to enjoy soaking in the hot water. If it were for Japanese guests, the bath would have been a large unisex one, since the Japanese don't view nudity the way we Americans do. But, for us and our American sensibilities there were two baths. A larger one for women and a smaller one for men. Each had a shower for actually washing yourself and there was a pool, about fifteen or sixteen inches deep, filled with warm water for the long, relaxing soak. By common agreement a family would use one or the other, locking the door to the hallway to keep the soak a family affair. For Stanley it was like playing in a swimming pool.

The lodge would provide transportation if you wanted to go to the town, Nagano, to shop and explore. This was almost as interesting to me as it was to Estelle. I had been in Japan for eight or nine months and was used to shopping in small Japanese shops, of the size and type we would call "Mom and Pop" stores back home in America. My interest was because the ones I had been going into were in Tachikawa or Tokyo or Hachioji, areas which had been completely destroyed during the war and had been rebuilt. But Nagano was located farther north, beyond our bombing range, plus there were no vital targets in the area. So the town was really a pre-war town, at least as far as the buildings were concerned,

I guess the Japanese in our Tachikawa/Tokyo area had become used to seeing large numbers of American service people. But, in Nagano we were something of a novelty. Especially Stanley. His hair was still mostly blond and he was fair-skinned. Compared to the cute little Japanese children and their black hair, he was a distinct novelty. Most of the shopkeepers made a big to-do over him and he received frequent small trinkets as gifts, usually accompanied by a gentle pat on the top of his head.

The Japanese toy shops were little wonder-lands for toys for children, especially boys. I assume that most of the toys were made in small shops by a worker who was ingenious at finding materials to use in making the toys. Some of the cars, which had little inertia motors, would reveal the source of some of the material. Pick up a little car and hold it up close to your eye. On the inside of the car you could frequently see the original packages' painted logo—Schlitz, or maybe Budweiser. A beer can reborn as a toy sedan!

Our leave-time together passed much too swiftly and soon I

had to return to duty. Estelle and Stanley would remain at the Akakura but I could visit on week-ends, unless I happened to be scheduled to fly. It was a rather strenuous commute. I would leave Tachikawa late Friday afternoon and go by local train to the central Tokyo train station. I believe its name was Ueno. There I would board a steam train for Nagano. When Estelle arrived, we had sleeper car accommodations for the trip. But my trip would be by coach in trains much like our American trains of the 1930's. Straight backed double seats with a back that would hinge forward or back to match the coach's direction of travel.

The Army's Camp Drake was a few stops north of the downtown Tokyo station. The Camp housed some elements of the Army's First Cavalry Division and their militant MP's. The car we would be riding in was peopled mostly by Air Force junior officers headed for Nagano as I was. We always were mindful of our conduct until we reached the stop for Camp Drake. At that stop, usually two or three First Cav MPs would board the train and walk down the aisle, suspiciously looking to make sure everyone was behaving and in proper uniform.

After the train left that stop, there would be no more MPs and we all proceeded to get comfortable for the all-night ride. On earlier trips someone had discovered that the seat backs could be lifted up and freed from the seat assembly and could be used to bridge the space between seats, making a flat surface which all of us could sleep on. I think that the Japanese conductors saw it as a sort of conspiracy game between us and the MPs and they sided with us in the conspiracy. It wasn't the most comfortable bed in the world but it was much better than trying to sleep sitting up. The conductors would alert us in time for us to replace the seat backs the next morning.

After several week-ends of commuting visits, Estelle decided to come down to Tachikawa. My room in the BOQ had two beds in it but my nominal room mate, Vern, was never in it. She was able to stay there several days, then the Billeting Officer suggested that she should probably go back to the Akakura. He said it would probably be okay if it were just her but with Stanley included it would be better if she left. He was very nice about it and she returned to the Akakura.

Soon the next move came. At the beginning of the Occupation when the military was setting up bases, the Army established an Air Base at Osaka. The base's name was Itami. Later the need for an operating base there ended but when they built the base the Japanese had built a nice group of family houses. With no tactical air unit at Itami, the houses were no longer needed locally. So they were made available for families waiting for on-base housing at their own base. We were happy to make the move. I still had the weekly commute but Estelle and Stanley would be living in a nice house now rather than a hotel room.

Since I would only be in the house on week-ends we arranged for a live-in maid for company and a bit of protection. The maid had her own little room. I don't think that she was a great deal of company because she was very young and her command of English was very limited. Estelle told me that one night when I was not there, in the middle of the night there was a moderate earth quake. It didn't damage the house—thanks to the Japanese builders' skill in making buildings able to resist moderate quakes. The girl started screaming when the quake started and continued screaming. Estelle went into her room when the shaking stopped and found the girl had pulled the covers up over her head and was afraid to come out. Stanley slept through the whole event.

Someone in headquarters at Tachikawa set up a weekly commuter shuttle for those of us with families at Itami. In this service, a C-46 would leave Tachikawa around mid-afternoon on Friday and carry us commuters to Itami. Then on Sunday afternoon the C-46 would come over to pick us up. During the Berlin Airlift, someone had started carrying candy to the little Berlin children. The operation gained the name "Little Vittles Express." Some wit at Tachikawa parodied that name and called our operation the "Little Diddle Express".

Although I liked and continued to use the Friday afternoon C-46 flight, I discovered a different way to get back to Tachikawa in time for work on Monday. We could ride Japanese trains at no expense to us. Nothing was needed for local trains. If you would have occasion to ride the long distance trains, you could get your organization to publish orders authorizing you to travel on a continuing bases. I found that I could catch a train in Osaka late Sunday afternoon, ride a sleeper coach all night and arrive in Tokyo early Monday morning and an early morning commuter train would get me to Tachikawa in time for the Monday morning duty formation in Squadron Ops. Probably I didn't gain much more than an additional hour or two with my family but it was a bit more adventuresome.

After living a few weeks in the Osaka area we were able to get a house in the Washington Heights housing area in Tokyo and now I ceased to be a week-end-only family man. It was a nice little house. Before leaving Itami Estelle had been given a replacement maid. This one had a little more fluency in English than the first one and when Estelle told her that we would be moving to the Tokyo area, Toshiko (or "Judy" as Estelle called her) asked if she could go to Tokyo and work for us. Since she couldn't travel on an Occupation train, we gave her Yen to buy herself a ticket to Tokyo. After we moved into the house in Tokyo we expected Judy to show up reasonably soon afterward. Several days passed with no Judy. Finally she did show up and explained her absence with a story that she had been visiting her brother who lived in Tokyo. Later Estelle found that Judy could not be depended on to take care of Stanley outside of the house. He was only three and a half years old and Estelle found him wandering around the housing area alone with no Judy in sight. After that, Judy was history.

Judy's replacement, Taka was as reliable as Judy was unreliable. Taka was a young single mother and had a young daughter who was tiny and cute, almost like a little doll.

By the time we moved into Washington Heights it was late fall. I remember one exciting afternoon we had in our new house. Chestnuts were popular in Japan as they are in parts of this country. I had absolutely no experience with chestnuts (we Southerners are more into peanuts and pecans!) and although Estelle had had them, she had never fixed them. We bought some and took them home to roast. Little did either of us know that if you roast chestnuts in the oven, you are supposed to pierce them with a knife to give the steam an escape hole. Innocently, we put the un-pierced chestnuts into a pan and put them into our oven. A little later the excitement began as the individual chestnuts started to explode like little fire crackers. I think we were able to rescue a few of them to eat but the rest created a big mess in the oven. Estelle and I cleaned up the grossest part of the mess but Taka had to do the final detail cleaning.

I had felt an occasional earthquake tremor earlier but none of them had been of much consequence. We had our first real one on Christmas Day. The three of us were up fairly early to check on Santa's loot and then Estelle fixed a late morning breakfast. I was sitting at the dining table with a second cup of coffee and Estelle had gone into the kitchen for some reason. Stanley was over by the Christmas tree, playing. The living room and dining room were really parts of one big area. I was watching Stanley play and after a sip of my coffee, put the cup back down on the saucer. Only, the saucer was moving around on the table and I could feel my chair shaking. I looked over at the Christmas tree and it was swaying back and forth; all of the ornaments and silver rain swaying with the tree. Estelle rushed back into the room and we looked at each other, wondering whether to rush outdoors or if it was all over. After a few seconds we decided that it must be all over, since there were no more tremors. Although in the future we would feel lesser tremors, this was the worst one I felt. I don't know how it compared with the one Estelle experienced in the house at Itami.

In later weeks we found that we would be getting on-base housing at Tachikawa. Finally! But before we moved, we found that we would be having our second child, probably in late spring of 1950.

When the Berlin Airlift ended in 1949, our squadron started getting its C-54 aircraft back, a few at a time. I had never flown in one before and the plane was a pleasure to fly. Four engines, a roomy cabin with fully insulated cabin walls and at last a decent work table for the Navigator! I don't remember the exact speeds of the two planes but I do remember that the C-54 was not significantly faster than the rugged old C-46s. But in comfort for the crew and passengers, it was miles ahead.

I never did feel that I knew what was going on with my ground job in the PX Warehouse. The squadron operations officer had first claim on my time and I spent so much time flying I never was any more than nominally in charge of the Warehouse. When we had a change of Squadron Commanders, the new Commander persuaded headquarters to put me on flying as my principal duty and put a non-rated officer in the Warehouse job. To do it, I believe he cited a flying regulation which provided that if an aircrewman logged three hundred hours of air time in three consecutive months, he had to be grounded for rest. When they changed my assignment, I think that I would have hit the three hundred hour mark early in the third month and that waved a red flag.

The change made life a lot easier. Report for an early morning duty call in Squadron Operations to find out if you had any small work detail for the day. Or more often, if you were scheduled for a local check flight, usually to swing a compass. If none of these, then just stay available on base, like at the Officer's Club, the PX, or home (that is, if home was on-base quarters.) If you had been scheduled earlier for one of the scheduled flights for that day of course you didn't go to the duty call.

Flying in a Troop Carrier squadron, one of the members' biggest collective prides was that in Troop Carrier, you flew in even the worst kind of weather. One morning a few days after a new pilot reported into the squadron from State-side it was pouring rain at the duty call. At the roll call this pilot was not present for duty. Somebody called his BOQ and told him to get himself over to Squadron Ops immediately. When he came walking in a few minutes later, the Operations Officer asked him why he wasn't with us at roll call. He said, "I looked out my BOQ window and saw how hard it was raining and didn't think we would be flying any today."

His answer brought a resounding horse laugh from all of us in the room. Someone said (in a very loud voice), "Hell, man. This isn't Air Training Command or MATS. This is Troop Carrier and we fly in any kind of weather!" The newcomer was properly chagrined.

A LONG FLIGHT

After World War II ended, the United States continued to keep a rudimentary air field operating on Iwo Jima. After the war, the first time we landed there was while our squadron was still flying the C-46s. I believe manning for the whole island was probably about fifty men. On this trip we picked up a small load to fly back to Japan. It was a casually planned load, more to take advantage of the fact that we were in a C-46 going back to Japan empty. The people who loaded the several boxes apparently were not professionally trained cargo handlers. During our take off, the motion-sensations inside the cargo portion of the plane seemed a little bit different. After we were air borne, the pilot wanted very much to know what was in the boxes of cargo which were sitting on the floor back near the big entrance door. They were just sitting on the floor and not secured with tiedown ropes, the way an experienced cargo handler would load them. His inspection found that the boxes were filled with books, a fairly dense type of cargo. The pilot was unhappy with the loading and said that at lift-off from the runway, the horizontal tail plane had stalled out and he felt lucky that he was able to keep the plane under control. If he had realized how heavy the few boxes were, he would have insisted that they be loaded forward, nearer the aircraft's center of gravity. Then he wouldn't have had to struggle to get a tail-heavy plane safely into the air.

On another, later trip, we had a little bit of a layover, about two or three hours. The pilot on this trip borrowed a jeep from someone in Operations and we decided to drive up the rudimentary road to the top of Mt. Suribachi, the site of the famous flag-raising picture and the inspiration for the flag-raising sculpture. The road was reasonably passable, at least for an Army Jeep. At the top we stopped by the small marker commemorating the event. It was a beautiful, brilliantly sunny day and the view from the top, out over the calm Pacific was spectacular. A lonely, peaceful place now with only memories of the bitter struggle that occurred there in 1945. At the beginning of that visit, when we were landing, for us there was a more emphatic reminder of the battle. As we were preparing to land, the control tower instructed the pilot to "Be sure and land on the right side of the runway. There's a hole on the left side of the runway."

We assumed that the reference was to a pot-hole, maybe the result of a sudden, heavy rain. As we passed the hole, though, we could see that it was no pot-hole. It was a big crater-like hole. Apparently one of the 500 pound bombs dropped during the fighting, or a 16 inch shell from a battleship's big guns did not explode when it hit and had buried itself in the soft, volcanic dirt. It had been sitting underground, brooding, for about five years, then suddenly of its own accord decided to explode.

* * *

Estelle and I were very happy with our new on-base quarters at Tachikawa. The building itself was a duplex with four housing units to each building. The two end units were two-bedroom apartments, all on the ground floor. The two center units were also two-bedroom apartments but they were two story. Our unit was an end apartment. Best feature of all was that it was right next door to the commissary. By this time we owned our first car but since Estelle did not drive yet, she could walk next door to the Commissary any time she wanted to without having to wait until I was available to drive. In future months she would find the location especially handy for that reason.

The wait for the birth of our second child came to an end in the middle of May, 1950. Although any childbirth experience is a major physical event for the mother, the result was a happy one for us. We now had a healthy baby daughter, who was named Kathryn Elizabeth by her proud mother.

There had been a succession of Japanese maids with the various quarters we had been assigned before we moved into the one at Tachikawa. When you lived in government quarters, instead of paying rent, Finance just withheld your Quarters Allowance from your pay. In occupied Japan, you had a Japanese maid or housekeeper as part of the housing package. The maid's wages were paid by the Japanese Government. If you wished, you could also have a second maid for about ten dollars a month, though her pay came from your own pay allowances. You were expected to feed the maid or maids a lunch and the saying was that it was more expensive to feed the second maid than pay her wages. Some wives were stingy about feeding the maids but Estelle had grown up in a household where Polish traditions of hospitality ruled and she insisted that the maids eat the same food we did.

We finally ended up with two maids we became quite fond of. Number one maid, who was classed as a housekeeper, was Masae. She was from a family that had been a little more prosperous than the average and she had a much better grasp of English. I believe her father or uncle had been a college professor. Masae told Estelle some events that had happened to her family during the war. She had been studying piano and her piano was lost in the fires and her uncle was killed by the same fire bomb which destroyed her home. Several of her brothers were part of the crew of an aircraft carrier. Their carrier had been involved in a big battle in which all the other carriers had been lost. When their carrier limped back to Japan, she said that the ship was sent to a navy base in northern Japan and her brothers, as well as all the rest of the crew, were confined to the base and completely isolated for the remainder of the war. Their family did not even know if they were alive or dead until the end of the war. This was in line with the Japanese Government's policy of telling the Japanese public only about victories, never about defeats. I was not present when Masae told this to Estelle but I guess that the big battle would have to have been the Battle of Midway. She also told about her uncle who had been in the Japanese Army in Burma. He survived the war but when the war ended, he was stranded in Burma and had to find his own way back to Japan. In turn, Estelle told about how her own brother, Peter, had been killed in the fighting in Normandy shortly after the invasion of Europe.

I believe that the second maid's name was also Masae but to prevent the confusion of two Masaes we all called her "Fuji". Fuji had less command of English than Masae did and I believe that she came from a farming family. She was hard-working and the two Masaes got along well together.

With a healthy four year old youngster, an equally healthy newborn infant, and two excellent maids we were living a busy and happy life. Then Squadron Operations came up with a complication. A long flight. Not RON (Remain Overnight) but a really long one.

Although we were now flying C-54s exclusively, there were still some of the C-46s around. Headquarters (above our base) decided that although they wanted a few twin engine airplanes in the various bases' Base Flight Sections, it would be better if the planes were C-47s instead of C-46s. The C-47s were simpler to maintain and more pilots had been trained to pilot them.

The airfield at Tachikawa was actually two separate bases. On the west side of the runway was our base, Tachikawa Air Force Base, home to our Troop Carrier Wing. On the east side of the runway was another base, JAMA (Japan Air Materiel Area). JAMA was a big supply and maintenance base, serving all the Air Force Bases in Japan.

The changeover in aircraft types involved JAMA sending C-46s back to the States with a ferrying crew from JAMA and the ferrying crew returning with a C-47. JAMA apparently had enough pilots of their own to provide pilots for the ferry crews. But they apparently had no Navigators so they borrowed Navigators from Tachikawa. One of the borrowees was me.

I was not enthusiastic about the idea. First, I had to leave Estelle with our newborn infant. Second, even if it weren't for that the trip itself didn't enthuse me. I had navigated the whole route in B-29s and knew how long the distance was. To make it less appealing, I remembered that the B-29's cruising speed was forty or fifty miles an hour faster than either of the two twin-engine planes. And the California-Hawaii leg of the flight was twenty two hundred miles. In a Gooney Bird (C-47) you could start that leg of the flight clean-shaven and by the time you finished you would probably need another shave. But I had always had a personal policy toward flights—never volunteer for one and never try to get out of an assigned flight. That policy would save my life a month or so later.

The twin engine planes could not carry enough fuel in their built-in tanks for the flight. That meant that they would have to have ferry-tanks installed inside the plane. These would be installed for the ferry flight and after they were installed, we—the ferry crew—would make a test flight to make sure they worked properly.

For our test flight the ferry tank was filled and secured in its place in the cabin right next to my navigator desk. The tank was about the size and shape of an old fashioned six-foot long bath tub. I felt a little dubious about all the additional weight of the fuel in the tank but the plane made it into the air with no problems. Of course at the take off the engines were using fuel out of the plane's built-in fuel tanks.

After a few minutes of normal flight, it was time for the pilot to test the flow of fuel from the ferry tank. The tank had a vent hose leading from the tank out through one of the plane's windows. When the pilot switched from the plane's built-in tanks to the big ferry tank, apparently the vent hose had been installed improperly and the tank began gushing aviation gasoline out of the vent connection, all over the outside of the tank and onto the plane's floor.

I think I probably set a speed record in reaching the cockpit and shouting for the pilot to switch the pumping operation off. He did so immediately and the gush of fuel stopped but now the whole floor of the cargo compartment was awash in gasoline. The pilot reached for the VHF microphone and paused before using it. We wondered if the radio would create any kind of spark to ignite all the gasoline. Then, he called in a "Mayday" to the tower which cleared us for an immediate emergency landing.

Fortunately we were immediately over the field and at a low altitude. I don't know what was wrong with the fuel tank but it must have been something simple to fix because the fuel system gave us no problems on the whole long trip. But the experience made me distrust the whole ferry tank system. I was a smoker at the time and even though the flight engineer said it would be safe to smoke after take off I didn't have any cigarettes while airborne for the whole trip. That in itself was a major health benefit but at the time I considered it a hardship!

The routing of the trip was a familiar one, a replay of the old B-29 flights. Tachikawa to Guam; Guam to Kwajalein. In a B-29 the next leg would have been from Kwajalein to Hawaii. But since we were now flying in a twin engine plane instead of a four engine plane, we had to stop at Johnston Island, a little smidge of an island along the route and refuel. The long flight from Hickam in Hawaii to San Bernardino, California was long but uneventful.

Since the two pilots had been eagerly anticipating taking leave in the States, I had to take leave also. I use the words "had to" because I wanted to be back with my family in Japan. I hitched a ride on an Air Force plane back to the old Brookley Air Force Base at Mobile, Alabama and took a train from there to Cullman. Of course I enjoyed being with my family again but unfortunately didn't have my two children along for the grandparents to cuddle.

Since hitching rides on military planes is chancy as to when and if you get a ride, I took a train back to California when it was time to leave. It rounded out my cross country train riding experience. When going to Japan earlier, I had traveled the northern route—via Chicago. This time it would be the southern route—via New Orleans. Both routes were long and tiring and the night time portions were boring.

We started the long grinding return flight to Hawaii from the air base at San Bernardino and in addition to keeping up my navigation log I started making what would be a long string of POMARs. I don't remember what the acronym stood for but it was an hourly radio report to the ground stations reporting our position and the meteorological conditions we were experiencing.

All of the equipment on the Gooney Bird operated normally and we didn't experience any bad weather.

I believe that the flight took approximately twenty hours. At Hickam, I reported in to the weather office to answer any questions which they might have. This was standard procedure. One of the Meteorologists said, "We were plotting your position reports on the big map and were starting to wonder if you would ever make it here." I replied that we were starting to wonder that also!

Number one priority for us at Hickam was sleep. With twenty hours of flying time, preceded by several hours of preparation for the flight, it had been more than twenty-four hours since we had slept. But with a day and night of rest, we were ready to start the next leg, the flight to Kwajalein with the intermediate stop at Johnston Island.

When we reported to Base Operations at Hickam, the pilot proceeded to file the flight plan and I went to Weather for weather information on our route. The copilot happened to buy a copy of the Honolulu newspaper, planning to read it during the flight. When we were airborne he skimmed through most of the non-local news. He told us that there was an interesting small news item which reported that there were reports of military activity by the North Korean Army along the border with South Korea. Not many details but it did cause us to wonder about it. At the time we were probably more interested in the story than the paper's Hawaiian readers, since we all lived much closer to Korea.

The flight to Johnston Island was uneventful until our landing. At the time the volcano, Mauna Loa on the island of Hawaii (the Big Island!) was erupting. Johnston Island was several hundred miles west of the volcano but the trade winds were carrying clouds of fine dust from the volcano over Johnston Island. When we descended to a lower altitude to land, we found that you could look straight down fairly clearly but vision out ahead was minimal because of the dust. The pilot had to abort his first approach to the runway because of the limited visibility and go around for a second shot at landing. The second approach was successful. After taking on fuel, we were ready to resume the flight to Kwajalein.

Kwajalein had changed quite a bit since we passed through in our B-29 during the war. The change was an improvement but it didn't alter the fact that Kwajalein was still a rather small place. A rock, to use the GI slang for a small island. This trip was missing the feeling I had during the first trip that I was in the doorway to the war and the future might hold unhappy things. This time I was happier, with the prospect of returning in two days to a good wife and two great children.

Our flight from Kwajalein to Guam was in characteristically beautiful tropical sunshine. Long, but not as long as the flight to Hawaii had been. Smooth air and a plane where everything was working perfectly. No worries, other than the problem of a little boredom with the perfection.

When we landed at Guam, we found that the base was buzzing with activity. There was no problem with refueling our plane or securing it for the night. But everybody seemed unusually busy. We had dinner in the Officers Club and sensed the tension among the other diners, all local personnel.

We asked some of the diners at the table next to ours about the unusual activity. They told us that the local tactical aircraft (B-29s, my old friends) were being deployed. Their destination was supposedly secret but with the Communist activity in Korea, the two most likely destinations would be either one of the airfields on Okinawa or Yokota AFB in Japan. We learned later that it turned out to be Okinawa.

Next morning we took off on the last leg of our long trip, the flight to Tachikawa. The weather was beautiful for this leg of the trip, as it had been the previous day, and we landed at Tachikawa in mid-afternoon.

Of course Estelle's and my reunion was a happy time for us and both children were still in good health. It was wonderful to be home again. We were still outside in our front yard, enjoying being together again when a jeep drove into our driveway. It was Frank, the Squadron Operations Officer from my Squadron. I had become a little more closely acquainted with Frank when we both were living in Washington Heights in Tokyo.

Frank was apologetic for running me down in the first few minutes after I reached home. But he said that he was desperate for Navigators. He said that both squadrons had been flying every available plane for three or four days and some of the crew-members were ragged from fatigue. They had been evacuating dependents and civilians from Kimpo Air Force Base in Korea to Itazuke AFB in Japan. That distance was only three hundred or so miles but the planes were making several round trips a day. Frank said that he knew I had been flying for several days and would be within my rights to refuse him but could I and would I take an early flight the next morning? Briefing time would be four-thirty AM. I didn't feel I could refuse, so I agreed to take the flight.

Estelle was not too happy that I had agreed to the flight. But, since I had been isolated from the emergency in Korea while I was en route home, she was more aware of the plight of the Americans in Korea, especially the dependents. As a good service wife she accepted our abbreviated reunion as one of the disappointments service wives must face willingly.

POLICE ACTION—
THE BEGINNING

The briefing for the flight was perfunctory. The weather en route and in Korea were the primary interest to me, since they involved my navigation. I don't believe the pilot was given a firm destination, since Kimpo AFB was now in Communist hands. Kimpo was the only American Air Force Base in Korea. As well as I can remember his order was to fly to Korea and somebody there would say where to land. There would be no passengers, only cargo. And, as I learned when we entered our plane, the cargo was artillery ammunition. A full load of it. Being a dense load, it didn't take up a great deal of space.

The abbreviated preliminary briefing over, we went to our C-54 plane. The pilot and copilot made their preflight inspection of the plane and found everything in order. The inspection included a brief check of the cargo which seemed to be securely loaded and tied down. When the pilot started the engines, it was still dark and we taxied out to the end of the runway. Tachiwawa's North/South runway was about fifty one hundred feet long, I believe. Too short for a B-29 with a war-time load but adequate for our C-54s. We would be taking off going north. The pilot gave the engines full power and it felt normal to me, though in the darkness I couldn't see much. After we were in the air, I unbuckled my belt and went up to the cockpit to watch the pilot's instruments during the climb south to the Oshima beacon. Not that I was essential to that part of the flight; I just liked to watch what was happening. The pilot seemed a little tense and after a few minutes, told me about the take off. He said that the plane didn't seem to want to fly even when the airspeed indicator showed normal take off speed and he felt that we were considerably overloaded. We just barely cleared the trees growing near the perimeter fence. There was not much we could do now and we knew that by the time we reached Korea, the engines would have burned enough fuel to lighten the plane's overall weight.

As we climbed toward the Oshima signal it started getting light. Not affected by the daunting take off, the plane's engines were all running smoothly and the weather promised a clear, smooth flight to Korea. Every time I passed the tied down cargo, the large artillery shells, I would eye them uneasily. I wasn't used to a load like that. Somehow they seemed different from the bombs we carried in the B-29s. Bombs I understood; artillery shells I didn't!

We were going into a combat area, presumably. The other crew members who had been flying in the flights evacuating the civilians from Kimpo told me that the North Koreans had made a few attacks on our C-54s, flying Russian made YAKS. None of the C-54s had been shot down or anyone wounded but a lucky shot for the North Koreans would be an unlucky shot for us.

This would be combat again, aerial combat, and I felt that combat in World War II somehow didn't prepare me for what we were going into this time. Flying into airspace that may be shared with enemy fighters, our own fighter planes would be armed with their own machine guns. And bombers, such as the B-29 and B-26 would have their own defensive turret-mounted machine guns. But a transport type has no defensive guns. There was only one defense for a transport and not a very comforting one either. It was to fly at tree-top level. A fighter pilot has his hands full when trying to shoot another plane down. First, flying a high performance plane into a position where he can shoot at his target, remembering that he aims his guns by aiming his plane. And, second, being on watch in all directions to see if his enemy (our "little friends"!) were on his own tail. Pursuing a transport flying at tree-top level, any slight miscalculation by the fighter pilot could end up with his colliding with the ground. It was a defense of sorts for the transport plane but a chancy one, since the transport could also make a miscalculation and end up as a pile of aluminum on the ground.

Of course while we were flying safely over Japan, we could fly comfortably at our normal flight altitude, usually either eight or nine thousand feet. The weather continued to be nice and we continued normally and comfortably. This had to change, though, after we left Japan and were crossing the Korea Strait toward Pusan. As we approached Pusan we descended much lower, probably to around a thousand feet. After leaving Pusan, we dropped down to about three hundred feet, our tree-top altitude, and started wandering around the southern part of Korea at that altitude.

"Tree top" altitude is a somewhat elastic term, depending on what type plane is involved. For a single engine Cessna it would possibly be as low as a hundred feet. But we were in a four engine transport and for us three hundred feet was not a really safe cruising altitude. The pilot was talking lengthily to someone over the VHF while the rest of us were nervously glued to the plane's windows. I used the plane's astrodome, normally used for celestial observations but now the only spot where we could see what or who was on our tail. We seemed to have the sky to ourselves though and flew generally north. Finally, the pilot said, "We are going to land."

"Where?" I asked. I knew, in a sort of general way, where we were.

"At Taejon."

I scanned my map around Taejon. "I don't see any airfields on the map near Taejon. What is it, an old Japanese field?"

"Negative. It's a grass field."

I had flown from a grass field in my brief days in pilot training. But we were flying little two-seat Stearmans there. I had never been through a landing or take off in a transport plane from anything except a paved runway.

"Did you call the tower yet?" I asked.

"There isn't any tower. Just an Army team with a radio."

I guess that I mentally expected the grass field to wipe us out and save the North Koreans a few bullets. But the landing itself was surprisingly smooth and uneventful.

The pilot called the flight engineer and me up to the cockpit where the copilot handed each of us a grease gun. "Grease Gun" was GI slang for a mass-produced sub-machine gun about the shape of a Thompson sub-machine gun. I didn't even know that they were aboard.

"Go back and open the cargo door while I'm taxiing. A jeep is going to meet us but we need to find out if it is our Army or the North Koreans."

The engineer opened the cargo door and the pilot slowed down and made a quarter of a circle turn while stopping. The plane carried an old fashioned step ladder to use in exiting the plane if there was no airport-type stair rolled up. But we did not lower the step ladder, pending our meeting with the ground people.

There was no one near the plane; we were all alone in a grassy expanse of field. The engineer and I nervously checked our grease-guns to make sure a round was chambered and the safety was off. I had fired a Thompson once but never one of the grease-guns. Finally we could see a jeep speeding toward us. As it approached, we could see that the passenger was an Army Captain (US Army, thankfully!) and a Korean Driver wearing green fatigues. We assumed that the Captain was an advisor to a unit of the South Korean Army and we lowered our step ladder.

The Captain wanted to know what we had for him. When he learned that it was a plane load of artillery shells, he shook his head sadly. "I can't use them," he said. "No guns!"

"What I desperately need is motor oil," he continued. "For my trucks. Do you have any?"

"Nope!" our pilot said. "No vehicle oil. The plane has a fifty gallon reserve tank of airplane oil. But it's built into the plane. If we can figure how to pump it out do you have anything to put it in?"

"Afraid not."

It was a big disappointment for both of our parties. The Army Captain had several Korean GI's nearby and he volunteered their assistance in unloading the plane. This was much more help to us than we had been to him. It had been difficult to get the overloaded plane air borne from Tachikawa's paved runway. Now we were somewhat lighter by the amount of gas we had used flying. But even though we were lighter it would be dicey if we tried taking off from a grassy field carrying the artillery shells.

With the artillery shell cargo removed, the plane had no trouble with taking off. Now we would be flying back to Tachikawa after a stop at Itazuke AFB to refuel. There had been no sign of any enemy YAKs and as we flew toward Pusan the pilot started climbing gradually to a more comfortable altitude. But we still watched carefully in all directions.

The flight back to Tachikawa was uneventful and I was happy to be back with Estelle to resume our happy reunion. She told me that during the day she had walked over to the Commissary and met a Mrs. McPherson. Mrs. McPherson thanked Estelle several times for my agreeing to take the flight. Her husband, Gerald, was a Navigator and had been flying almost continuously and was almost exhausted. He was able to get a little sleep before having to take off again on a flight later in the day. The flight he was on would have been the flight I would have been on if I hadn't agreed to take the earlier morning flight.

We learned later that the plane that Gerald was on was not as lucky as we had been. Their tree-top flying had ended disastrously when they crashed into a mountain side and of course everyone aboard was killed instantly.

It was then that I told Estelle about my own personal philosophy of never volunteering for a flight and never trying to get out of one that I was scheduled for. It had saved me from being on the ill-fated flight. Her comment was physical rather than verbal—a long hug and a long thankful silence.

POLICE ACTION—
DAYS OF CONFUSION

There was much confusion in the early days of the Korean War. I don't know if things were any different up at Group or Wing level. But down at the Lieutenant/Captain level in the Squadrons we could only guess what was happening at the moment or would happen in our immediate future.

The next move was for most of our planes to go to Itazuke AFB empty and stand by. Itazuke was the Air Force Base in Japan that was closest to Korea. It was more or less across the Korea Strait from Pusan, Korea. At Itazuke we all congregated in the small combination Operations and Terminal building. Normally on our scheduled passenger or freight flights we were expected to dress in a Class A uniform. But with the emergency conditions prevailing, all of us wore flight coveralls (flight suits). This made waiting around for action a little more comfortable. There weren't enough seats and standing continually, even leaning on the wall, would get tiresome. The floor was moderately clean and soon many of us were stretched out on it. I guess we looked a little slovenly but no one tried to make it a time for spit and polish. At the time none of us had had much sleep and we had no idea what the rest of the day would bring. Of course if you were really, really tired you could have gone out to your plane and stretched out on one of the long canvas seats. But in the plane you would not be close to where things were happening so most of us just lounged around, waiting for something to happen.

At the time our C-54s were the largest cargo aircraft, at least among the ones in general service. It was a wonderful plane to fly in. But it was mainly a four engine passenger plane. There was a large side cargo door but loading any cargo, other than palletized freight presented serious loading problems. To get a vehicle in, the vehicle had to be lifted in through the side door and then turned ninety degrees to the left so it could be rolled forward. The working space was so constricted that you couldn't use the vehicle's wheels to back-and-fill into the sharp left hand turn. Maybe you could on a jeep but nothing larger than a jeep. We would have been in hog-heaven with the later C-130 Herky Birds where you could just drive a vehicle in and tie it down. But this was years before their time.

As far as we knew, no Americans had been committed to intervening action in Korea. Maybe fighter planes or bombers but at our level we had no way of knowing. It was certain that the Army had not gone in. At least not yet. We would know if they had because we would be providing the Army's airlift. But if the Army elements involved were to be elements of the 25th Infantry they may have been traveling at the time by train from Osaka, over several hundred miles toward the middle of Honshu.

Finally some activity started. Planes started being loaded and taking off. Our plane was not one of the earlier ones. Finally, when it came to be our turn, we found our load would be one of the lighter ones. It was one Army weapons carrier truck (a small truck, the next size up from a jeep), the truck driver, and the truck's one passenger, an Army Major General. He was General Dean, I believe, the Commander of the 25th Division.

The airlift would be from Itazuke, across the Korea Strait to Pusan. There was an airstrip at Pusan with a paved runway, an old, pre-WW II Japanese field. It would be our destination. Not a good destination but about the best available at the time.

The actual distance of the flight was not great, probably about an hour's flying time, assuming there was only one plane involved. But it would be different now with planes from two Troop Carrier Squadrons all trying to make the run at one time. We reached Pusan in normal time and started circling the field, waiting for our turn to land.

Our turn to land did not come. A rudimentary control tower

(probably a jeep!) had been set up on the ground and before our turn came, the controller directed all of us in the air to return to Itazuke. The Japanese airfield was old and had probably been constructed to handle mostly single-engine Japanese aircraft. Our four-engine C-54s, fully loaded were too heavy for the old Japanese paving and the runway started breaking up.

I believe that General Dean went over in a later flight in a C-47, a much lighter plane but I don't know where he landed. I always felt sorry for the General and his later experiences. He was forced to commit his Division to the fighting in bits and pieces as they came in to Korea and before long he was captured. He was the highest ranking American POW in the Korean action.

On one of our flights to Itazuke in these earliest days we had taken a load for Itazuke and were getting ready to return to Tachikawa. There was a C-47 waiting to go into Korea. It had two Pilots and no Navigator. Neither of the two Pilots had ever flown into any part of Korea and the Aircraft Commander was reluctant to try it without a Navigator. Somebody volunteered my services (it wasn't me!). They wanted to go to Taejon and land at the grassy field where we had landed. I found the field for them and when we left they dropped me off at Itazuke. I hitched a ride back to Tachikawa on one of our C-54s.

Gradually some order came into the flights into Korea. Thanks to either Army Engineers or Navy Seabees (I don't know who to thank) landing strips were thrown into existence in Korea. Using conventional paving it couldn't have been done so quickly. But, with PSP it was not only practical, it was done. PSP was a World War II invention which was used many times in the Pacific to throw up airfields in a hurry for fighter planes or transports. PSP was an abbreviation for "Pierced Steel Planking". It used strips of heavy steel, about twelve or fourteen feet long and six or seven inches in width. There were little claws along the sides so that when the strip was laid down, it could be interlocked with the strip next to it. I felt more at ease landing on a PSP strip than on the grassy fields.

I never did learn how the 25th Division was moved into Korea.

Our few plane loads certainly did not take the bulk of the Division over and we could never have handled their larger vehicles and artillery nor could the airstrips in Korea. It must have been on Navy ships; after all, the distance from Kyushu to Pusan was relatively short. They did get across and found themselves in a position where they were pitifully outnumbered. In spite of the serious odds facing them, they and possibly other Army or Marine units finally stopped the advance of the North Koreans and set up a defensive perimeter which held its own successfully until the well known Inchon landing took place.

The pace of our own Troop Carrier effort slowed down from "Frantic" to "Routine Hectic". We were now in a routine support role, busy but not unusually dangerous.

The main source of news for us was the Armed services newspaper Stars and Stripes. The regular readers of state-side newspapers probably knew more about the day-by-day events of the war than we did in Japan, since Stars and Stripes, as good as it was, was a low-budget house organ. But I guess we were reasonably informed with day by day anecdotes.

One series of interesting anecdotes concerned the exploits of the B-26's. We looked on them as something of a home team, since they had been based at Johnson AFB, one of the three Air Force Bases in the immediate Tokyo area. Some of their missions were daylight mission. The more fascinating stories were about their missions where the crews reported successes in destroying targets at night. Their strikes were described as Night Intruder missions. We wondered if their planes were equipped with some new and secret night flying equipment. The stories never told and we could only guess.

More and more, we Navigators felt we had slipped into a more minor role in the Troop Carrier flights. The flights were mostly to Itazuke AFB in Japan and Naha AFB in Okinawa and the pilots could handle their own navigation easily. There were fewer longer over-water flights where a Navigator did more to earn his keep. This situation must have come to the attention of the command levels above our base. Where our Wing was fat on Navigators, the

B-26 Wing was in a Navigator-short situation. Higher Headquarters decided to equalize the situation. Their solution involved sending ten or twelve of us Navigators, selected more or less equally from the 22nd and the 6th, to the B-26 Wing. I was among those transferred.

13TH BOMB SQUADRON

We Navigators who were transferred found that the 3rd Bomb Wing, our new local headquarters, had two bomb squadrons, the 8th Bomb Squadron and the 13th Bomb Squadron. Half of us went to each squadron; my new squadron would be the 13th. Fortunately I never was superstitious about the number thirteen. The squadron had been initially activated in World War I where they flew Spads. After that war the squadron was inactivated and was reactivated in later years. The squadron insignia was a little on the macabre side. It was a skeleton, standing, holding a scythe which had four drops of blood dropping from the blade and underneath it was our nickname, "Grim Reapers".

Although the Wing was technically based at Johnston AFB in the Tokyo area I found that they were currently operating on a semipermanent basis from Iwakuni RAAFB. Iwakuni was a home base to a P-51 squadron of the Royal Australian Air Force and we would be a tenant of their's. The Australian P-51s had been moved to operate from a base closer to the war. I guess that most of the Australian family dependents went back to Australia because we found that the Australian family quarters were now being used as American BOQs.

Iwakuni was located on the Inland Sea, probably forty or fifty miles down the coast from Hiroshima. It had been a Japanese air base before and during World War II.

Without any delay we were given a familiarization introduction to the B-26 bombers we would be flying. I decided right there that I didn't like the plane. Later I became impressed by the plane's capabilities as time passed and my experience with it accumulated. But actually liking it was something that never came to me.

Even the designation of the plane frequently causes confusion.

Air Force types of planes were supposed to be identifiable from the prefix of their type number. "B" with a number meant it was a bomber. "P" with a number meant it was a pursuit plane (now it's "F," meaning fighter). "C" meant it was a cargo plane and "T" identified it as a trainer. When the letter designations started, there was another category, "A" for attack plane. Our current B-26 was originally called an A-26 and it evolved from an earlier A-20. Later, the "A" classification was discontinued and our A-26 became a B-26. This created a confusing situation which continues today because there already was another B-26, an entirely different plane. "Our" B-26 was manufactured by the Douglas company. The "other" B-26 was manufactured by the Martin company. To this day when I mention that I flew some in the B-26, I have to explain that it was the Douglas B-26, not the Martin B-26.

The B-26 was a bit of a flying arsenal. In our squadron there were two versions of the plane. The "glass nose" version had a Plexiglas enclosed nose which housed a Bombardier position, complete with a Norden bombsight. There were only a few of these in the squadron, about two or three. The majority of the ones in the squadron were the "hard nose" model. Instead of the glass-enclosed nose, the hard nose model had machine guns in the nose section. Most of the planes had eight machine guns in the nose while a few had only six guns there. Additionally, there were six machine guns enclosed in the wings, three on each side. All of these guns were fixed in place, the pilot aiming the guns by aiming the plane itself, using a sight image before his seat in the cockpit. When he blasted away at a target, it was with the force of either twelve or fourteen fifty caliber machine guns. In addition, there was an upper turret and a lower turret, both turrets controlled by one gunner whose station was immediately behind the bomb bay. In addition to the guns, there was a bomb bay which carried about six or eight bombs, usually either 500 pounders or 260 pound anti-personnel fragmentation bombs. As if this wasn't enough, the plane could also carry a bunch of five inch aerial rockets (equivalent to a five inch artillery shell, I believe) or two 260 gallon tanks of jellied gasoline—both munitions slung underneath the wing.

While the armament of the plane was impressive, as a Navigator, I was unhappy with the navigator station. There wasn't one, really! As originally conceived the glass-nosed model would carry a Bombardier-Navigator who would lead a flight of the hard-nosed planes into a target area. The flight would pass over the target, the Bombardier-Navigator aiming with the bombsight and the remainder of the formation toggling their bombs out when they saw the leader's bombs drop. Then the flight would break up with the hard-nose planes diving down individually to strafe the target with their guns or rockets.

There was only one pilot for the plane. There was a seat to the right of the Pilot—the normal place for a Copilot seat. But there were no flight controls at this seat, which was called a jump-seat (I have no idea where it got the name). Under original planning it was occupied usually by a crew chief or someone going along to sight-see. Under the current practices this had become the Navigator's seat and station. Not like the Navigator desk on a bomber or transport plane where the Navigator had his own instruments. Here my desk would be my brief case perched across my knees. The few instruments a Navigator needs to use were the ones on the pilot's instrument panel—Airspeed Indicator, Altimeter, Compass, Radio Compass. No Driftmeter because a Pilot doesn't use a Driftmeter so therefore I wouldn't use one either! And an Astrodome to use when doing Celestial? Forget it. Celestial would be a forgotten skill now. Loran joined Celestial as a missing asset.

Precision bombing with a bombsight? Forget that too. In the hard nose model the pilot aimed the bombs by flying straight toward the target at a thirty to forty degree dive angle, using the same sight he used to aim the guns. At the point in the dive where the pilot thought the bomb would hit his target he would release the bomb, hoping that he had chosen the right time and that he (read "we") would still be high enough so that we wouldn't be hit by any of the bomb fragments or anything blowing up on the ground. In our squadron terminology this technique was called dive bombing, although I'm sure any experienced Navy dive bomber pilot would laugh at our name for it. It was a matter of skill. A few of the pilots were good at it. A few not very good. The rest were in between; occasionally one would get a good hit but occasionally one would bring his plane home full of holes from fragments of his own bombs. And, sadly sometimes one wouldn't come home at all.

Attacking a ground target with either the guns or rockets involved the same diving approach. I was more impressed with the machine guns than with the rockets. The rockets would mess up a target very well—if they hit the target. The machine guns were more accurate.

While our B-29s had just barely enough power to get airborne safely with a maximum load, you couldn't fault the B-26s for that. For all the weight it could carry, it was a rather small plane. It had two Pratt-Whitney R-2800 engines, basically the same engines we loved in the old C-46s. Losing an engine's power in a B-29 at take off was a catastrophe; it was not a big problem with a B-26. We learned that one night in a takeoff from Iwakuni with the full load of fuel and munitions. Right after take off, one of the engines had some sort of malfunction and the pilot feathered the propeller on that engine immediately. In spite of the dead engine, the pilot found the plane could still climb respectably on the remaining one engine. We salvoed our bombs over the Inland Sea and made a normal landing. That is, a landing that was normal until the pilot tried to turn off the runway onto the taxi way and found that the plane wouldn't taxi on one engine. The one engine just made the plane turn around and around in a tight little circle. They had to tow it with a tractor to a parking spot.

The BOQs for us were the family quarters occupied earlier by the Australian families. There were ten of us assigned to one small two story unit. Five guys were upstairs and five of us were downstairs. Three of us were on cots in the living room and two more on cots in the former dining room. The only other room downstairs was the tiny kitchen.

There was one Japanese maid assigned to each two officers. Their duties were to do their officers' laundry, their bed linen and collectively keep the quarters clean. Everybody got along harmoniously with everybody else, fortunately. But privacy was an unknown thing for us in the crowded quarters. If you undressed, out of necessity you just undressed without any attempt at modesty. The Japanese maids seemed to think nothing of it and most of us Americans got used to it.

The Japanese were an interesting lot. The oldest was "Old Mamma-san". Next was "Young-Mamma-san". The youngest of the group was "Baby-san", probably about seventeen or eighteen years old. The one assigned to me was Fumiko. Last of all was one we called "Rosebud", not a Japanese name but we never learned her real Japanese name. With the exception of Fumiko's name, all the other names we used were easy-to-remember tags we started using.

The one in the group with the best command of English was Young Mama-san. But the one who was the most interesting of the group was Old-Mama-san, a woman who was probably in her sixties or maybe even her seventies. She had a minimal grasp of English but that didn't stop her from getting involved with us in longer conversations. She liked to talk and usually there was at least one of us ready to listen. Of course none of us had any Japanese language grasp beyond the ten or twenty words most Americans usually picked up. A simple exchange of ideas with Old Mama-san involved much grasping for words and sometimes a call on Young-Mama-san for help.

In these surroundings having the maids was something of a mixed blessing. It was nice to always have clean socks and underwear and freshly washed and pressed khakis. But when you had been awake all the previous night on a mission, peace and quiet for a few hours would also have been a blessing too, one which usually was in short supply in our crowded quarters.

When we started our first missions with the 3rd Bomb Wing, one of the squadrons would fly daylight missions for a whole week while the other squadron would fly night missions. After the week the assignments would change and if you had been flying daylight missions, you would change over to night missions. After a few weeks of this alternating, Headquarters decided it would be more efficient if one squadron would fly daylight missions all the time and the other would fly night missions all the time. Our squadron, the 13th, became the full time night flyers.

Before the war started there was an outbreak of smallpox in Korea. This was back when we were flying from Tachikawa. Orders were put out which said that if you were going into Korea, you must show evidence (i.e., a shot record) that you had received a smallpox vaccination within the past thirty days. No exceptions! So, whenever you were scheduled for one of the Korea flights, you made sure to bring your shot record with you to the briefing. No shot record? There was always a standby medic ready to give you a smallpox inoculation.

When we were transferred to the B-26 Wing, the 30-day shot requirement was still in effect. At that time it was early fall. It was still very warm at ground level but the air had started to get a cold nip to it at the low altitudes where we flew, especially over Korea which was several hundred miles north of us. For this reason, some of us had stopped wearing cotton flight coveralls when on a mission and had started wearing the all wool flight coveralls. I had just had a small-pox inoculation the day before we took off on a daylight mission. The wool flight suit was comfortable over Korea. Unfortunately, a typhoon had moved in from the Pacific south of us and it headed for Iwakuni. We flew our mission but our landing was diverted to Itazuke AFB to escape the hurricane. The move turned into a three day stay at Itazuke while the typhoon passed over Iwakuni. Of course we flight crew members spent the time at Itazuke wearing the same clothes we wore when we took off on the mission; in my case the woolen flight suit. The ground air temperature rose with all the tropical air which had blown up from the Pacific south of us and we (the ones of us in woolens) sweltered. My smallpox inoculation was on the arm just below the part protected by my cotton tee shirt. The woolen sleeve rubbing over the inoculation for three days in summer heat made the inoculation "take" with a vengeance. (For those who have never had a smallpox inoculation, "take" was the term used by laymen when the inoculation showed a reaction, in most cases a crusty sore which resulted in a scab, followed by the traditional scar.)

The typhoon did not do a great deal of damage to the base. But the town of Iwakuni was not so lucky. The town's big landmark was the Kintai Bridge, a very Oriental-looking bridge over a wide, shallow mountain stream. The bridge was washed away by the rainfall of the typhoon. The bridge had been built several hundred years earlier and had been kept in repair with the repair crews scrupulously keeping the bridge in its original medieval form.

KOREA!

Having flown B-29 Missions against Japan, and then later, B-26 missions against Korea, I frequently mentally compare the two assignments, particularly the differences.

Because the B-29 missions were usually about thirteen or thirteen and a half hours long, they frequently spread over two days and with the time the ground crews needed in between missions, we were scheduled either every second or third day.

The B-26 missions were usually about six or six and a half hours long. But you were frequently scheduled on a mission every day. The longer airtime in the B-29 was offset by the fact that you could get up and move around. In the B-26 you didn't even unbuckle your safety belt the whole time you were airborne. At least the Pilot and Navigator didn't; I think the Gunner may have been able to move around a little bit.

Of course both types of missions took place in the days before modern aerial refueling began; now flights in modern fighter planes in some instances have become endurance sitting contests.

I'll mention one personal problem but only briefly. Our missions usually ran from five and a half hours to six hours. My own personal maximum time between comfort stops usually was about four and a half hours. Since the plane had no relief facilities at the Navigator position, the last hour or two of a mission usually involved varying degrees of personal discomfort and it doesn't take much imagination to guess what the first order of business always was after landing.

Since the missions were always or most always squadron efforts, the briefing was always a squadron briefing instead of a group briefing. Crew assignments were not permanent and one of the first things I always wanted to see at the briefing was which pilot would be my aircraft commander. A few of our pilots were "Tigers", especially aggressive in pushing strafing attacks. These were the favorites of the Intelligence Officers who would look forward to getting lurid accounts of their strikes at the debriefing. Another few were extremely unaggresive. I flew with one of these once and his idea of strafing was to do it from an altitude of seven or eight thousand feet. That way our target didn't even know we were shooting at him! The majority of the pilots were in the middle group, reasonably aggressive.

By this point in the war, the Army had stabilized its defense perimeter to some extent, although conditions could vary from day to day. One of the most important things in the briefing was to see on the big wall map of Korea where the Bomb Line was. It was marked on the map with push pins and red yarn. Anything on our side of the bomb line would not be attacked. Anything on the Communist side of the Bomb Line was fair game. For us, the "anything" would be anything that moved, usually a truck or train.

Most of my missions were night missions and on these our planes flew individually. Each plane would have a separate departure time, the squadron objective being to have some of our planes over the Communists at all times during darkness. Your assigned take-off time would be anywhere from dusk until two or three hours before sunrise. The very late take-offs were miserable because you could not get much sleep before your take off and by the time you returned to your quarters it was well into the following morning's daylight.

At Tachikawa we had speculated about what new night tracking device the B-26s were using to locate targets in darkness. We found that the answer was very simple. It was nothing mechanical or optical. It was just the crews' own eyes and learning to use them at night. Night vision!

Assuming that a person has reasonably normal eyesight, you can cultivate and develop your ability to see things at night. First of all, you need about a half hour to an hour of fairly complete darkness before you can start to distinguish things at night. That is about the time it took to fly from Iwakuni to the target area.

Second, you don't look directly at the object you are interested in because with night vision, the eye's acuity is better around the sides of your field of vision than at the center. The plane's instruments were lit by a lighting system which did not interfere with your eye's night vision accommodation time. The Navigator needs light to read his map and make entries in his log. For this, we used the standard GI two cell flashlight, the old olive-drab colored plastic one. But these had an added feature, a red plastic lens filter. For some reason (which I'm sure the medical people can explain) red light does not interfere with your night vision. So now the Navigator is working on his lap-desk, reading his map like an owl by a dim red flashlight! But it worked, though in varying degrees. For us, we found that targets were easiest to find and attack when the moon was about half full. With a bright full moon, the enemy vehicle drivers could drive with no lights and were hard to find from the air. When there was no moonlight, the vehicle drivers had to use their headlights but the pilot also had problems in attacking because in nearly complete darkness it was hard to see the ground and ground obstacles when strafing.

My own very personal, very unofficial opinion is that the biggest value of our night intruder missions was that it made the enemy drive without lights, slowing them down a lot and probably causing lots of accidents—from fender-benders to run-off-the-road accidents. This was at a time when they probably also had problems in the daytime too from our fighters and our own B-26 "day flyers".

After their initial attack much of the material the North Koreans needed came from China, delivered by way of Manchuria. The dividing line between Manchuria and North Korea was the Yalu River. I'm not familiar with what the American newspapers were saying about the war but I'm under the impression that the Yalu River figured in many news stories. At night the Manchurian countryside and the Korean countryside were in almost stark contrast. We would fly up to within a mile or two of the Yalu, hoping to catch a convoy which had just crossed the river over into Korea. In the darkness you could see over into Manchuria and the roads were strings of lights, like beads on a necklace, trucks on their way to Korea in most cases. At the Yalu, the lights were always doused and the Korean countryside was a little like black velvet with not a light to be seen. Occasionally when the moonlight was just right, if you flew down to very low altitude you might be able to see individual trucks and make an attack.

Trains were an important part of the North Korean transportation system and they were a favorite target for our pilots. If no trains could be found, then the rails themselves became targets, especially for the daylight missions. In the war in Europe a favorite target was the rail marshaling yards with their intricate network of tracks. The Korean marshaling yards were much smaller than the European ones but they were attacked frequently.

After several marshaling yard attacks which had been successful it was noticed that the railways seemed to be repaired in a short amount of time. Intelligence learned—probably through photo interpreters, that the Koreans were stockpiling rails, ties and ballast and with abundant manpower at hand, repairs could be made in minimum time. So our tactic changed too—hit the rail lines out in the boondocks and force the enemy to haul the repair materials out to the boondocks too.

I flew a couple of missions with one of the squadron's most aggressive pilots. I don't think that Bob was really a blood-and-guts killer at heart. Actually he was a quiet, soft-spoken individual. I think it was more that he was one of those occasional super-competitive individuals who always wanted to turn whatever he was doing into a competition and he was always determined to win it at all costs.

On this particular mission, it was an especially dark night, probably a new moon. Prowling around over a wooded area at what seemed, to me anyway, to be an uncomfortably low altitude, we found a locomotive. In World War II one of the more exciting scenes in the Army filmed news reels was pictures taken by fighter aircraft with their gunpoint aiming cameras, scenes where our fighter bores in on the German train, firing machine guns until the locomotive blows up in a cloud of steam and smoke. Bob wanted this one to blow up and he started making strafing passes. Bob was a good shot and I'm sure he was hitting the locomotive but it wouldn't blow up. He kept making more and more strafing passes, each one a little lower than the one before. Finally, on an especially low-altitude pass in the pitch darkness there was suddenly a slightly darker shadow directly ahead of us and almost simultaneously we felt or heard a thump. The plane continued to fly, apparently normally but Bob decided that it was time to go home. I couldn't resist needling him—"Bob, you attack targets like you had bayonets on the nose guns and you were making a bayonet charge!"

Back at Iwakuni the ground crew found that there was a long crease along the belly of our plane and one of the propellers had a nick in it and needed changing. We had flown through the top of a North Korean tree! The ground crew painted a little silhouette of a tree on the nose of the plane to represent one North Korean tree attacked! We all treated the incident lightly and with humor. But in truth, if the path of our plane had been three or four feet lower, it would have been the tree's trunk we hit instead of the smaller top branches and that would have been the end of our crew.

Because of the peculiarities of the Occupation where the Japanese government was paying the housekeeping expenses of the Occupation bases, we at Iwakuni were in the unusual position of being able to make long distance telephone calls back to our families at Tachikawa. At no expense to us. Surprisingly, the tonal quality was pretty good, much better than our calls from Tachikawa across Tokyo Bay to the small base at Kisarazu had been. I and most of my fellow Navigators from Tachikawa would call our wives at Tachikawa every evening; as a consequence the wives usually knew when you were flying on a mission. A highly unusual situation for wives of American combat personnel. Usually the talk was small talk, personal conversation between husband and wife. During the first call after our crew's encounter with the tree, Estelle told me that on other nights she didn't worry too much but for some reason that particular night she had a strong premonition that this mission would be different. Normally when she went to bed, she prayed, using the Rosary beads I had sent to her from Travis AAB when I passed through on my way to Guam during World War II.

She told me that the premonition was so strong that she couldn't sleep and kept repeating the Rosary prayers over and over. Then, she said she had a sudden feeling that everything was all right; she felt at peace and soon fell asleep. We compared times and to us it seemed that her feeling of relief came about the time the incident ended and we started the flight back to Iwakuni.

We did not have any sort of news source where we could learn what was happening in the overall war picture. Our most up to date news about the progress of the war was the changes in the Bomb Line on the wall map at briefing time. I remember one briefing where there was the usual Bomb Line just beyond the Army's defense perimeter but another Bomb Line had been added, one surrounding the city of Inchon. No explanation to us, just the word "Don't bomb or attack anything inside this circle!"

We took off normally and found that, as usual, Korea on the Communist side of the Bomb Line was inky black. Except when we came within visual range of the Inchon Bomb Line the whole countryside there was a blaze of light. Almost like a little Tokyo at night. Of course it was the Inchon landing area. On succeeding nights the Bomb Line showed dramatic changes each night, going north at each change.

The effect of the United Nations air superiority showed up most dramatically at night. The enemy had to drive their vehicles in complete darkness or risk being attacked from the air. But the UN forces could move whole convoys at night with headlights on at full beam and not worry about night intruder planes. Apparently we night intruders had no counterpart on the other side in the war.

KOREA 2

One of the strongest memories of the Korean missions, at least for me on my tour was the cold, starting with the flights in late October or early November. The B-26 did not have any insulation on the aluminum cockpit walls which ended about waist level—above that it was Plexiglas of the large canopy. There was no heating system of any kind.

In late summer and early fall, the temperature inside the plane was not a factor and with the big glass clamshell canopy the view at times could be spectacular, like when you flew through a thunderstorm and you could see lightning all around you and the occasional blue glow of St. Elmo's Fire around your prop tips and antennas.

But when winter arrived the cold sometimes seemed as bitter an enemy as the flesh and blood enemy. There was only one way to deal with it; layers of clothing and even that didn't seem to do much beyond preventing frostbite. Looking at a map you can see that Korea is not too far from Siberia.

On these winter flights I wore about as much clothing as I could and still be able to walk. On a typical flight, to dress I would start out with a regular tee shirt and boxer shorts. Over that a pair of Long John underwear, both tops and bottoms. Next an old lambs wool civilian sweater. Over that next was a cotton flight suit (coveralls) and then a wool winter flight suit. Socks were first a pair of nylon uniform socks, then on top of that a pair of black cushion-sole wool socks, then a pair of high-top GI shoes (Little Abners). This finished my dressing in the BOQ. There would be more to come in the Personal Equipment Section on the flight line.

In Personal Equipment the next layer would be a two piece

electric heated flight suit, then over that a B-15 bomber jacket with pants of the same material and fleece lined flying boots. Over all this clothing there were more layers of equipment to be added. A yellow Mae West life preserver—in case you landed in water if you bailed out. Then a parachute with an inflatable dingy boat attached to it; the dingy boat pack constituting your seat cushion in flight. If you tried to walk wearing the chute harness the dingy would bang on your butt every step you took. Somewhere in all of that clothing and equipment came your shoulder holster and 45 caliber automatic pistol. And to help you discharge your Navigator duties, your leather briefcase with your maps, log, pencils, dividers, protractor and the old faithful GI flashlight.

It could have been worse—if we were flying fighters or heavy bombers there would also have been an oxygen mask. But the B-26 was strictly a low altitude plane so that item was not necessary. Most of us would wear a uniform cap on our head and fitted the earphones over that. I'm amazed that we could even climb into the plane with all that clothing and equipment. Mounting a B-26 was a little bit of an athletic feat in itself. Sitting in the cockpit you would be about twelve or fifteen feet above the ground. To get there, the plane had little recessed niches in the side of the fuselage and you climbed in, like a beginner rock climber. Once in, you had to get connected—plug in the electric suit, the earphones, your throat mike and fasten the seatbelt.

Now in, you waited while the pilot tended to his pre-start chores before starting the engines. The canopy was hinged like a clam shell and stayed open until the pilot had both engines started and running. With both engines running normally to the pilot's satisfaction, we would be ready to taxi. In day light the clam shell canopy would stay open until we were ready to take off because in sunlight on the ground the cockpit soon became a hot little greenhouse. Just before turning onto the runway for takeoff, the pilot had to give both engines a power check. This was true for all propeller driven planes but in the B-26 it was a miserable assault on your ears. The Pilot's and Navigator's seats were only about six or eight feet from the tips of the propellers and when the pilot tested the engines, one at a time, at full power and RPM's it was uncomfortable, almost painful on your eardrums. Your only defense was to hold your earphones tightly against your ears. At least the Navigator could get a little relief that way; the poor Pilot needed his hands for the controls to guide the engines through the power check. Once the power check was completed to the Pilot's satisfaction, you closed the canopy, turned onto the active runway and started the take off run. With the canopy closed and the slipstream pushing the prop noise to the rear, it seemed almost calm by comparison.

Wearing an electrically heated flying suit you would think that that automatically assured you of a warm, toasty flight. Far from it. We were always warned—"Don't turn the temperature of the electric suit up to where you feel warm. You'll start to sweat and that could cause a short circuit in the suit and you'll get burned!" I would set the temperature control on mine so low that sometimes I'm sure it wasn't even getting any electricity in the coils.

We had one unusual Pilot flying missions with us. He was an exchange British RAF pilot—I'm not sure now what his name was or what his rank in the RAF was called. I remember him as "Commander Bodine", though with the passing of so many years since 1950 I probably am not remembering the name and rank correctly. Commander Bodine was a good pilot and handled the B-26 well.

I flew one night mission with Commander Bodine; for me a memorable mission. We were a memorable crew too—Bodine the RAF Flight Commander, Thompson (that's me) the Navigator from Alabama, and a Gunner, who to us was a voice over the intercom. The Gunner had an unusual speaking voice; at first I thought that he was drunk but later in the flight I concluded that he couldn't have been drunk; it was his accent, an unidentifiable accent. I'm sure that Bodine probably thought my accent was odd also.

It was one of the darker nights and we couldn't find much vehicle activity. When that happened we normally would drop a single bomb on a town to disrupt any possible Communist troop activity. We picked a town to drop a single bomb on. Since it was being dropped for psychological effect rather than on a specific target, Commander Bodine elected to drop the bomb from level flight rather than making a dive bomb approach. He set the circuits so that only one bomb would drop, opened the bomb doors and pressed his release button on the yoke.

The Gunner's duty was to shine his flashlight into the bomb bay and tell the pilot, over the intercom, if the bomb had cleared the bomb bay. This time he had bad news for the Pilot. "Sir. The bomb didn't clear. It's hung up!"

When Bodine asked him to describe what the situation was, the Gunner said that the front lug of the bomb had dropped free of the bomb shackle but the bomb was still hanging by the rear lug. To add to our problems he said that the arming wire had slipped out of its hole in the fuse's propeller and the propeller was starting to spin slowly in the breeze coming into the bomb bay. We all knew that after the propeller had turned a certain number of times, it would fall off the bomb fuse and then the bomb fuse would be in a fully armed condition so that any bump on it could detonate the bomb. Up front the only thing the Pilot could do was fly as smoothly as possible and the only thing the Navigator could do was say a few fervent prayers.

The Gunner started working, using a long screwdriver, his body partly out into the open bomb bay. He grunted a few progress reports over the intercom but we had little idea of what he was doing. Then he reported to the Pilot, "Sir. I secured the propeller on the fuse so it can't spin." Now if the pilot could get the bomb to fall free from the back lug, we would all be okay.

"Stay clear of the bomb bay," Bodine instructed the Gunner over the intercom. "I'm going to see if I can get it to drop."

"Negative, Sir," the Gunner answered. "I'm securing it with a long screwdriver. Let's find a target to drop it on!"

I never could figure out clearly just what the Gunner had done, except that I knew most of it involved his having much of his upper body out in the open bomb bay, a thing that most of us wouldn't want to try ourselves.

After landing and after the debriefing, the three of us adjourned to the GI Messhall for the traditional after-mission breakfast of bacon and eggs. As we ate, none of us talked about our bomb incident. Instead, the Gunner and Commander Bodine got into a discussion of their favorite planes. The Gunner talked enthusiastically about his favorite, our own B-26. Bodine allowed that it wasn't a bad plane but his own all-time-favorite was the British Mosquito. "Just one bomb," he said. "But it was a big four thousand pound cookie!" I didn't feel like joining the comparison. They probably wouldn't have wanted to hear my views favoring the C-54! Or the B-29 either.

I flew quite a few missions with John. (I remember his last name but would rather not use it out of concern for his privacy.) John was a good pilot and his aggressiveness matched my own tastes. Aggressive enough to make it worth flying the mission but he never took it to extremes. I remember one mission with him especially well. At least the debriefing after the mission. There were two procedures common to all of our debriefings. First, there would be a medic from the hospital who would give the crew their combat ration. The combat ration was a shot of whisky, usually of some unknown brand. The shot had several beneficial effects. After the winter missions your body was still chilled and the whisky made you feel a little warmer. You were tired and tense and sleepy. While a few individuals might have been talkative, without the whisky most of us probably would have grumped out noncommital information to the Intelligence Officer making the interrogation. The main feature of course was the interrogation by the Intelligence Officer. His would be the report for the record of what the crew had seen and had done.

On the mission which I remember especially well, when we went to the debriefing room, there was another crew being debriefed ahead of us. Our crew took seats near the table where the medic was giving out the combat ration. The medic was a very young GI, probably around nineteen years old. He handed each of us our little cup of ration and we sat, sipping it slowly and relaxing. The ration he gave us was the first out of a new bottle. Normally most interrogations didn't last very long and we expected to be called over to the Intelligence Officer at any moment. But he kept on talking with the crew ahead of us. John, our pilot, said to the Medic, "Say, that wasn't too bad. How about another one?"

"Sure," the Medic replied and he poured a second shot for each of the three of us and we started sipping again. Meanwhile, the interrogation of the other crew continued as we sat sipping our second ration. The second ration cheered our crew and we found the wait becoming tolerable. This routine continued. None of us kept score but I would guess that our crew must have had four or five shots apiece before it was our turn to be interrogated. Since we were all tired, hungry and sleepy, I doubt if the Intelligence Officer learned anything of value from our crew. This makes me wonder what it was that the crew ahead of us had found in Korea. Our's had been an especially routine mission so I guess they must have found their action in an area we didn't fly over.

One unusual thing about the night intruder missions was their somewhat unstructured nature. With the heavy bombers, you took off, flew to a pre-planned area, dropped your bombs or did whatever else had been planned and returned home. Fuel planning was a little more cut and dried than with the intruder missions. With the intruder missions, as the Pilot prowled around in the North Korean darkness, he had to remember that home to us was Iwakuni, back in Japan, and he had better head for home while he still had enough fuel to make it. Usually the pilots would gauge it pretty well and come home with low fuel but still enough to make it comfortably. Occasionally a crew would get too much interested in their target and find when they were landing that they were almost out of gas.

One crew cut it a little too close and ended up in trouble. The Pilot was a new one and had moved into one of the rooms upstairs in my BOQ. I didn't know the guy very well, other than he lived upstairs in our building. When they returned to the base, he was really running on fumes. Iwakuni's runway ended two or three hundred feet from the beach (with the Inland Sea) and there was a low seawall running along the beach, one about two or three feet high. The plane ran out of fuel when the Pilot was flying his final approach, while he was several hundred yards before reaching the seawall. With no engines running the B-26 doesn't perform very well as a glider and as the Pilot tried to stretch his glide over the seawall, he ran out of altitude and his wheels hit the seawall. Nobody was injured in the crash but the plane was wrecked. The old cliche was "any landing you can walk away from is a good landing." By that standard I guess it qualified as a good landing. The Pilot was not injured physically but it was a terrific blow to his own self-esteem. He walked back to our BOQ, probably mentally kicking himself the whole way. He was carrying his big canvas bag full of winter flying clothing and at the top of the outdoor steps to the BOQ he didn't put the bag down to open the door—he just gave the door a tremendous kick. The door, a light fragile one, shattered and he continued walking up the stairs to his room, not saying a word to anyone. This happened in either late November or December and the weather was definitely winter weather. My bed was right by the front door and for the two nights before Air Installations could send a crew over to fix the shattered door, I felt like I was a winter camper.

None of the Pilots I flew with ever came home with tanks dangerously empty. But we did have one fuel episode that sort of gave us a brief scare. The B-26 had several fuel tanks which the Pilot could draw fuel from at different times. Standard procedure when a Pilot was strafing a ground target was to have the engines run from the tanks with the most fuel in them. We had found a target, not a spectacular one but still it was one which called for an attack. The Pilot forgot to switch the engines over to the fullest tanks and we made several passes at the target, diving down close to the ground on each strafing pass. On one pass the engines used up the last of the fuel in the tank they were running on and the engines stopped briefly. Luckily the Pilot realized the problem and quickly switched to a fuel tank that had fuel in it and the engines immediately began running again. Sheepishly, he turned to me and said, "Sure got quiet there, didn't it?"

One aerodynamic characteristic of the B-26 was always in the back of your mind in winter flying, especially when the weather was bad. The plane would not fly with any ice on the wings. In this respect it was not able to fly in weather a cargo plane, with its de-icer boots on the wings, could fly through. There was only one way to deal with weather where there was the possibility or likelihood of icing conditions and that was—don't even think about trying to fly through it or over it!

On one winter mission we had spent considerably more time than we should have up over North Korea and the Pilot decided to land at the new Korean airfield at Taegu to refuel. It was a miserably cold night, damp, windy and the temperature on the ground bordering the freezing point. We all knew well about the plane's reluctance to fly with ice on it and conditions that night were near the point where frosty ice would form on the ground. Not a good night for flying but we all wanted to get back to Iwakuni and sleep in a bed instead of on a cot in a transient's tent at Taegu. The Pilot came up with what he though might help prevent trouble; it was a fiendish idea, at least the Gunner and I thought it was a little later.

Somehow the Pilot managed to get two buckets of isopropyl alcohol (used in the propeller de-icing system of cargo planes). Also two very scruffy looking dirty rags. The Pilot's idea was that the Gunner and I would each take a bucket of alcohol and a rag, climb up on our plane's wing (about ten or fifteen feet above the ground) and wipe down the leading edge of the wing with the alcohol.

With the cold, raw breeze blowing, the alcohol made our hands feel colder and the cold aluminum of the wing felt even colder. Though we didn't put the thought into words, both the Gunner and I thought it was a miserable, futile thing to do. But in the back of our minds was all that we had heard about the dangers of wing icing on B-26s, so we made a halfway effort to wipe down the leading edge of the wing, at least to about half way out toward the wing-tips. We made a safe take off a few minutes later. Probably our alcohol rub didn't contribute a thing to the safety of the take-off. But we don't really know; maybe it did help.

Flying as close to the ground as we did searching for targets at night, you were sure sometimes of what you were seeing and at other times you hoped you were really seeing what you thought you were seeing. It was something like driving at night down a deserted country road at about thirty or forty miles an hour with your headlights off. You hope what you see is what is actually ahead of you and there are no dark black horses or cows in the middle of the road.

On one night mission we had cruised around out in the countryside of North Korea without finding a target. The Pilot decided that we should fly around at the same altitude over Pyongyang, the capitol of North Korea. The whole city was blacked out and most of the buildings seemed to be one or two story buildings. We could see several grayish smokestacks which looked like they were about three or four stories tall, probably small factories. The Pilot dive-bombed a bomb toward one of these. I was looking out to the side of the plane and when the bomb exploded the flash showed that in addition to the medium-height gray smokestacks, there was also a number of black smokestacks which were considerably taller than the gray ones. In fact they were taller than the altitude of our plane and quite invisible in the darkness. I gave the Pilot a frantic warning over the intercom to climb higher and after we leveled off about five hundred feet higher, I told him what I had seen. He decided to drop another bomb from that altitude and by its flash we both could see the big tall black stacks. Neither the noise of our engines or the sound of the bombs had stirred up any sort of reaction from the enemy. We were sure that the B-29s had probably bombed the city days before our visit and any more of our single bombs would be almost like beating a dead horse. So, we headed back out to the open countryside to look for trucks or locomotives. They were more our speed.

One mission is still memorable to me. Not because of any damage we inflicted on the enemy. In fact, we didn't see anything at all warlike during much of the flight. In North Korea most of the people lived on the western side of the peninsula. The eastern part is mostly mountainous and if you flew over that part there were hardly any targets to be found, other than the town of Wonsan. This mission was in December during the middle of an unusually cold snap. We flew up north of Wonsan in an area with few towns of any size at all. It was a bright full moon night and the ground was covered with what looked like a heavy, new snowfall. We flew several miles up a valley along a road following the lowest part of the valley. There were ridges of hills on either side of us, not really high ridges but they were higher than our altitude. The scene was deserted, just us and the snowy valley. With the good visibility of the full moon and the bright snow underneath we could probably have seen anything larger than a pedestrian. We saw nothing that could have been considered a target. Just the snow covered trees and the small country road. It was a beautiful sight and I was happy that we didn't find any military target. It was too much like a winter painting or a snowy Christmas card and too peaceful to bring the war in and spoil it all.

TACHIKAWA—AGAIN!

For bomber crews, starting with World War II (I guess!) the anticipated routine was for a crew to fly an established number of missions and that would end their combat tour. I don't know what criteria was used to set the number of missions. I suspect that it probably included the amount of flying hours in a typical mission for that theater of operations, plus the mortality rate, i.e., "high", or "low", and of course the availability of trained replacements. When I was flying most of my B-26 missions, the tour length hadn't been set and some of the crews started getting restless about the uncertainty. Several days before Christmas, I went on sick call for some minor complaint. The doctor gave me a prescription for whatever the condition was. But he spent several minutes looking at my face closely. I believe that he thought I was getting combat-fatigue. I assured him that although I was fatigued, it was just plain old garden-variety fatigue, not combat fatigue. I told him that if you were up until three or four every night flying missions and if you returned each time to where there were five of you sleeping in one big room with five Japanese maids coming in to work and chatter at seven-thirty; you had to give up on the idea of getting enough really restful sleep. He seemed to agree with my reasoning but that still didn't give me a full night sleep any night.

Under some other condition (which I can't remember!) when Christmas 1950 approached I was lucky enough to get a few days leave to go back to Tachikawa and spend the holiday with Estelle and the children. Usually you could hitch a ride on an Air Force plane if you were going back to the Tokyo area. My friend, Bill was given leave at the same time I was. At Tachikawa, Bill was in the 6th Squadron while I was in the 22nd but at Iwakuni we were both on the first floor of the same house and had gotten acquainted.

Bill and I were disappointed that there were no planes headed our way but that wasn't the only way we could travel. There was the Japanese railway system. We saw that it was either go back to Tachi by train or not get home in time for Christmas so we took the train. The Japanese railway system was still pretty good (by 1940's standards) in spite of the bombing of World War II. But, we had to go by day coach. Bill and I were both tired and feeling the effects of days and weeks of minimum sleep, so I guess we were not too talkative. We sat on a seat facing a couple of Army Officers. One was a bird Colonel and not inclined to be especially talkative. His seat-mate was an Army Captain who was the most talkative of the four of us.

Bill and I were secretly amused by the Army Captain. He seemed to be trying to impress the Colonel by addressing him in the third person every time he had something to say, which was rather often. "What did the Colonel think of the last town we passed through?" Or, "Does the Colonel think we will reach Osaka on time?"

Bill and I weren't used to this type of formality. During World War II relations between different ranks had become much more straightforward, at least in the Air Corps. Officer positions on bomber crews could consist of any rank from Second Lieutenant to full Colonel. Communication over a plane's intercom system was necessarily informal and addressing a senior officer in the third person would have been ridiculous. Bill and I laughed (but always inwardly) when the Captain made one of his pompous statements. I guess the Army duo thought we were a couple of clams but we were just a couple of fatigued Lieutenants counting the hours until we joined our families. Bill's wife had had a baby at the Station Hospital at about the same time that Estelle had given birth to our daughter.

Our leave, like most leaves, passed all too quickly and soon we were back at Iwakuni again. The Chinese intervention in the war had changed what for a time was a routine operation for our crews.

We were still flying the same type of missions but the emphasis of the action seemed to change more frequently and now was almost entirely in the original area of North Korea. And it was still bitterly cold on each flight. After the war I talked with men who had been with the ground forces and they felt the cold even more than we did. We aircrew members could warm up back at Iwakuni but for them the cold went on and on with no welcome relief other than an overheated tent.

With many of us at or near the fifty mission count, a tour length was announced. It was fifty missions. I had reached fifty-two missions and the B-26 portion of the war was over for me. Some of the crew members, mostly Pilots I think, opted to continue flying. I assume that in most cases the Pilots volunteering were hoping for promotions. Promotion chances for Navigators appeared to be much more limited and we of the Tachikawa group of Navigators were more interested in rejoining our families and resuming flying in the vastly more comfortable C-54s.

In each case, although we had been completely transferred out of our respective squadrons, when our group returned, we were returned to the squadron we had been in before the transfer. There were changes in our squadron and we no longer had our extremely popular squadron CO, "Curly" and there was a new Operations Officer also.

Most of the regularly scheduled flights still continued: Misawa, Itazuke, Naha (Okinawa) and occasionally Clark in the Philippines. But there were many, many more flights into Korea now. Passengers, supplies, general freight. And coming back, now there were frequent Medical Evacuation flights.

The medical evacuees of course were troops who had either been wounded in the fighting or in accidents. I'm not familiar with what the routines were for these patients before we picked them up. In all cases on flights I was on the individuals' conditions were stabilized to the point where they could be expected to stand the non-stop flight back to Tachikawa. Some would probably be getting their further treatment in the military hospitals in the Tokyo area. Others would be transferring to MATS planes for the long air-evac flight back to the States. But even though their medical condition had been stabilized, they were still patients on litters and in most cases probably suffering considerable pain and anxiety.

The litters were suspended in rows three or four litters high along each side of the plane. The earliest patients brought aboard the plane had to lie and wait while the following litters were brought on and secured and I'm sure that the wait didn't contribute anything to their mental comfort. Of course there were Medical people who would tend to their charges during the flight.

After all the patients were loaded and secured, we of the flight crew would board the plane and prepare for take-off. I found that this boarding was much more emotionally charged than taking off on our bombing missions had been. You boarded through the door in the back of the plane and walked up the aisle in the middle, bordered on each side by layers of stretchers with patients in them. No moans or cries, at least on any of the air-evacs I flew. But you could sense the pain and tension as you walked toward the cockpit area, the patient's eyes following you, probably wondering what would come next. On our B-26 missions, there were never any wounded the way it was in the heavies, especially the flights from England in World War II. For us, you either came back whole and sound, or you didn't come back at all as happened to several Pilots and Navigators I knew. Being this close to wounded men, many of them, was a new and sobering experience. I was glad that we could help and wished that we could do more than hurry the trip for them.

Fortunately on the air-evacs I flew there were no medical emergencies during the flights. The take offs in Korea were in field conditions and probably not very dramatic. But the landings at Tachikawa were more dramatic. Of course the Tower knew when an air-evac flight was coming in and they started the emergency-vehicle protocol for the landing. As you landed, you could see that fire trucks and ambulances were lined up along the runway, several hundred yards apart. We sometimes joked that they were ghouls, waiting for a disaster, and would be disappointed by a safe landing. But it was a smart precaution because they would be right at the scene if an accident occurred.

While we of the Iwakuni-Navigator group had been away, we found that the Catholic Chaplain, Father Maher had kept in close touch with the families in Tachikawa. Estelle told me that he would regularly visit for a few minutes with the wives, usually in the morning or mid-afternoon for coffee. She told me also that she asked him to call her before he came over for a social visit to let her know that it was a social visit, rather than an official visit as the Duty Chaplain. She felt that if she had gone to the front door without this preliminary warning and saw the Chaplain and another Officer, she would automatically assume the worst, i.e., that it was a visit to inform her that something serious had happened to me.

The B-26 tour ended when I reached the mission count goal for that duty. Later, at Tachikawa, the overseas tour ended as a normal overseas tour would. Most of us would be going back to the States to Langley Air Force Base, Virginia, to be instructors for combat crews coming over to the 3-rd Bomb Wing. Several of us from the Iwakuni group flew back to the States on the same plane and Father Maher saw us all off at Haneda Airport in Tokyo. He gave a small religious medal to each family member of his flock and we knew that we would be in his prayers and best wishes. He had been a good friend and it was like having family to wish us a good trip. A few months after reporting back to Langley, we heard that Father Maher had died in an aircraft crash. He was acquainted with a Missionary working in Korea and he learned that the Missionary was having trouble traveling to minister to his flock. Father Maher bought a surplus Army jeep and arranged to have it flown to Korea. He was accompanying the jeep to give it to the Missionary when their plane crashed.

After a few months as an Instructor Navigator at Langley Air Force Base, I went off flying. Looking back to the B-29s, the B-26s, the C-46s and C-54s, it had been an interesting and exciting experience flying, even as a Navigator instead of the Pilot I had hoped to be. There would be a couple of short term non-flying assignments before becoming an Auditor with the Air Force Auditor General organization. With them I enjoyed being first a Staff

Auditor and later Resident Auditor at several bases. But enough; the experiences of a ground-pounder Auditor have no place in this recollection of flying experiences so we'll just leave that to my reminiscences with my Bean Counter Associates.

APPENDIX

Slang, Jargon, Abbreviations

AO—Airdrome Officer. A detailed job for pilots. The AO performed many of the Base Operations Officer's routine tasks when the Base Operations Officer was off duty. e.g. Signing pilot's clearances, checking the operations of the runways, tower, fueling facilities, etc.

AUGUR IN—When applied to a plane, it meant a crash in which the plane was in a spin (tailspin). When applied to a person it meant going to bed and sleep when fatigued.

AWOL—Absent Without Leave. A court martialable offense.

AOCP—Aircraft Out of Commission, Parts. Status of a plane which cannot be flown for lack of a needed part.

AOCM—Aircraft Out of Commission, Maintenance. Status of a plane which cannot be flown until certain maintenance is done on it.

BED CHECK—In a training situation, a check by one of the training staff to ensure that all the trainees were in quarters and in bed. In a combat situation, "Bed Check Charlie" would be a nuisance raid by an enemy plane, usually after midnight to disrupt sleep.

BIRD COLONEL—A full Colonel (0-6). A term used only in conversation to distinguish the person from a Lieutenant Colonel. The rank insignia for a Bird Colonel was an eagle, hence the name. The Lieutenant Colonel in a similar situation would be a Leaf Colonel, his rank insignia being a silver leaf.

BITCH—To complain. Most American troops considered bitching one of their inalienable rights. A saying among some commanders was that if the troops were bitching, then all was well but if they stopped bitching then things were taking a really bad turn.

BOMB LINE—For planes flying in an area close to the fighting front, a line shown on the briefing map. Crews were not supposed to attack anything on our side of the bomb line, anything beyond the line was fair game.

BOUGHT THE FARM—Died, usually suddenly. An old military term, usually used when a person dies in combat or in an accident.

BUG OUT-Leave a place quickly and usually without ceremony.

CHICKEN—Originally "Chicken Shit"—a term for a petty exercise of authority for no realistic reason. Example: "I'll be glad when I'm out of this chicken outfit", or "My last CO was a good one but this one is a real Chicken." Shortly after WW II the term "Chicken" was seized on by teen-agers who gave it an entirely different meaning. In their usage it usually meant someone who was less brave (foolhardy?) than his competitor and frequently resulted in pointless competitions of nerve, sometimes ending tragically.

CHOW HOUND—The person or persons who are always waiting for a mess to start serving. e.g., "Let's go to eat early so we can beat the chow hounds."

COMBAT RATION—A shot of whisky given to aircrewmen after a combat mission by a Medic.

DETAIL—A temporary work assignment in addition to the individual's regular job description. EXAMPLES: Officer of the Day, Airdrome Officer, Inventory Officer, Accident Investigation Board Member, Charge of Quarters, Kitchen Police, Guard Duty, Court Martial Board, plus many more possible Details.

DINNER KEY—For those Cadets in the Army's Navigation School at Coral Gables, "Dinner Key" was the name of the Pan American Seaplane Passenger Terminal in Miami.

EAGLE FLEW—a slang term for payday.

FEATHER MERCHANT—A civilian, usually one with some connection with the Air Corps.

FIGMO—An acronym, spelled out "F—It! I Got My Orders!" It supposedly described the attitude of a person who has received his orders to return home to the states and is reluctant to do anything he can get out of doing. Most Officers realized that although they might use the term in social banter, they couldn't be too uncooperative because the CO could have the last laugh when they made the person's final performance evaluation.

FIRST SHIRT—The first sergeant of a squadron. The man who "got things done". In a squadron with an effective organization, the first sergeant backed up the commander's authority and the commander backed up the first sergeant's position and authority.

FIX—In the Navigator's vocabulary, a "fix" on a map was a location with more validity than a dead reckoning position. It could be a Celestial Fix, a LORAN Fix, a visual Fix, or a Radar Fix.

GEORGE—A nickname for a plane's autopilot. Aircrewmen would frequently say (with affection) that George was the best pilot in the Air Force.

GI—Literally, "Government Issue" but in usage a term with almost unlimited uses. e.g.s (1) to clean thoroughly, as "we had to GI the barracks every Friday"; (2) an enlisted man, particularly in the Army; (3) non-GI clothing was any article of outer wear which was not compatible with the uniform; (4) the GI's was a term for diarrhea—in less-polite company the GI shits; (5) plus many, many more usages.

GROUND POUNDER—Air Corps slang term for non-flying Army troops usually implying Infantry. A variation was "Gravel Agitator".

GUARD HOUSE—The base confinement facility, i.e., the jail.

HEADS UP, or HEAD_UP—In non-Air Force usage, "Heads up" meant being especially careful or observant. In Air Force usage the meaning was exactly opposite. It meant doing something which could end up disastrously, especially when flying. e.g., "I really had my head up that time and am lucky to be alive today." Originally it was "I had my head up my ass," but in politer company the shortened form was usually used, the user knowing that the listener knew what he meant.

JUG—Could have one of several different meanings, depending on the context. e.g.s (1) a P-47 fighter aircraft; (2) a cylinder on a radial aircraft engine; (3) a bottle of whisky, especially in states requiring patrons to take their own bottle to a night spot (Texas comes to mind); (4) a woman's bosom (plural).

LET DOWN:— A descent by an aircraft from higher altitude, usually directed by either a control facility or other external direction. A "Nylon Letdown" was a slang term for a parachute bail out.

MAE WEST:—A life preserver worn by aircrew members. Bright yellow, made of rubberized fabric. Worn over all clothing but underneath the parachute harness. It had two short cords at the base. If the user parachuted into water, he would pull the short cords and two carbon dioxide cylinders would inflate the life vest. Named after the bountifully endowed movie actress of that name.

MAY DAY—A term in voice-radio calls to indicate a serious emergency for the caller. Equivalent to SOS in maritime use.

OD—Officer of the Day. A detail job for junior officers. The duties varied from base to base but could include monitoring incoming communications, notifying the commander of unusual events, handling minor emergencies, etc.

ODs—Literally "Olive Drab". The official name for the color of the enlisted wool uniform. Wearing OD's meant wearing the wool blouse (coat) and trousers.

OVER THE HILL—To desert. A much more serious offense than AWOL.

PROVOST MARSHALL—The officer responsible for ground security and law and order. Usually also the commander of the Air Police Squadron.

RON—Literally "Remain Overnight"—a flight to another base where the crew spent the night.

RED ASS—Frequently "The RA's". A term used by subordinates for a situation where someone superior to them seems to be especially irritated with them or even with the world itself.

SACK—A bed or cot. Originally the term was "fart sack" but in later days the single word sack was used.

SAD SACK—Originally "Sad Sack of Shit", later shortened to just Sad Sack. Specifically, an individual who always comes out the loser in any encounter. "Sad Sack" was also a cartoon character in a series of cartoons appearing in military publications.

SEXTANT—The optical instrument used by a Navigator to measure a celestial body's height above the horizon. Our instructors in Navigation School said that technically the instrument we used was an OCTANT, (or Bubble Octant), not a true Sextant. The maritime Sextant measured the distance of the body above the horizon. Since in flying the horizon is much more vague than it is to a mariner, our Bubble Octant (Sextant to us!!) substituted a bubble floating in a small circle of liquid as its horizon.

SMI—Saturday Morning Inspection.

SNAFU—Situation Normal-All Fouled Up. (Originally the "F" word was used). A condition where planned things don't go as planned or where no one knows what is happening or what to do next. The purists among complainers would complain that there were three degrees to the term:

1. SNAFU (Situation Normal, All Fouled Up.)
2. TARFU (Things Are Really Fouled Up.)
3. FUBAR (Fouled Up Beyond All Repair.)

TOUR—A punishment in cadet training. A tour was having to walk at attention in Class A uniform for one hour. A "tour" could also be used to identify a period of duty at some geographic location.

TS/TS CARD—TS stood for "Tough Shit", usually applied when a person is the victim of an unfortunate event. In the popular mythology, everyone had a TS CARD and when they were the victim of such a happening they could have the Chaplain punch their TS card for them. If an individual felt that he had had more than his share of such events, he would frequently complain that his TS Card had been punched so much it looked like lace.

USA JIMA—Affectionate name sometimes used by occupation troops in Japan for the United States. Sometimes it was "USA JIMA-Land of the big, BIG PX" Originated, probably, from seeing so many Japanese place names which ended in "-JIMA".

WIDOW MAKER—A plane that had a bad reputation for being involved in fatal crashes. One of the more widely known was the Martin B-26 (not to be confused with the Douglas B-26, a different plane.) Oddly, while the Martin B-26 was called "The Widow Maker" in training situations, in actual combat in Europe its combat losses were less discouraging than the B-17s and B-24s.

BVG